Gender Myths v. Working Realities

Gender Myths v. Working Realities

*Using Social Science to Reformulate
Sexual Harassment Law*

Theresa M. Beiner

NEW YORK UNIVERSITY PRESS

New York and London

NEW YORK UNIVERSITY PRESS
New York and London
www.nyupress.org

© 2005 by New York University

Library of Congress Cataloging-in-Publication Data
Beiner, Theresa M.
Gender myths v. working realities : using social science
to reformulate sexual harassment law / Theresa M. Beiner.
p. cm.
Includes bibliographical references and index.
ISBN 0–8147–9917–5 (cloth : alk. paper)
1. Sexual harassment—Law and legislation—
United States—Sociological aspects.   2. Law and the
social sciences—United States.   I. Title: Gender myths
versus working realities.   II. Title.
KF3467.B44   2004
344.7301'4133—dc22   2004013754

New York University Press books are printed on acid-free paper,
and their binding materials are chosen for strength and durability.

Manufactured in the United States of America

10 9 8 7 6 5 4 3 2 1

To the book orphans—
Erin, Ryan, and Daniel Gauger

Contents

Acknowledgments

No book is completed without the help of many people. My helpers came in two varieties: those who helped with the actual content of this book and those who provided moral support during a long and sometimes grueling process. One person fits in both categories. Nancy Levit guided me through the publishing process, read chapters of my manuscript, and provided moral support throughout this project. I would not have known where to start without her help, for which I'm truly grateful.

Others also helped by reading chapters and providing me with helpful feedback. Thanks to Margaret Stockdale, David Schwartz, Nancy Levit, James Arnt Aune, and Vicki Schultz for providing valuable comments on various chapters. Jim Aune, in particular, is someone whom I have found inspirational as a teacher and scholar. In addition, the NYU Press's outside reviewers, including Margaret Stockdale, provided valuable comments on the entire book, and I benefited from the research of one of Dr. Stockdale's students, Dawn M. Ohse. Others listened as I ran ideas, theories, and solutions by them. This is a group of colleagues I value highly: Erica Beecher-Monas, John DiPippa, Robert Chapman, and Kelly Olson. My husband, Timothy Gauger, also listened and provided feedback as I reasoned through many arguments aloud in his presence.

This book benefited from various presentations made and feedback received at several conferences, including the Law & Society Association's annual meetings in 2002 and 2003 and a symposium sponsored by the UALR Law School. I also received feedback from my own colleagues at various faculty development sessions throughout the past two years. Two chapters of the book benefited from previous publication (and editing) by student-run law reviews. In particular, portions of chapter 1 were published in the *Southern California Law Review* and portions of chapter 5 were published in the *William and Mary Journal of Women and the Law* and the *UALR Law Review*. I was aided by the work of several valuable research assistants, including Erin Vinett, Debra Reece, April Minor, Christopher Brockett, Emilie Leibovitch and Danna Young, who in particular had the unenviable job of cite checking this book. Laura Anderson tirelessly tracked down all non-legal sources, and Kathryn Fitzhugh provided research support. Finally, my secretary, Cheryl Bigelow, not only typed various revisions but also very graciously listened to me puzzle through various problems I encountered in writing this book.

This project also was supported by my institution—the University of Arkansas at Little Rock William H. Bowen School of Law—both financially and timewise. Financial support was provided by the school through several summer research grants as well as a sabbatical semester. It was supported by two deans—Charles Goldner and Rodney Smith. Dean Smith is responsible for getting this whole project started. I still remember the meeting I had with him to explain that my summer research project—a single law review article—seemed to be turning into three articles. Dean Smith's comment was "Those aren't law review articles; that's a book." It seems he was right.

I am grateful to the fine editorial staff at the NYU Press for believing in this project and providing excellent editorial support. In particular, I'd like to thank Alison Waldenberg, Deborah Gershenowitz, Jennifer Yoon, Betty Seaver, and Despina Papazoglou Gimbel for their support.

Finally, there is a group of people who provided moral support as I struggled through this project. Included in this group are friends, colleagues, and family members. My students as well always provide me with inspiration. My friends Sandy Moore and Stacy Fletcher were always supportive and also pitched in to read chapters. My colleague Gene Mullins was always there to encourage me. And, of course, there is my family, who includes the group to whom this book is dedicated: the book orphans—Erin, Ryan, and Daniel Gauger. All three kids endured extra days in extended care and summer camps so that Mom could "get the book done." In addition, my husband, Timothy Gauger, was very patient and supportive throughout this entire project. Finally, my Mom and Dad, Marylin and Raymond Beiner, who volunteered to watch children for me and, along with my sister, Loretta Torpey, never failed to ask how the book was "coming along," further encouraging me to keep plugging away. Yes, Ryan, the book is finally done.

Introduction
What Law Can Learn from Social Science about Workplace Sexual Harassment

Sexual harassment is a persistent workplace problem that is experienced by working women and, to a lesser extent, working men. For example, in its last study of sexual harassment in the federal workplace, the United States Merit Systems Protection Board (USMSPB) found that 44% of women and 19% of men reported having experienced some form of unwanted sexual attention at work in the two years prior to the survey.[1] Other studies support the continued persistence of sexual harassment in the American workplace, with estimates that anywhere from 40% to 80% of working women have experienced sexually harassing behavior at work.[2] In addition, the Equal Employment Opportunity Commission (EEOC) has seen a consistent rise in the number of charges of sexual harassment being filed, although this trend has leveled off recently.[3] Just this past year, the EEOC leveled charges against Procter & Gamble for sexual harassment at a Dial soap factory. The irony in this case is that the EEOC recently had commended the company for its equal opportunity practices.[4]

Aside from its prevalence, sexual harassment costs both businesses and its targets considerably. For example, the USMSPB estimated that sexual harassment cost the federal government alone $327 million during the period April 1992 through April 1994.[5] Its targets incur costs not only to their careers but also to their personal lives as well as their physical and psychological well-being. Thus, even though the Supreme Court recognized sexual harassment as a viable theory of sex discrimination under Title VII of the Civil Rights Act of 1964 in 1986, it persists as a costly and disturbing workplace phenomenon.

The law's efficacy in combating this workplace problem has not been what it should or could be. The development of sexual harassment law has been rather anomalous as compared to other areas of the law. There are famous instances of social science being used to reform legal standards,[6] but it is unusual for the law to lead the way in reform before social scientists have defined the particular human behavior that warrants legal attention. Yet, the courts developed sexual harassment law without the benefit of years of study by social scientists. As Catharine MacKinnon stated: "Sometimes, even the law does something for the first time."[7] With sexual harassment, it was the law that led and social scientists who played catch-up. In a sense, the courts were guessing about how sexual harassment operated and how best to address it through the legal system.

What this guesswork has led to in many instances is a legal standard that places targets of harassment under a microscope and dismisses the defendant's behavior as trivial. The courts all too often resort to stereotypes of female-male interactions. This is not unusual for human beings faced with ambiguous legal standards. Without the help of social science or clear standards, some courts have defaulted to stereotypes. Thus, all too often a plaintiff, in order to have an actionable claim, must be a chaste and demure woman. However, in spite of her stereotypical timidity, she must be bold enough to complain of sexual harassment as soon as it occurs, or else risk losing her claim. If she yells back at her harasser, shows any signs of "un-ladylike" behavior, or waits too long to complain, her claim will be questioned, and, in some cases, thrown out because she is not the right type of plaintiff or has not behaved as a worthy plaintiff should. At the same time, courts seemingly sympathize with employers, dismissing harassing incidents as mere horseplay, beyond the employer's knowledge or control, or inconsistent with the employer's often half-hearted efforts to implement an anti–sexual harassment policy.

Social science reveals that in many instances these assumptions are wrong. This book attempts to bridge the gap between what social scientists have discovered about sexual harassment in the workplace and the current legal standards that frequently misapprehend how sexual harassment functions as a form of sex discrimination. It has taken more than twenty years for this incongruity to reveal itself. Even today, social scientific study of sexual harassment is still considered to be "in its infancy";[8] however, there is sufficient data to begin to examine how the legal standards stack up against the reality of this disturbing workplace phenomenon. Social scientists began to focus on sexual harassment in the late

1970s after the publication of two influential books: Lin Farley's *Sexual Shakedown: The Sexual Harassment of Women in the Working World* and Catharine MacKinnon's *Sexual Harassment of Working Women.* These two books, as well as the promulgation of the Equal Employment Opportunity Commission's Guidelines on Sexual Harassment, caused both social scientists and legal scholars to focus on sexual harassment in the workplace.[9] The lower federal courts had begun to develop harassment law in the context of racial and ethnic harassment.[10]

Since the late 1970s, social scientists have scrambled to study the contours of workplace harassment, including how frequently harassment occurs,[11] whether male and female perceptions of harassment differ,[12] and how women respond to harassment.[13] More recently, social scientists have begun to focus on harassment of people of color.[14] I will consider how harassment may differ or be exacerbated by other statuses, such as race, to the extent that there are studies and cases reflecting this. This is extremely important because recent studies suggest that the incidence of harassment of women of color may be much higher than that of white women.[15] After twenty years of study, some patterns have begun to emerge in social scientific study that are very helpful in understanding how sexual harassment happens, how targets respond to it, and what people perceive to be sexual harassment.

I use the term "social science" throughout this book, but most of the studies used were produced by psychologists, sociologists, and related behavioral theorists. Notably absent are economists. I ignore economics for a number of reasons. First, many articles (indeed, whole books) examine employment discrimination laws from an economics perspective.[16] Second, economics uses methodologies different from those used by other disciplines.[17] Finally, although law and economics theorists have much to say about employment discrimination law generally, they have little to say about sexual harassment in particular.[18] Instead, psychologists and sociologists have led the way in understanding sexual harassment.

Social science studies provide valuable information that the courts, jurors, employers, and workers can use not only to understand sexual harassment better but also to develop legal standards that will actually reflect (or consciously choose not to reflect) how sexual harassment happens, is perceived, and affects workers. This book is a first step in suggesting reforms to reflect that science. In it, I review legal standards and social scientific findings that have implications for the current legal standard. Then I propose potential reforms to the standards that better reflect the phenomenon, with due consideration for what employment discrimination laws are designed to do. I also suggest areas in which more social science research would be helpful for lawyers and judges trying to set legal standards. It is my hope that by taking a hard look at what both social scientists and judges have done in the area of sexual harassment, this book will enlighten both groups and ultimately result in workplaces that are more hospitable for workers.

Studies reveal that the most prevalent form of sexual harassment involves men harassing women. This book focuses on that form of sexual harassment. However, I am in no way suggesting that men are not likewise harassed. Having focused initially on sexual harassment of women by men, social scientists are just beginning to explore sexual harassment of men.[19] There are more consistent and reliable findings relative to male-on-female harassment than any other form of harassment. Thus, the possibility of drawing conclusions from the data and applying these conclusions to legal standards is greatest for this type of harassment. One recent study has indicated that male-on-male sexual harassment may be as prevalent as male-on-female sexual harassment. The former kind of harassment in the workplace may operate differently (and, perhaps, have less impact) than the latter. In the area of same-gender harassment, more harassment occurs among males than females.[20] Thus, the particulars of male harassment require further study.

The format of each chapter is designed to maximize understanding by both social scientists and legal professionals by encouraging social scientists to consider legal doctrine and by causing legal professionals (including judges and lawyers) to consider social science. In each chapter I begin by discussing in depth the particular element of the claim for sexual harassment from a legal perspective. I not only cover the Supreme Court's precedent but also consider trends and issues arising in the lower courts. Although the Supreme Court has issued several decisions on sexual harassment law, the number pales in comparison to the number of cases that are coming through the lower federal courts. Given the rate of certiorari grants, these courts are the main decision makers in sexual harassment cases. Therefore, how they evaluate these claims is of the utmost importance to the efficacy of the law, as well as to the rights and interests of litigants. From there, I go on to examine the findings of social scientists regarding how sexual harassment actually occurs in the workplace. Finally, I suggest reforms to the legal standard such that the courts can address sexual harassment in a more realistic manner.

Another aim of this book is to help employers and others who deal with workplace sexual harassment to better understand how sexual harassment is thought of in the legal system and how it functions in the workplace. Listening to popular opinion about sexual harassment reveals a sense of confusion. It seems that people, including human resource managers and sometimes the courts themselves,[21] believe that they do not know what sexual harassment is and are confounded by what is considered appropriate and inappropriate workplace behavior. Part of the ambiguity in this area may well stem from the nature of the legal standards developed by the courts.[22] Terms such as "severe or pervasive" and "alter the conditions of employment," both of which are included in the legal standard for sexual harassment, are vague. This has left the lower courts to develop, on a case-by-case basis, the law based on the particular facts involved. Indeed, the Supreme Court essentially has told them to do just that. Far from being inappropriate in this setting, it makes sense for courts to judge harassment on a case-specific basis, considering the entire context in which the harassment occurs.[23] However, this does not seem to furnish workers and the courts with much guidance.

Given the case-by-case analysis supported by Supreme Court precedent, it seems that by now—the Supreme Court recognized the cause of action eighteen years ago[24]—there would be some consensus about the nature of what is legally cognizable as sexual harassment. Procedural problems, however, have left much of sexual harassment law's development in the hands of a single trial judge or, less often, a panel of appellate judges. Indeed, surveys of employment lawyers as well as empirical study of decision making in these cases reveal that sexual harassment plaintiffs have a tough time in court. Many sexual harassment cases are resolved by pretial motion, never revealing how a jury might assess the situation. Courts grant summary judgment, motions to dismiss, and, even when a jury has returned a verdict for the plaintiff, sometimes overturn that decision using judgment as a matter of law.

Throughout this book the procedural posture of the case is emphasized. Even though the Civil Rights Act of 1991 places factual determinations in these cases before the jury, many plaintiffs do not have the opportunity to present their case to the jury. Instead, studies suggest that pretrial motion practice in sexual harassment cases is on the rise. In a recent study of cases decided in the ten years following *Meritor v. Vinson* (through 1995), Juliano and Schwab found that in 64.9% of reported district court cases, there was a pretrial motion on the substance of a claim.

Of these, plaintiffs won 52.5% of the motions. In addition, in 3.8% of the cases, pretrial motions were made on procedural or evidentiary issues. Of these motions, plaintiffs won 79%. Overall, district court judges decided 54.1% of the cases studied on pretrial motions without a trial. These authors also noted this practice is on the rise. During 1986–1989, half of the opinions they studied were at the pretrial stage, whereas three-quarters of the decisions studied during the 1990s were at the pretrial stage.[25] It is not unreasonable to hypothesize that the increase in these motions is due at least in part to defense perceptions that they can be won.

A rise in pretrial motions may not seem all that problematic. The Juliano and Schwab study shows plaintiff win rates on these motions are greater than 50%. However, there is reason to believe that these win rates may be inflated. Juliano and Schwab used only reported decisions in their study. Seigelman and Donohue have demonstrated that leaving out unpublished decisions may skew results in several respects, including inflating plaintiff win rates.[26] In their study of all employment civil rights cases filed in the Northern District of Illinois between July 1, 1972, and December 31, 1986, 80% of the cases did not produce a published opinion by the district court.[27] Thus, including unpublished decisions in the Juliano and Schwab study might have dropped plaintiff win rates significantly.

It could well be that pretrial motions are granted and denied appropriately, saving both the litigants and the courts the time and expense of trial. This book suggests the opposite: that judges are taking cases away from juries when issues of fact exist. Various decisions are examined throughout this book in an effort to show that judges in some instances are granting these pretrial motions improperly. In the course of ruling on these motions, courts have decided some very questionable cases summarily, using, for example, the objective standard that "no reasonable person" could find the alleged behavior to be sexual harassment.

There is also reason to believe that these plaintiffs might fare better in front of juries. Using data from the Administrative Office of the United States Courts for fiscal years 1979 through 1989 regarding case outcomes in bench trials versus jury trials, Clermont and Eisenberg found that plaintiffs fare better before juries (winning 39% of the time) than before judges (winning 20% of the time).[28] Although this data does not tell us about jury trials in Title VII cases because at the time jury trials were unavailable for such cases, it does suggest an overall lower win rate in job-related civil rights cases in which the fact finder is a judge.

The appellate courts may not be as inclined to vindicate plaintiff's rights when these lower court decisions are made incorrectly. Juliano and Schwab's study showed similar appellate win rates for plaintiffs and defendants,[29] but a report by Clermont and Eisenberg that relies on a study by Clermont and Eisenberg of official government data generated by the Administrative Office of the United States Courts in all cases decided after trial during 1988 through 1997 found that "employment discrimination plaintiffs do dramatically worse than defendants on appeal."[30] The appellate reversal rates are telling: plaintiffs obtain reversals in 5.8% of the cases they appeal, whereas defendants obtain reversals in 43.61% of the cases they appeal. Plaintiffs' abilities to preserve decisions in their favor in these cases is worse than that of any other litigant with the exception of "other civil rights" cases, which included police misconduct cases, First Amendment cases, and other discrimination cases.[31] This held true for cases decided on pretrial motions as well.[32] Juliano and Schwab looked at appellate data for sexual harassment cases specifically and found that plaintiffs won on appeal 39% of the time, counting all reported cases studied (including cases reported in Westlaw and Lexis databases), and 45.2% of the time if only officially published opinions were considered.[33] These findings support Siegelman and Donohue's work suggesting that plaintiff win rates go down if unpublished decisions are included. Eisenberg and Clermont have suggested that federal appellate judges may be exhibiting an anti-plaintiff bias.[34]

There are also some disturbing recent studies showing the influence of race, gender, and political affiliation in the decision outcomes in sex discrimination cases that have implications for harassment cases. In a recent study of federal courts of appeal decisions from 1981 to 1996, political science professor Nancy Crowe found race, gender, and political party correlated with judges' voting behavior in sex discrimination cases. In particular, in nonunanimous cases a white male Republican judge voted for a sex discrimination plaintiff only 28% of the time, whereas, for example, an African American Democratic judge voted for a sex discrimination plaintiff 93% of the time. White female Republican judges voted for sex discrimination plaintiffs much more often than their white male counterparts—53% of the time. In addition, the implications of political affiliation were clear. White male Democratic judges voted for sex discrimination plaintiffs 76% of the time—a much higher percentage than the 28% ascribed to their Republican judicial counterparts.[35] The Crowe study shows a relationship between a judge's race, gender, and political affiliation and the outcomes of sex discrimination cases and clearly has implications for sexual harassment cases, a subset of the cases Crowe studied.

A more recent study, by Carol Kulik and her colleagues, revealed the relationship between a judge's personal characteristics and outcomes in hostile environment cases specifically. They found that younger judges and Democratic judges were more likely to find for plaintiffs even after controlling for the effects of the factual circumstances of the case.[36] This study and Crowe's reveal how crucial judicial selection is to the efficacy of these claims.

Unfortunately, Crowe's study does not stand alone in reflecting judicial bias toward sex discrimination and other civil rights claims. Racial and gender bias task forces likewise support the existence of judicial bias directed at employment discrimination cases. Task forces from the District of Columbia, the Eighth, Ninth, and Second Circuits particularly looked at employment discrimination cases and found judicial administration of those cases problematic.[37] Thus, employment discrimination plaintiffs (including sexual harassment plaintiffs) are confronting a variety of obstacles in successfully pursuing claims in court. One obstacle specifically addressed in this book is the inadequate nature of the legal standard.

A. *The Basics of the Sexual Harassment Claim*

Before discussing in depth the various elements of a sexual harassment claim, it is useful to give a brief overview for those who are unfamiliar with the nature of the legal standard. Sexual harassment claims come in two varieties: quid pro quo claims and hostile environment claims. A quid pro quo claim is cognizable when an employee's "submission to the unwelcome advances [of a supervisor] was an express or implied condition for receiving job benefits or her refusal to submit resulted in a tangible job detriment."[38] A hostile environment occurs "[w]hen the workplace is permeated with 'discriminatory intimidation, ridicule, and insult' . . . that is 'sufficiently severe or pervasive to alter the conditions of the victim's employment and create an abusive working environment.'"[39]

The elements of a hostile environment claim, although varying in particulars from circuit to circuit, generally include (1) an employee was subjected to unwelcome harassment;[40] (2) the harassment was based on the employee's sex; (3) the harassment was "sufficiently severe or pervasive" to alter a term, condition, or privilege of employment;[41] and (4) a way to impute liability to the employer.[42] Some courts have added a fifth element: that the plaintiff be a member of a protected class.[43] However, this element adds nothing to the claim, given that the plaintiff must already prove that she was harassed based on her sex. The fourth element, imputing liability to the employer, varies depending on whether the alleged harasser is a coworker or a supervisor. In the case of a coworker, the plaintiff must show that the employer knew or should have known of the harassment and did not take "prompt and effective remedial action."[44] In the case of a supervisor, the employer will be vicariously liable, subject to an affirmative defense created by the United States Supreme Court in 1998 in the *Faragher* and *Ellerth* cases, which are described in detail in chapter 5.

The elements of the hostile environment claim as well as the lower court interpretations of these elements are examined individually in each chapter of this book. These elements form the overall structure of the book. I look at each element of the claim, how the courts are interpreting it, review relevant social science studies, and suggest reforms based on social science.

B. Methodological Difficulties

This book relies heavily on social science in suggesting reforms to the legal standard, but it is important to understand some of the limitations of that use in the legal system. The fit between social scientific studies and legal rules is not perfect. This should not be surprising. Social scientists and lawyers have very different missions, but that does not mean that the work of social scientists is inapplicable. It means that one should be thoughtful about using social science in the legal system and acknowledge any limitations.

To begin with, there are several methodological problems involved in adopting into the court system social science explanations of harassment. Indeed, the use of social science in the courts is not without its detractors.[45] First, social science relies largely on correlational studies. For example, it cannot prove what "causes" sexual harassment; however, it can provide information as to whether there is a correlation between, for example, a supervisor's attitude toward sexual harassment and the rate at which sexual harassment occurs in the workplace. Although a correlation may not explain why sexual harassment occurs, the accumulation of many studies showing such an effect certainly suggests something about the environment in which sexual harassment is likely to occur.

Second, many studies rely on data generated by studying college students. This is understandable, given that sociology and psychology professors have easy access to such populations, but they may not be the best populations to use to study sexual harassment. Many college students have limited work experience and limited experience with harassment. Often, they have not faced a situation in which their ability to eat, house, and clothe themselves depend on their jobs. Thus, some studies show that working people define more behaviors as sexual harassment than do students. However, this is not universally true. Most studies show that younger people define sexual harassment more narrowly,[46] yet some studies have not found differences in definition between student and working populations.[47] Hence, additional research is needed to examine more fully this purported discrepancy. Because some studies support these differences, studies based on working populations are used where possible. It also is indicated where a study discussed involves undergraduates so that readers may consider this potential methodological difficulty in the course of reading this book.

One of the more reliable series of studies of working populations is that of the USMSPB.[48] The USMSPB studies survey federal government employees and therefore do not suffer from the possible deficiencies of undergraduate-based studies. The USMSPB study suffers from a bias problem (i.e., it asks subjects to assess whether certain behaviors are sexual harassment). However, it does provide a good look at a large working population. I rely on the USMSPB studies throughout this book.

In addition to the problems outlined above, there is a problem of terminology. What social scientists refer to as harassment may not be what the courts consider to be sexual harassment.[49] Indeed, there is little consensus even among social scientists about precisely which behaviors are encompassed within the term "sexual harassment." Thus, it is not always clear that the behaviors social scientists study would meet the courts' definition. For example, the courts rely on the severe or pervasive standard. There are very few studies of sexual harassment by social scientists that incorporate that standard. However, social scientists do seem to study behaviors that are sufficiently severe or, if repeated enough, would create hostile environments based on the pervasiveness of the behavior, which is consistent with the legal standard. Therefore, their findings do have relevance to sexual harassment as the courts assess it. In addition, if workers are interpreting behaviors as sexually harassing in situations in which the courts are not, this suggests that there may be a problem with the legal standard.

This book is not immune from this problem of terminology. I have chosen to use the term "sexual harassment" instead of "sex harassment" when referring to these behaviors. The reason for choosing the former term is because of its common usage by courts and social science researchers. Yet, behavior need not be "sexual" in nature to be actionable. Instead, derogatory acts and words that are directed at a person because of her sex can be actionable even though they have no sexual connotation. Law professor Vicki Schultz coined the term "sex harassment" to encompass more behaviors in the claim.[50] While her term is in some ways more accurate, for the sake of clarity, "sexual harassment" will be used throughout this book.

Acknowledging definitional problems, some researchers have made an effort to tailor their research for use in the legal system. Wiener et al. have developed what they term "social analytic jurisprudence"—an analysis that "combines empirical investigation of social and psychological reality with traditional legal analysis."[51] These scholars make an effort to understand legal doctrine and "pose research questions in a way that bears directly on the legal issues that give rise to the questions."[52] Their research has been helpful in the debate over the reasonable woman standard, discussed in chapter 2. As more social scientists focus on the issues arising in the courtrooms, more and more studies relevant to the development of sexual harassment law should become available, providing data that may be more directly relevant to legal assessments of what is harassment and how best to prevent it.

Another problem is that social scientists from diverse disciplines are studying harassment, which results in a variety of theories with differing methodologies. Also, social scientists have not been studying sexual harassment all that long—a little more than twenty years.[53] Some conclusions are still preliminary in nature.[54] This means that there is still a great deal more that needs to be done, including such fundamentals as refining and testing the definitions of sexual harassment.[55] Further, there is little research discussing the implications and interaction of sexual harassment with race, ethnicity, and socioeconomic status, as well as sexual harassment of men and same-sex harassment.[56] Such research is critical, given that courts have struggled in some cases involving harassment that incorporates both race and sex, often disaggregating different forms of harassment as distinct and separate phenomena.[57] Bearing these caveats in mind, it is clear that social science does increase understanding of sexual harassment in a manner that could be helpful to the courts.

C. Using Social Science in Sexual Harassment Cases

Even though the fit might not be perfect, social science still holds great promise for informing the legal standard. Judges and jurors could find it helpful in assessing various elements of the claim, including the assessment of what the "reasonable person" finds harassing,[58] understanding how targets respond to the harassment, as well as the extent to which employers can influence work environments to make sexual harassment less likely. In addition, policy makers, whether they be appellate courts, legislatures, or the EEOC itself, could find it helpful in setting new standards or in reforming old standards of sexual harassment.

Right now, many important assessments related to sexual harassment claims are left in the hands of individual trial judges or, in some cases, panels of appellate judges. Without using this research, judges are left to impose their own, sometimes stereotyped, views of what is and is not appropriate workplace behavior, their own interpretations of the target's behavior, and their own assessment of the extent of the employer's liability for workplace harassment.[59] This has led courts to make essentialist assumptions about the manner in which the "perfect" sexual harassment target should behave. As social science shows, many targets do not meet this idealized standard of "appropriate" feminine behavior.

Because it is often a judge who is making these decisions at the summary judgment or judgment as a matter of law stage of the process, social science information should help judges overcome the above stereotypes in deciding whether a case would be more properly decided by a jury. There is reason to be more concerned with a single judge's judgment than with that of a truly representative jury. The Juliano and Schwab study showed that plaintiffs are only barely more likely to win a jury trial (54.6%) than a bench trial (45.7%), but their study did not incorporate all unreported cases.[60] A recent study of California employment discrimination jury verdicts by law professor David Oppenheimer using Bureau of Justice Statistics, which includes all cases, suggests that jurors are much more sympathetic than judges are to employment discrimination plaintiffs.[61] In addition, many cases are won and lost at the pretrial motion stage (plaintiffs lose these motions 54.1% of the time).[62] Accordingly, plaintiffs are losing before judges not only at trial but also during pretrial motions. Both types of fact finders, however, could benefit from a fuller understanding of how sexual harassment functions in the workplace. Jurors could consider social science in their fact-finding function; judges could use it in formulating legal standards (including making evidentiary decisions) that better reflected the manner in which sexual harassment occurs in the workplace. This should lead to the law's becoming more effective in eliminating this form of workplace discrimination.

How, as a practical matter, would jurors use this information? It is possible for an expert psychologist or psychiatrist to submit expert testimony about, for example, how women react to harassment to help explain that a plaintiff's failure to use a reporting system was a reasonable one.[63] There are several problems with allowing jurors to use social science in this manner. First, it runs the risk of changing the role of the jury from that of fact finder to that of policy maker. Generally, it is the legislature and, in some instances, the courts that consider the policy implications of creating a new rule of law.[64] Second, jurors often have trouble discerning which expert information is well-grounded. Even though the Supreme Court's scientific-evidence decisions in *Daubert v. Merrell Dow Pharmaceuticals, Inc.* and its progeny[65] leave the initial gatekeeping function in the hands of the trial judge, this does not mean that juries will not have difficulty assessing the opinions of two competing experts. Rather than focusing on the validity of the experts' conclusions, jurors could be influenced by the persuasiveness of the particular expert.[66] This seems to be a problem with any proffer of expert testimony, but it is especially problematic in the social sciences, where issues of causation are difficult to assess and individual differences in people are not necessarily accounted for in the studies. Still, there is no doubt that such information could be helpful in assessing, for example, the reasonableness of the particular plaintiff's response to harassment. Further, if a judge does a proper *Daubert* assessment of the evidence, it should have enough reliability to be considered by the jury.[67]

Social science could well be useful to the jury, but perhaps Congress, state legislatures, and the courts are in the best position to make the changes suggested throughout this text. Congress and the courts both have more policy-making authority than do juries.[68] Because many of the changes I am suggesting would benefit from court-wide application, a definitive interpretation by the Supreme Court or amendment by Congress would be the best way to implement many of these suggestions. However, it is not unreasonable for a trial or appellate court to consider them as well in the appropriate case. The ability of courts to consider information that was not part of the record at trial on appeal is somewhat controversial, yet courts routinely do so.[69] Commentators have criticized the courts' use of social science evidence both generally and in specific contexts on a variety of grounds. Still it seems more reliable for the courts to consider this data than to do what they appear to do in the area of sexual harassment: make assumptions about the manner in which people behave. As one commentator put it, "[t]he formulation of law and policy, both in the judicial process and in the administrative process, obviously gains strength to the extent that information replaces guesswork or ignorance or intuition or general impressions."[70] Some information, even though imperfect, is better than guesswork. Right now, much of sexual harassment law is based on such guesswork. Unfortunately, all too often this results in a fixation on the behavior of the plaintiff, distracting the courts from the real issue at hand: the behavior of the harasser and its alteration of the workplace environment. The law in this manner, rather than stopping harassment, allows it to flourish.

1

Making a More Realistic Assessment of What Is Sufficiently Severe or Pervasive to Constitute Sexual Harassment

One of the most problematic elements of a sexual harassment claim is determining what behaviors actually reach a level that is actionable. Indeed, what constitutes sexual harassment at work in the public's mind, according to legal and journalistic pundits, is anything but clear. This confusion is supported by human resources professionals, who say that the biggest problem they have with sexual harassment is that employees do not know what behaviors constitute sexual harassment.[1] However, is the conduct that constitutes sexual harassment really so unclear? Are people really at such a loss, at such a lack of understanding, about what constitutes appropriate and inappropriate interpersonal workplace behavior? Or, is this simply a myth—a type of legal urban legend—that has very little basis in fact? Most important, if indeed a myth, is it one that the judiciary has been complicit in creating by rejecting plaintiffs' cases where reasonable people would believe there is sexually harassing conduct involved?

Given that the Supreme Court recognized the cause of action for sexual harassment eighteen years ago, one would expect to see some consensus from the lower courts about what behaviors constitute sexual harassment so that employers and workers would know what was appropriate in the workplace. However, other problems have made such a court-arrived-at consensus difficult to reach. Very few sexual harassment cases are actually litigated to a final jury verdict. Thus, workers and employers have not had as much guidance on what "reasonable people" (in the form of jurors) believe is harassing. This might leave a false sense that there is no evidence about what behaviors people deem harassing.

There is, in actuality, considerable evidence about what behaviors people believe constitute sexual harassment in the workplace. Further, with respect to a range of behaviors, there is agreement among workers about which behaviors they find harassing. This evidence comes from social scientists, who have been studying the types of behaviors people perceive as sexually harassing and the factors that influence this perception. These studies reveal some areas of ambiguity and confusion but also show a surprising amount of consensus—and consensus about behaviors that some courts have rejected as being actionable. The preliminary findings from this data suggest that the courts have not interpreted this element of the claim in a manner that is consistent with what many reasonable people believe is sexually harassing.

In this chapter, I make the case that courts should permit more cases to go to the jury to assess whether the harassment is severe or pervasive enough to alter the conditions of the plaintiff's employment. I begin by considering what current sexual harassment law is on this element and how lower courts are interpreting it. In doing so, my emphasis is on how some courts are applying the standard—not on the standard itself. I then review the work of social scientists regarding perceptions of what constitutes sexual harassment and discuss the implications of that research on the manner in which courts assess whether harassment reaches the "severe or pervasive" level set by the Supreme Court.

Unfortunately, the findings of social scientists are not necessarily adaptable wholesale into the legal standard. I consider the limitations on the use of social science in the courts in the particular context of the severe or pervasive standard. After considering these limitations, I show that social science provides a great deal of information about what people perceive as harassing. Indeed, it appears that judges often get these assessments about harassment wrong. Reasonable people believe that conduct is sexual harassment in situations that courts fail to recognize but, instead, summarily dispose of using dismissal for failure to state a claim, summary judgment, or judgment as a matter of law. Thus, the perceptions of judges on what constitutes harassment to the reasonable person do not always square with what reasonable people perceive as harassment.

A. The Severe or Pervasive Standard

1. Supreme Court Precedent

In its first decision involving a sexual harassment claim, the Supreme Court in *Meritor Savings Bank, FSB v. Vinson* stated that to be actionable, the behavior or behaviors in question must "be sufficiently severe or pervasive 'to alter the conditions of [the victim's] employment and create an abusive working environment.'"[2] Since this case, the lower courts and, to a certain extent, the Supreme Court itself have grappled to give meaning to this standard, landing all over the map in their results. Thus, some courts have held that a single incident, if sufficiently severe, can give rise to a claim; other courts have examined multiple incidents of behavior, including physical touching, and found it insufficiently severe or pervasive to be actionable.[3]

Along with setting this standard, the *Meritor* Court also held that a plaintiff need not face "tangible, economic barriers" in order to have an actionable claim.[4] The Supreme Court further clarified the standard in *Harris v. Forklift Systems, Inc.* The *Harris* Court was faced with a split in the circuit courts on whether the harassment had to seriously affect the psychological well-being of the plaintiff in order to be actionable. The Court explained that a Title VII violation occurs "[w]hen the workplace is permeated with 'discriminatory intimidation, ridicule, and insult . . . that is sufficiently severe or pervasive to alter the conditions of the victim's employment and create an abusive working environment.'"[5] In reiterating this standard, the Court rejected what it considered the two extreme approaches of making every utterance of an epithet actionable and of requiring that the conduct produce "tangible psychological injury."[6] In doing so, the Court adopted both an objective and subjective approach to the determination.

First, the conduct must be "severe or pervasive enough to create an objectively hostile or abusive work environment—an environment that a reasonable person would find hostile or abusive."[7] Several courts have reinterpreted this standard in light of the status of the target of harassment. For example, several lower courts have adopted a reasonable woman standard in the context of sexual harassment of a woman.[8] In addition to the objective standard, the *Harris* Court also held that the target must "subjectively perceive the environment to be abusive."[9] The Court reasoned that if the target does not subjectively find the environment abusive, the conduct does not alter the terms, conditions, or privileges of that person's employment enough to make it actionable under Title VII.

The Supreme Court did note that it was not creating a "mathematically precise test."[10] Instead, whether behavior amounts to sexual harassment should be viewed from the totality of the circumstances. In this regard, the Court specifically set out several factors for the lower courts to consider, including "the frequency of the discriminatory conduct; its severity; whether it is physically threatening or humiliating, or a mere offensive utterance; and whether it unreasonably interferes with an employee's work performance."[11] Noting that "no single factor is required," the Court did explain that the harassment's effect on the plaintiff's psychological well-being is relevant to whether the plaintiff found the environment abusive; however, harassment need not "seriously affect" the plaintiff's "psychological well-being" to be actionable.[12]

One of the Supreme Court's more recent cases on harassment law emphasized the contextual nature of the severe or pervasive determination. In *Oncale v. Sundowner Offshore Services, Inc.*, the Court explained:

[T]he objective severity of harassment should be judged from the perspective of a reasonable person in the plaintiff's position, considering "all the circumstances." In same-sex (as in all) harassment cases, that inquiry requires careful consideration of the social context in which particular behavior occurs and is experienced by the target. A professional football player's working environment is not severely or pervasively abusive, for example, if the coach smacks him the buttocks as he heads onto the field—even if the same behavior would reasonably be experienced as abusive by the coach's secretary (male or female) back at the office. The real social impact of workplace behavior often depends on a constellation of surrounding circumstances, expectations, and relationships which are not fully captured by a simple recitation of the words used or the physical acts performed.[13]

The context of the alleged harassment, according to the Court, is key to determining whether the incident qualifies as actionable harassment.

The *Oncale* Court also settled two questions that had been lingering in the area of harassment law. One issue—and the primary holding of the case—was whether same-sex harassment is cognizable under Title VII. The Court clearly held that it was.[14] Second, the Court resolved whether the alleged harassing behavior must be of a "sexual" nature. Some lower courts had held that harassment need not be of a "sexual nature" to constitute discrimination,[15] but this had not been a universal rule. Thus, if a supervisor treated women in a demeaning—but not necessarily sexual—manner but did not treat male subordinates the same way, it was unclear whether such behavior could constitute sexual harassment. The Court in *Oncale* explained that such behavior, often referred to as gender harassment, was actionable: "A trier of fact might reasonably find such discrimination, for example, if a female victim is harassed in such sex-specific and derogatory terms by another woman as to make it clear that the harasser is motivated by general hostility to the presence of women in the workplace."[16] Thus, harassment based on dislike of persons of the particular gender (though not sexual in nature) is actionable if it is sufficiently severe or pervasive to alter a term, condition, or privilege of employment.

Finally, in a recent per curiam decision, the Court in *Clark County School District v. Breeden* visited the issue of whether a single incident of relatively minor behavior could support the first element of a related Title VII claim, retaliation for complaining about harassment. In particular, the Court addressed whether the plaintiff reasonably could believe that the employer's conduct was unlawful, i.e., constituted sexual harassment. The case revolved around a discussion of job applicants' psychological evaluations. One applicant's report included a comment that the worker had once said to a coworker, "'I hear making love to you is like making love to the Grand Canyon.'" The plaintiff's supervisor read it aloud, commenting that he did not know what that meant. Another employee at the meeting said he would tell him later, and then both men laughed.[17] Based on this one incident and her complaint about it, the plaintiff alleged that her employer retaliated against her. The Court found her claim meritless, in part, because "no one could reasonably believe that the incident recounted above violated Title VII."[18] In reaching this conclusion, the Court reiterated its position that "simple teasing, offhand comments, and isolated incidents (unless extremely serious) will not amount to discriminatory changes in the 'terms and conditions of employment.'"[19] The Court appeared swayed in part by the routine nature of sexually explicit statements arising in the course of plaintiff's review of job applications and plaintiff's position that this did not bother her. The Court characterized the exchange between her supervisor and coworker "as at worst an 'isolated inciden[t]' that cannot remotely be considered 'extremely serious,'" as the Court's language in other cases regarding actionable single incidents requires.[20]

Given Supreme Court precedent and the nature of the single incident involved in *Breeden*, this result is hardly surprising, although there is irony in it. As shown in chapter 5, the Court has insisted that targets of harassment report harassing behaviors as quickly as possible so that the employer might correct the situation before it reaches the "severe or pervasive" level. Here, the plaintiff did just that. However, because she reported before the harassment reached an actionable level, the Court held her retaliation claim inadequate. She was penalized, essentially, for following the Court's earlier rulings. Also, this decision does not appear to undermine the position of lower courts that a single incident, if sufficiently severe, can give rise to a claim. This incident was simply too minor in the Court's opinion to even arguably reach that level. How the lower courts will interpret this case remains to be seen. However, the lower courts' interpretations of other Supreme Court precedents described above reveal some judicial skepticism directed toward these claims.

2. Lower Court Interpretations of the Standard

Because the vast majority of sexual harassment claims are resolved by lower federal courts, trends in their interpretation of the severe or pervasive element have a direct effect on a plaintiff's ability to succeed. Some courts appear very sympathetic to sexual harassment claims; some judges have been hostile toward the claims, resulting in dismissal on the pleadings, summary judgment, and judgment as a matter of law against plaintiffs in questionable cases. Indeed, the gender bias task forces revealed judicial hostility toward these claims and other "women's cases."[21] Disposition by a judge rather than a jury could well be significant in the vindication of employment rights; studies suggest that in job-related civil rights cases, plaintiffs fare better before juries than judges.[22]

Lower courts have taken the Supreme Court's pronouncements on the severity or pervasiveness standard and run with them—often to the detriment of seemingly meritorious claims. Part of this trend in the lower courts may be the result of dicta in Supreme Court precedent. Although Supreme Court decisions in this area appear friendly to plaintiffs, dicta within them suggest that the bar for what is actionable harassment might be high. As one commentator pointed out:

The Court [in *Oncale*] declared that Title VII does not prohibit "genuine but innocuous differences in ways men and women routinely interact with members of the same sex and of the opposite sex." . . . This approach is consistent with earlier rulings intended to protect employers from a barrage of claims by hypersensitive employees and from employees who believe that any workplace triviality that offends someone rises to the level of actionable harassment. "We have always regarded that requirement as crucial, and as sufficient to ensure that courts and juries do not mistake ordinary socializing in the workplace—such as male-on-male horseplay or intersexual flirtation—for discriminatory 'conditions of employment.'"[23]

As a result of these cases, incidents of harassment that are termed "innocuous" are not actionable. Some lower courts, as I describe below, have taken these bits of dicta and used them as a basis for summary disposition in some very close cases involving more than merely "innocuous" incidents.

Thematically, the lower courts are using several strategies to dispose of sexual harassment cases before and, in some cases, after they reach the jury. Vicki Schultz has already recounted difficulties in the lower courts for plaintiffs bringing gender harassment cases.[24] In addition, courts simply downplay the severity of the conduct in order to conclude that no reasonable person could find it sexually harassing. They also engage in what I call the "divide and conquer" approach, whereby rather than looking at the effects of all incidents as the "totality of the circumstances" standard requires, they break the incidents apart in a piecemeal fashion, essentially concluding that each individual instance is insufficient, while failing to consider the cumulative effect of all the incidents. Finally, they rely on faulty precedent. Subsequent courts will use one extremely close case to justify summary disposition in succeeding close cases in the same circuit, thereby expanding that case's reach. Sometimes courts use a combination of these strategies in an effort to dismiss cases. Examination of these cases reveals how, as a practical matter, some courts eliminate arguably meritorious cases or, at least, cases that should be left to the jury.

A. UNDERMINING THE SEVERITY OF THE HARASSMENT

One of the most common rhetorical strategies lower courts use to dispose of sexual harassment cases is simply to declare that no reasonable person could find the behavior sufficiently severe or pervasive. Courts do this in two ways. First, courts simply say that it does not meet the standard with little explanation or downplay the severity or frequency of the harassment. Second, courts set the bar of what is actionable harassment so high that few claimants could reach it. Perhaps it is easiest to understand this phenomenon by way of example.

In what was an obvious instance of downplaying the severity of the harassment, the court in *Hosey v. McDonald's Corp.* granted the employer's motion for summary judgment. In *Hosey* a female supervisor at a McDonald's restaurant made unwanted sexual advances toward a male employee whom she did not supervise. Specifically, she asked him out on numerous occasions and made offensive comments to him, including telling him "'she would like to know what it felt like to have me inside her.'"[25] She also touched him offensively on ten occasions, including grabbing his rear end and pinching him. The district court, with the Fourth Circuit affirming, found these incidents insufficiently severe or pervasive to be actionable.[26] The court explained that "[w]hile [plaintiff] may have thought such conduct improper, Title VII does not prohibit teenagers from asking each other out on dates."[27] This case, including the number of incidents, seems to be about more than teenagers asking each other out on dates. The plaintiff was subjected to repeated acts of a sexual nature, which included offensive touching. By reducing the incidents merely to "teenagers . . . asking each other out on dates," the court downplayed both the severity (the physical touching) and the pervasiveness (repetitive nature) of the behavior. This, in part, laid the foundation for summary judgment in this case.

Courts have granted summary judgment in several cases involving sexual touching. For example, in *Saidu-Kamara v. Parkway Corp.*, along with derogatory comments made to the plaintiff throughout her employment, an assistant manager at the plaintiff's place of employment also touched the plaintiff's breasts while making suggestive comments, offered her financial help if she would go out with him, offered to take her to a local hotel to have a "good time," as well as patted her buttocks and breast.[28] Acknowledging that the behavior was "loathsome and inappropriate," the court still granted summary judgment because four of the principal incidents occurred over an eighteen-month period. This led the court to dismiss them as "sporadic and isolated."[29] Other courts have likewise thrown out cases involving physical touching.[30]

EEOC v. Champion International Corp. provides another example of a situation in which the court downplayed the severity of the harassment as well as created a high bar of severity. The plaintiff, an African American woman, confronted a male coworker who was poking two female coworkers with a stick. When the alleged harasser saw the plaintiff observing this behavior, he shouted at her, "What the fuck are you looking at!" and allegedly told her he would make her job more difficult. He then shouted at her, "'Suck my dick, you black bitch,'" while dropping his pants and holding his penis (the "'Butram incident'").[31] In addition to this incident, another coworker told plaintiff that he wanted to hang plaintiff in a cornfield and that if she brought any "gang-member" friends to work, he would bury them in a cornfield. Finally, a fellow African American employee found a Ku Klux Klan card posted on the inside of a beam at the factory. The card was eventually shown to plaintiff by one of her African American coworkers.[32]

There was some factual discrepancy about the primary incident of harassment, but the court evaluated plaintiff's claim based on her account, which is appropriate at the summary judgment stage. Indeed, "[i]n moving for summary judgment, Champion contends that . . . even if the incidents Jackson asserts occurred as she alleged, they do not rise to a sufficient level to constitute harassment actionable under Title VII."[33] The court agreed with the defendant:

> In the present case, the only event or behavior the EEOC can point to as the basis of a sexually hostile work environment with regard to [plaintiff] Jackson is the Butram incident. Taking the evidence in the light most favorable to the EEOC, Butram's behavior was deplorable and even offensive, humiliating, and threatening to Jackson. It very well could have interfered with her work performance at the time. There is no evidence, however, from which this court can draw a reasonable inference that Butram's sexual harassment of Jackson was sufficiently severe or pervasive to alter the conditions of her employment and create an abusive working environment. This single incident, which was of very limited duration and included nothing but expressive behavior, with no follow-up or repeat, is simply not enough to violate Title VII as sexual harassment.[34]

The court here overlooked that a single incident, if sufficiently severe, can form the basis of a sex harassment claim. The court held similarly on the

claim of racial harassment, stating that even though the incidents involved (the derogatory statement and Ku Klux Klan incident) were "deplorable and even offensive to" plaintiff, the derogatory statement was a
single incident and the Ku Klux Klan card "does not by itself rise to
within anywhere near the same level of severity hypothesized" in another
case discussing racial harassment and Ku Klux Klan activity.[35]

Finally, the court did not see the link between the incidents. Being
called a "black bitch" is about more than sexual harassment. It has racial
harassment implications as well. By ignoring this link, the court was able
to separate the incidents, finding that neither constituted actionable harassment. In addition, the cumulative effect (pervasiveness) of the incidents was ignored. In setting the severity bar so high, the court also has
made it very difficult for plaintiffs in single-incident cases to get to the
jury.

Other courts have ignored the pervasiveness of the harassment, resulting in dismissal of the case. For example, in *Gregory v. Daly*, the Second
Circuit reversed the granting of a motion to dismiss by a trial court where
it was clear that the plaintiff had alleged sufficient facts under federal notice pleading standards to state a claim for sexual harassment. The Second Circuit described the disturbing allegations in this complaint:

> Daly made "demeaning comments about women." Later, Daly made
> further "demeaning comments of a sexual nature," engaged in "behav-
> ioral displays of a sexual nature, and made unwelcome physical contact
> . . . of a sexual nature" with Gregory [the plaintiff]. In particular, Daly
> asked Gregory if she knew what a "sexual perpetrator" was, explained
> "in graphic detail[ ]" how a rape may occur, told her "how easy it is to
> rape a woman," and "described sodomy and anal intercourse relating to
> boys in detail." Gregory further alleges that Daly repeatedly came into
> her office, closed the door, and stood uncomfortably close to her, despite
> her requests that he move away.[36]

The trial court characterized the complaint as containing nothing more
than accusations of "demeaning comments" that were insufficient to
reach the severe or pervasive standard required in sexual harassment
cases.[37] Again, the trial court downplayed the severity of the allegations
as well as ignored the repeated nature of the incidents. The Second Circuit reversed this decision, but all the parties incurred the expense of an
appeal in this case. In addition, the appellate court used resources on a

case that, as explained later in this chapter, social science suggests should have gone to the jury.

Sometimes the courts operate in the opposite direction, with the court of appeals reversing a case in which the trial court upheld a verdict in the plaintiff's favor. *Duncan v. General Motors Corp.* presents just such a case. In it, the plaintiff was propositioned by her supervisor, whom she rebuffed. He then became critical of her work. In addition, plaintiff was required to use her boss's computer, which had a screen saver of a naked woman on it. He also would unnecessarily touch her hand when she handed him the phone. Her boss also asked her to sketch a planter that was shaped like a man wearing a sombrero to qualify for a job as an illustrator. The planter had a hole in its front on which the man's pants were sketched such that the cactus the planter contained would protrude as would a penis. The supervisor also kept a pacifier shaped like a man's penis on his desk. He created a poster (along with another worker) portraying the plaintiff as the president of "the Man Hater's Club of America" and later asked her to type a draft of the tenets of the "He-Men Women Hater's Club." She complained to "anyone who would listen" about his behavior.[38]

The jury found for the plaintiff on her hostile environment claim, awarding her a significant amount of damages. The court of appeals reversed, explaining:

> The evidence presented at trial illustrates that Duncan was upset and embarrassed by the posting and was disturbed by Booth's advances and his boorish behavior; but as a matter of law, she has failed to show that these occurrences in the aggregate were so severe and extreme that a reasonable person would find that the terms or conditions of Duncan's employment had been altered. . . . Numerous cases have rejected hostile work environment claims premised upon facts equally or more egregious than the conduct at issue here.[39]

After citing a series of cases that evidence a "race to the bottom" in terms of inappropriate workplace conduct that was not found actionable, the court characterized the behavior here as "boorish, chauvinistic, and decidedly immature," but still insufficient to meet the objective standard for actionable hostile environment—in spite of what the jury found.[40]

In all of these cases, the courts saw factual circumstances that presented close cases on the severity or pervasiveness element and found a way to resolve them before they got to the jury or overturned a jury's verdict for the plaintiff. Although sometimes this strategy was short-lived due to appellate court correction, in all of them the courts made assumptions about what is or is not sexually harassing and concluded that some disturbing and often repeated behaviors were not.

B. THE DIVIDE AND CONQUER APPROACH

Courts also have looked at individual instances of harassment, concluding they were not sufficiently severe or pervasive enough without considering the "totality of the circumstances." In other words, they failed to consider the cumulative effect of the incidents. Some courts have recognized this as an improper strategy, given the totality of the circumstances standard,[41] but that recognition has not stopped many courts from using the strategy.

Saxton v. AT&T Co. provides an example. In this case, the Seventh Circuit held that the plaintiff failed to raise an issue of fact as to whether a reasonable person could find that her supervisor's conduct created a hostile environment. The facts as described by that court indicate two overt sexually related acts. First, plaintiff Saxton's supervisor requested to meet with her at a club after work to discuss problems with her work performance. He placed his hand on Saxton's thigh several times and rubbed his hand along her upper thigh. After they left the club, he pulled her into a doorway and kissed her. Plaintiff objected to these actions. He also put his hand on her leg in the car on the way home. On another occasion, they went to lunch to discuss work. He stopped at an arboretum to take a walk. He lurched at her from behind some bushes, as if to grab her. Once again, plaintiff rebuffed his advance. After these incidents, the supervisor's attitude toward plaintiff changed. "[H]e refused to speak with her, treated her in a condescending manner, and teased her about her romantic interest in a coworker. In addition, [the supervisor] seemed inaccessible and on several occasions canceled meetings that he had scheduled with [the plaintiff]."[42]

The court found that the actions of Saxton's supervisor were not sufficiently severe or pervasive to raise an issue of fact for purposes of summary judgment. According to the court, the plaintiff's showing failed on several grounds. First, as to the two incidents of "undoubtedly inappropriate" behavior detailed above, the court held that they "did not rise to the level of pervasive harassment as that term has been defined by this court."[43] As to her allegations of getting the "cold shoulder" from her boss, the court opined:

> Saxton has offered no evidence that Richardson's conduct was frequent or severe, that it interfered with her work, or that it otherwise created an abusive work environment. Thus, although it might be reasonable for us to assume that Richardson's inaccessibility, condescension, impatience, and teasing made Saxton's life at work subjectively unpleasant, the evidence fails to demonstrate that his behavior was not "merely offensive," but instead was "sufficiently severe or pervasive to alter the conditions of [her] employment and create an abusive working environment."[44]

The court further reasoned that even if there were questions of fact as to whether Saxton's work environment had become difficult, the evidence was insufficient to raise an issue of fact as to whether a reasonable person would have found the environment hostile.[45]

The court disaggregated the two sexually oriented incidents from the later cold shoulder treatment that the same supervisor directed at the plaintiff. Yet, these incidents clearly were part of the total harassing environment that she experienced. They were related in time and by perpetrator and arguably resulted from the two earlier incidents. The court did not consider that the two forms of harassment—both based on gender—when combined might rise to the actionable severe or pervasive level.

The courts in several of the cases discussed in the downplaying of harassment section, above, likewise engaged in the "divide and conquer" approach to evaluate the incidents of sexual harassment. For example, the court in *Champion*, while acknowledging that even though the incidents involved (the derogatory statement and Ku Klux Klan incident) were "deplorable and even offensive to" the plaintiff, concluded that the derogatory statement was a single incident and the Ku Klux Klan card "d[id] not by itself rise to within anywhere near the same level of severity hypothesized in *Daniels*"—another Seventh Circuit case that tried to envision an actionable single incident by way of the hypothetical.[46] Again, the court refused to look at the two incidents together and ignored repeated behavior (plaintiff's being called "bitch" and "black bitch") in determining whether a reasonable person in the plaintiff's position would feel harassed based on race and/or sex.

Finally, the court in *Champion*, as other courts have done, disaggregated types of harassment. For example, if a plaintiff is harassed based on sex (i.e., being female) and based on race (i.e., being Black), the courts have considered both these categories separately. The courts seem unwilling to acknowledge that harassment can occur based on two protected statuses at once, i.e., the sexual harassment of a Black woman. In *Champion*, there were incidents of sexual harassment that had racial implications (the Butram incident), as well as acts of racial harassment. The differing forms of harassment can combine into a joint form of harassment based on a combination of both statuses.[47]

C. BAD PRECEDENT LEADS TO BAD PRECEDENT

In an individual appellate circuit, it takes only one appellate court upholding the granting of summary judgment, a motion to dismiss, or judgment as a matter of law in a case that should go to the jury to spur a number of succeeding cases of equally questionable outcomes. Some of the cases discussed previously have become such cases. For example, *Saxton v. AT&T Co.* has been relied upon by several courts in the Seventh Circuit to support summary judgment.[48]

In a glaring example of poor use of precedent, the Sixth Circuit Court of Appeals affirmed the granting of summary judgment by the trial court in a close case relying on *Fleenor v. Hewitt Soap Co.* In *Fleenor*, the plaintiff was subjected to repeated unwanted sexual advances and harassment over a two-week period. The harassment included a coworker's exposing his genitals to the plaintiff, threats to force plaintiff to engage in oral sex, and, on one occasion, the same coworker "stuck a ruler up Plaintiff's buttocks."[49] The court upheld the trial court's dismissal of the complaint for failure to plead a basis for imputing liability to the employer. The court in *Gwen v. Regional Transit Authority* relied on *Fleenor* to grant summary judgment to the defendant employer based on the insufficient severity or pervasiveness of the harassment.

In *Gwen*, the plaintiff provided evidence that a coworker had exposed himself to the plaintiff twice, and, during one of these episodes, made "'rude and inappropriate comments'" to her.[50] When the plaintiff's husband complained of the conduct to the plaintiff's supervisor, the supervisor replied, "Sounds like something Earl [the harasser] would do."[51] In addition to the exposure incidents, the plaintiff also stated that the coworker had been harassing her for some time. The court did not consider these additional incidents because they were raised for the first time in her response to the employer's summary judgment motion. The court of appeals, like the trial court, did not believe that the repeated exposure incidents were sufficiently severe or pervasive to make it to the jury and upheld summary judgment. In doing so, the court relied heavily on *Fleenor*, stating, "The co-worker harassment in *Fleenor* was both more severe and more pervasive than that at issue here."[52] It cited no other case for its position in this regard. Yet, *Fleenor* was not resolved on the severity or pervasiveness element but, instead, on the plaintiff's failure to provide a basis to impute liability to the employer. This is simply gross misuse of inapposite precedent.

The above is not the only example of bad precedent leading to bad precedent in the Sixth Circuit. The controversial case *Rabidue v. Osceola* continues to be cited in that circuit in spite of its apparent overruling by the Supreme Court in *Harris v. Forklift Systems, Inc.*[53] In *Rabidue*, the Sixth Circuit held that a plaintiff must prove severe psychological damage resulting from sexual harassment in order for it to be actionable. The Supreme Court in *Harris* clearly rejected this, stating that a plaintiff need not have a nervous breakdown before sexual harassment will be actionable. Yet, courts continue to positively cite *Rabidue* for its analysis of whether conduct was sufficiently severe or pervasive to be actionable in spite of its apparently being overruled by *Harris*.[54]

These cases show, then, that some courts believe fairly severe or repeated behaviors are not harassment. In granting motions to dismiss, summary judgment, and judgment as a matter of law, these courts are making the assessment that there is no actionable claim based on the allegations or that no reasonable juror could find these behaviors harassing. Social science, however, paints a different picture of what reasonable people find harassing.

C. Social Science on What "Reasonable" People Perceive as Harassing

Social science research has great potential to inform the manner in which the courts define what is sufficiently severe or pervasive enough behavior to be actionable as sexual harassment. This element is frequently litigated in sexual harassment cases. A great deal of social science research has focused on what sorts of behaviors people perceive as sexual harassment. Because the Supreme Court has based this standard on the perspective of the "reasonable person," social science research provides useful information about what such a "reasonable person" might perceive as harassing. Unfortunately, many courts are making this assessment at a preliminary stage of the litigation based on the one person's—the judge's—notion of what is offensive, with sometimes problematic results for the vindication of important federal employment rights.

The severe or pervasive standard is based on an assessment of what is harassing to the "objective" reasonable person. This is necessarily based on community standards of appropriate behavior in the workplace.[55] By taking these cases away from the jury, judges are impeding development of a community standard. This can lead to confusion for both employers and workers. If employers and employees do not know what a jury would find sexually harassing, how are employers to assess harassment complaints and how are workers to avoid behaviors that may offend coworkers? Instead, all too often such decisions are left in the hands of a single federal trial judge, who, given his status, may not be in the best position to make that assessment. The demographics of the federal judiciary, in this regard, are telling. The majority of federal judges are wealthy male Republican appointees. Their ability to empathize with the common worker may be reasonably questioned.[56] The end result in these cases may well be that plaintiffs who have meritorious claims—judged by a true community standard—are being thrown out of court unnecessarily. It is to be hoped that social science data on what people believe is harassing will help judges not rush to judgment in these cases but, instead, convince them that the issue might well be one for the jury.

1. Problems with Using Social Science Data

There are several methodological and conceptual problems with using social science perception data as the baseline for what "reasonable people" believe is harassing. Some problems are products of the nature of the studies. Some are a result of trying to translate social science into a legal standard. However, even given the problems, the data is better than courts using their own notion of what is and is not appropriate workplace behavior.

Beginning with a conceptual problem, using a consensus-based approach may be inadequate because of gaps between perceptions and how harassment actually operates. For example, studies show that many women who are being harassed would not necessarily identify their situation as harassment.[57] Still, it may make sense to set the legal standard to protect other women who experience these behaviors as harassing by making them actionable even though not all women (or men, for that matter) would perceive them to be so. This implicates the underlying policies of Title VII and precisely what this legislation is intended to accomplish, which is discussed in more detail at the end of this chapter.

Several specific problems with these studies are worthy of note. First, as discussed in the introduction, many use undergraduate students as subjects. Such subjects may tend to downplay what is harassing based on their lack of experience in the workplace. I use the USMSPB's study throughout this chapter as an example of results from a working population. Yet, this study, as well, is not perfect. Second, there is a problem of terminology. Behaviors categorized as sexual harassment by social scientists may not be the same sorts of behaviors that the courts characterize as sexual harassment. Few studies use the legal standard for assessing whether the scenario or particular behavior involved constitutes sexual harassment. For example, subjects are not asked whether, looking at the totality of the circumstances, the behavior is sufficiently severe or pervasive to alter a term, condition, or privilege of employment. Thus, study subjects are often left to rely on their own personal definitions of sexual harassment rather than the standard that the Court has provided.[58]

Although some studies have looked at the impact of the severity of the harassment on perceptions, few have focused on the effect of repetition of behaviors on judgments about what constitutes harassment. Yet, pervasiveness (which results from repetition) is one of the key components of the legal standard. However, if less severe behaviors were repeated, they at least arguably would meet the "pervasive" standard used by the courts. Similarly, social science studies often do not provide detailed contexts in which harassing behaviors might occur. Studies that simply ask whether a particular behavior is or is not harassment suffer especially from this inadequacy. This is problematic because the Supreme Court has emphasized the context in which the alleged harassing behaviors occur is of particular importance in assessing whether the behavior meets the legal definition.

The Supreme Court's position in this regard is not unreasonable. A pat on the back from a fellow female coworker for a job well done is very different from a pat on the back from a male supervisor accompanied by a leer. The result is that researchers often have studied sexual harassment in a vacuum. Real sexual harassment fact patterns are often complex. Rather than giving study subjects developed factual scenarios that reflect this complexity, researchers often give two or three lines of description of the alleged harassment. The assessors are not given both sides of the story but, instead, a fact pattern that they must accept as "true." In addition, they are given the perspective of the "omniscient observer."[59] Thus, these assessments, far from incorporating the "totality of the circumstances" approach that the Court requires, end up being assessments of sexual harassment without context or viewpoint. A recent study by Gutek et al. sought to remedy these difficulties by providing full fact patterns using both "sides of the story."[60]

These studies also suffer from response bias. By asking subjects whether the conduct in question constitutes sexual harassment, subjects will bring to their answers any sort of bias they might have with regard to sexual harassment—whether they are supportive of the legal concept or not. This has led some researchers to avoid the term "sexual harassment," instead asking subjects to assess whether conduct was "sexual" in nature or was "appropriate."[61] Most, however, simply ask whether the behavior is harassing or constitutes sexual harassment. Hence, bias can play a part in these evaluations. Yet, this is the question jurors (and judges during bench trials and motion practice) are asked to answer in the legal system. So, in a sense, although bias might well play some part in that assessment during research studies, it also will play some part in jury decisions. Finally, jurors might assess a situation differently when holding someone legally liable (with the potential for money damages) than when they are evaluating behaviors in a research context where it will have no real effect. Although it would be difficult to determine the degree of difference, it seems fairly safe to assume that jurors will be more circumspect in judging whether behaviors are legally actionable sexual harassment when there is actual liability involved than would a research subject. Still, given the consistency in some of the results of these surveys, they do provide a rough estimate of what sorts of behaviors people believe to be harassing. And, they are certainly a better approximation of what reasonable people believe is harassing than the view of a single trial judge.

2. Studies of Perceptions

Although studies have looked at the effects of a variety of factors that influence perceptions of sexual harassment, some factors have surfaced consistently from study to study as having an impact on that assessment. Louise Fitzgerald and her colleagues identify three factors prevalent in psychological definitions of harassment that have an effect on perceptions: (1) stimulus factors, such as frequency of harassment, duration of harassment, and the intensity of the harassment; (2) contextual factors, such as organizational tolerance of sexual harassment and "permissive management norms"; and (3) individual factors, such as "victimizaton history, personal resources, attributions," victim attitude, and control.[62] The last two factors will be considered in other chapters of this book. Stimulus factors are the particular focus of this chapter because they reflect the types of behaviors that people perceive as harassing.

Social scientists also have assessed the impact of other factors on whether particular workplace behaviors are perceived as sexual harassment. Included in their studies have been such disparate factors as education level, personal experience with sexual harassment, sex-role identity, attitudes toward sexual harassment, sexual orientation, the marital status of the harasser and target, feminist ideology, race and ethnicity, as well as other individual factors.[63] Indeed, too many discrete factors have been studied to discuss them in detail in the context of this chapter. In addition, research on many of these factors is still ongoing and findings are preliminary. Therefore, I will not discuss these findings here.

Social scientists have developed several different categorical approaches to what types of behaviors potentially constitute sexual harassment.[64] James Gruber developed the Inventory of Sexual Harassment (ISH). The ISH encompasses three general categories of harassing behaviors, including verbal requests, verbal comments, and nonverbal displays.[65] Within each category, Gruber identified subcategories of behavior that varied in severity. Fitzgerald et al. developed a model based on increasing severity that roughly models the division between hostile environment and quid pro quo sexual harassment. Known as the Sexual Experiences Questionnaire, or SEQ, these categories were developed to test forms of male-on-female sexual harassment. The SEQ identifies three general categories of sexual harassment: "gender harassment (i.e., lewd comments and negative remarks about women), unwanted sexual attention (i.e., unwanted touching and pressure for dates), and sexual coercion (i.e., sexual bribery and threats)."[66] Yet, other researchers have divided sexual harassment into different categories. Tata used the categories developed early on by Till, who, like Fitzgerald et al., created categories based on severity. These categories include (1) "gender harassment, or generalized sexists remarks and behavior"; (2) "seductive behavior, or offensive but sanction-free sexual advances"; (3) "sexual bribery, or solicitation of sexual activity by promise of rewards"; (4) "sexual coercion, or solicitation of sexual activity by threat of punishment"; and (5) "sexual assault, or gross sexual imposition."[67] The SEQ appears to collapse Till's third, fourth, and fifth categories into one, which is sensible, given the widespread agreement on this category of sexual harassment.

The USMSPB specifically has studied what sorts of behaviors people find sexually harassing as well as the incidence and type of sexual harassment that occurs among federal employees. The USMSPB breaks down sexual harassment into six behaviors: (1) "uninvited letters, telephone calls, or materials of a sexual nature"; (2) "uninvited and deliberate touching, leaning over, cornering, or pinching"; (3) "uninvited sexually suggestive looks or gestures"; (4) "uninvited pressure for sexual favors"; (5) "uninvited pressure for dates"; and (6) "uninvited sexual teasing, jokes, remarks or questions."[68] One category that the USMSPB may not adequately address that social scientists have included in their constructs is behavior commonly known as "gender harassment," or negative behaviors directed at someone because of gender but that do not have any "sexual" connotation. An example would be a male supervisor who dislikes working with women might consistently refer to women who work for him in a derogatory fashion. Stockdale and Hope conducted a study to determine whether the USMSPB survey does encompass the three SEQ forms of sexual harassment described above. They included behaviors (3) and (6) as examples of gender harassment. Considering several different models, they found that the three general categories used in the SEQ were the best fitting model of those tested.[69] The finding led them to conclude that the SEQ may be a better instrument for assessing both gender harassment and unwanted sexual harassment.[70] In spite of the USMSPB's failure to include as many types of gender harassment as it might, it does appear to cover some behaviors that could be characterized as gender harassment.

For purposes of organizing my discussion, I roughly follow the lead of the SEQ and discuss perceptions from severe to less severe behaviors. I also rely heavily on the USMSPB study, because it uses a working population and encompasses categories of harassment that fit within the SEQ categories. To the extent other studies use differing categories, I will endeavor to fit them in as well as possible with the most applicable category. Once again, more research needs to be done to fine tune the categories of harassment. As a general matter, the more severe the behavior, the more likely people will perceive it to be sexual harassment. In examining these categories, it is surprising just how much consensus exists on what constitutes sexual harassment.

A. THE OBVIOUS: SEXUAL COERCION

With so much emphasis in the press and commentary on the lack of understanding about sexual harassment, it is interesting that a great deal of consensus exists that more serious types of behaviors are harassing. These more obvious forms of harassment include sexual bribery, sexual coercion, and sexual assault. Studies of both working populations and students overwhelmingly show that people agree that sexual propositions tied to a job threat or a job enhancement constitute sexual harassment.[71] Sexual bribery and coercion as well as propositions tied to a job threat or enhancement, if perpetrated by a supervisor, are consistent with the quid pro quo category of harassment, which the Court has held creates strict liability for the employer. Yet, the Court has attached strings even to this form of harassment, as I more fully explain below. Thus, even as to behaviors that nearly all agree are sexually harassing, an adjustment to the legal standard based on perception data is necessary.

B. PHYSICAL TOUCHING AND THREATS

In addition, agreement exists on other behaviors that do not fit within the quid pro quo category. People believe that physical touching of a sexual nature, such as touching a woman's breast, constitutes sexual harassment. Behaviors that are more imposing—for example, are physically threatening or involve threats or coercion—are generally considered harassing and consensus exists on these. Rape as well as physical assaults are considered sexual harassment.[72]

The USMSPB studies support this too. Federal employees likewise consider pressure for sexual favors sexual harassment. The statistics are startling: more than 90% of the 8,000-plus federal employees who responded to the latest survey agreed that such behavior would "definitely" or "probably" constitutes sexual harassment. In addition, more than 90% of men and women agreed that deliberate touching or cornering by a supervisor "definitely" or "probably" constitutes sexual harassment. Ninety-six percent of women and 89% of men also believed such conduct if perpetrated by a coworker was "definitely" or "probably" sexual harassment.[73] This is consistent with other studies that have found that behavior including physical touching was considered harassing.[74] Hence, it has become increasingly clear that behaviors that involve physical touching or intimidation are considered sexually harassing by the average worker. Yet, from the case law examined in this chapter, not all courts have agreed with this assessment.

C. *"Ambiguous" Behaviors*

Social scientists posit that there is less consensus on other "more ambiguous" behaviors, although what they consider "ambiguous" seems to vary greatly. Included within behaviors that social scientists have categorized as ambiguous are sexual remarks, gestures, sexist jokes, requests for dates, gender harassment, and other behaviors. Many studies support the seeming lack of consensus regarding whether these behaviors constitute harassment. Still, often well over half of those surveyed agree that these "less obvious" behaviors can be harassment as well. And, trends in current research suggest that an increasing number of workers believe even ambiguous behaviors constitute sexual harassment. In addition, research suggests that certain contextual factors may affect whether these less severe forms of behavior will be deemed harassing.

In a study of undergraduate students, Terpstra and Baker found that a clear majority (70%–80%) considered directed gestures, propositions not linked to employment, putting an arm around someone, remarks, and unwanted physical contact of a potentially sexual nature to be instances of sexual harassment.[75] Other studies show similar results. For example, in a study of potential sexually harassing humor in the workplace, Hemmasi and his colleagues found that men and women agreed on which types of jokes were most offensive.[76] Likewise, Solomon and Williams found in a study of working students and verbal messages, evaluations were "overwhelmingly determined by message explicitness."[77]

The USMSPB likewise has charted growing agreement among federal employees that more ambiguous behaviors are perceived as harassment. Beginning its studies in 1980, the USMSPB has charted a shift in what federal employees believe constitutes harassing behavior, with the definition broadening. The greatest increases have come in what men consider sexually harassing. For example, in the 1980 survey, only 47% of men believed that suggestive looks and gestures from a coworker were "definitely" or "probably" sexual harassment. As of 1994, 70% of men surveyed considered such behavior "definitely" or "probably" harassment. The lowest percentage of agreement was in male respondents' perceptions that sexual teasing, jokes, and remarks by coworkers. Only 64% of men indicated that they "definitely" or "probably" considered these behaviors sexual harassment, but that is still more than 50%. In many instances, close to or more than 90% of respondents agreed that the behaviors studied were "definitely" or "probably" sexual harassment.[78]

A couple of caveats about applying results from the USMSPB to the population as a whole must be mentioned. First, the federal government is a particularly aware employer with respect to discrimination. For example, 92% of the federal employees responding said they were aware of sexual harassment policies in place. In addition, 87% of supervisors and 77% of nonsupervisory employees had received sexual harassment training.[79] Finally, the questions are posed as to whether the subjects "definitely" or "probably" believed that the behavior in question was sexual harassment. "Probably" is a classic wiggle word that, as used in the study, could have led to a lack of certainty on the part of respondents answering in the affirmative, i.e., that behavior "probably" constituted sexual harassment. However, even responding that behavior "probably" constituted sexual harassment suggests that the behavior at issue would at least be questionable to respondents.

In spite of a fair degree of consensus among federal employees on behaviors that constitute harassment, there still was anecdotal concern about more ambiguous forms of harassment. Comments in focus groups exemplify typical employee concerns about what does and does not constitute sexual harassment and the need for more precise categories of appropriate and inappropriate behavior. People were concerned that behaviors, when taken out of context, would fit some category of harassment when, from the context, they were not.[80] The Supreme Court has made the context in which harassment occurs extremely important. Thus, to the extent that the USMSPB surveys have divorced context from its scenarios, it tells less about harassment than it could.

Social scientists have found that several factors affect whether ambiguous behaviors are deemed harassment. Included in these factors are the frequency, intensity, and duration of the harassment. Studies have found that whether the behavior is repeated can have an impact on whether people perceive it as harassing. In addition, people consider behaviors less severe if they are not "targeted," i.e., are not directed at a particular individual.[81] Likewise, the more severe a behavior is judged to be, the more likely a perceiver will consider it harassment.[82] Thus, contextual factors matter and appear consistent with the Supreme Court's totality of the circumstances standard.

In a study of undergraduates aimed at perceptions of more ambiguous behaviors, Hurt et al. assessed the effects of severity of behavior, frequency of behavior, target response, and general context of behavior on perceptions of what constitutes harassment. The ambiguous behaviors studied ranged from those that were clearly appropriate (asking for help with work) to clearly inappropriate (trying to kiss and touch a subordinate in the elevator). Interestingly, the frequency of the behavior affected judgments about whether it was harassment only when the behavior hit a certain level of severity. As the researchers explained, "[T]he behavior had to be at least moderately severe before frequency mattered in considering a situation to be sexual harassment."[83]

Other social scientists have found the repeated nature of the behavior to have an impact on whether it will be perceived as harassing. In a study of 196 undergraduate students, Thomann and Wiener found

> that as an accused harasser's request becomes more flagrant and more frequent, decision makers are increasingly likely to perceive the incident to be a sexual advance. . . . For instance, when there are multiple occurrences of the incident, individuals are more likely to view the behavior as harassment, attribute a greater degree of responsibility to the alleged perpetrator, and recommend more severe disciplinary sanctions.[84]

Thus, as the behavior escalates in severity and frequency, it is more likely to be perceived as harassment. Combining the severity of the behavior with its frequency begins to give a clearer picture of what people perceive as sexually harassing. In addition, it suggests that jurors will assess harassment in a manner similar to the legal standard: based on its severity and frequency. Instead, it is the courts that are not being faithful to the legal standard.

D. Reforming the Legal Standard

One fundamental problem with the use of reasonableness in assessing the offensiveness of sexually harassing behavior is who is this reasonable person? Indeed, social science suggests that such an objective standard may not be achievable in this context. I have assumed, through my discussion of the data, that if there is some sense among a significant number of American workers about whether a certain behavior constitutes sexual harassment, the courts should give this common perception effect. In doing so, the descriptive standard emerging from the data was aligned with a normative standard. Although employing a descriptive standard has facial appeal, it is far from obvious that the law should employ such a standard.

It may be that the law should be more aspirational than the "reasonable person's" perception—based on social science data—of what is harassment. Perhaps this perception does not mesh with actual target experiences or simply reinforces norms that are discriminatory toward women. Given that women have possessed and continue to possess less power in American society than men, this consensus-based approach runs the risk of perpetuating already discriminatory norms, which are male-based. Law professor Jane Dolkart has argued that for this reason as well as others, reasonableness should be abandoned as an element of the plaintiff's claim, and instead the courts should use an affirmative defense based on the contextualized reasonable victim.[85] This contextual analysis allows for the plaintiff's particular circumstances to be considered. The concept of reasonableness and the impact of gender on this assessment is discussed in more detail in chapter 2. This chapter is concerned with the social science concerning what behaviors are perceived as harassing, an issue that involves a different set of data.

What is relevant to the discussion here is how to set a reasonable person standard that makes sense, given that it is highly unlikely that the courts will abandon reasonableness altogether. Much depends on whether reasonableness is set by a doctrinal, normative, or descriptive standard. By "doctrinal," I mean setting the reasonable person standard by what society decides *must (or must not)* be considered harassment. By "normative," I mean setting the reasonable person standard by what society decides, for policy reasons, *should* be deemed actionable behavior. By "descriptive," I mean setting the standard based on the reality as it exists in the workplace: actual perceptions of working people about what they perceive to be harassment.

By focusing only on studies of harassment victims, the standard also could be based entirely on the subjective target's or reasonable victim's perspective. Commentators have suggested this approach,[86] but there is less information available about actual harassment victims at this point. The approach here is based on a descriptive account that is broader than what at least some courts consider harassing, i.e., it is based on what be-haviors people (not necessarily those who have experienced harassment) perceive as sexual harassment. Even though more research is needed on actual victim perceptions, preliminary studies suggest that targets of ha-rassment are not peculiarly hypersensitive to harassment scenarios.[87] The approach taken here may hold more appeal for the courts, which already have discredited targets' accounts somewhat by separating out the "ob-jective" from the "subjective" standard. In effect, the courts are taking the position that some targets—hypersensitive victims—might subjec-tively perceive behaviors as sexually harassing where reasonable people would disagree.

Another reason for using the descriptive approach discussed here is that the courts appear accepting of descriptive accounts. It's a fairly com-monsensible way to approach the issue, given that the Court has adopted a "reasonable person" standard. One way to figure out what reasonable people believe is to survey them and ask them. Indeed, adoption of the reasonable woman standard itself came from studies that were based on the manner in which harassing behavior is perceived by men and women and the differences in those perceptions. Thus, it should be a more com-fortable stretch for the courts to look at general perception data to arrive at what the "reasonable person" deems harassing. I admit to being prag-matic in my approach. Absent a sweeping reconceptualization of sexual harassment by the courts, small steps tend to provide the best hope of af-fecting actual results in real cases. Until more data is available on actual target perceptions, this provides the best approach for reform.

Even considering the perception data, one might well be concerned about the 1, 10, 30, or even 49 percent of people who disagree that the behaviors in question constitute harassment. Once again, much depends on how the legal standard should be set. In sexual harassment cases, as in most civil cases, a plaintiff need only prove her case by a preponderance of the evidence. The Supreme Court has instructed that this "simply re-quires the trier of fact 'to believe that the existence of a fact is more prob-able than its nonexistence before [he] may find in favor of the party who has the burden to persuade the [judge] of the fact's existence.'"[88] As a practical matter, some judges translate this into percentages; this means that the jury must believe that there is a greater possibility than 50% that the plaintiff has proven his or her case.[89] Translating that into what rea-sonable people believe, is it reasonable to assume that if greater than 50% of survey respondents consistently perceive a particular behavior as sexual harassment that the courts should determine it to be so? Not necessarily. Some hesitation in accepting this comes from the methodological limitations already mentioned regarding these data (i.e., lack of context, use of students, inherent bias in surveys). However, it should influence courts when considering whether summary disposition—either through a motion to dismiss, motion for summary judgment, or judgment as a matter of law—is appropriate in the particular case if it involves behaviors that social science surveys reveal most people perceive as harassing. If surveys indicate that a majority of people surveyed believe a particular behavior harassing, let the jury decide, given the context, whether it constitutes harassment in the particular case. Of course, the samples discussed above were not surveys of "most Americans." Indeed, they are limited by the populations studied. That's why the USMSPB studies are particularly helpful; the government surveyed federal employees nationwide and had a large number of survey respondents (8,000+).[90] Thus, it provides a pretty good litmus test of what behaviors people perceive as at least arguably harassing.

As for the 1, 10, 30, or even 49 percent who disagree, well, that's in the nature of any legal standard. There will always be those who do not believe the particular conduct is (or should be) actionable. Tort law suffers from similar problems with respect to the determination of negligence. People who do not believe such behaviors are harassing, i.e., "thicker"-skinned plaintiffs, will not sue if such behaviors are directed at them. Although this means that the occasional "clueless" harasser may cause his company to become liable for sexual harassment (given that he evaluates his behavior as nonharassing and therefore may engage in such conduct), the point of sexual harassment law is to allow women and men to work in a nondiscriminatory environment. Some individuals may create such an environment unwittingly, but the legal system need not accommodate their minority view over that of the majority who would recognize the behavior as harassing. Social science data can provide information that supports that majority position and helps substantiate the reactions of most workers as not those of the hypersensitive plaintiff but, instead, as those of the common "reasonable person." At least it should result in fewer dismissals before the case goes to the jury and more consistency in outcomes.

Certainly, it is better to use this social science data than what many courts are doing now. All too often the courts' accounts appear based upon the individual perceptions of trial judges instead of considering the empirical research described above.[91] Indeed, at present a decided gap exists between what judges consider to be harassment and what the "common person" who social scientists have studied considers to be harassment. Thus, although it might be preferable to have a standard that is actually based on what affects the "terms, conditions, and privileges of employment" from the target's perspective,[92] given the gap between common perceptions of what is harassment and what judges are doing in real cases, I would settle for (at least for the time being) setting the standard with reference to the body of empirical knowledge about how the common person perceives harassment. This level lowers the bar for actionable conduct in comparison to where many courts currently are placing that bar and should allow more plaintiffs to reach a jury.

1. The Reasonable Person versus Judges

The social science data described above shows a high degree of agreement that certain behaviors constitute harassment. Some courts have yet to acknowledge these behaviors as sexual harassment, and some have actually granted summary judgment in cases involving these behaviors. Obviously, severe behaviors—such as propositions tied to job detriments or enhancements—are considered by most subjects to be sexually harassing. Because these behaviors (at least where the threats are carried out) constitute quid pro quo harassment, the courts find defendants strictly liable in these cases. This is consistent with social science perception data. There is some discrepancy between courts and perception data in cases involving uncarried out threats, an issue discussed in more detail in chapter 5.

Law Professor Vicki Schultz has noted that, unlike courts, employers have in some instances included too many behaviors in their definitions of sexual harassment.[93] A more detailed discussion of the implications of social science for employers is provided in chapters 4 and 5, but it is worth noting here that employers may be prohibiting behaviors that are ambiguous.

Yet, courts confronted with moderate to ambiguous behaviors are neither ruling consistently nor necessarily fairly. In many instances, a high degree of agreement exists that these less severe behaviors (at least, if repeated) constitute harassment. For example, a large percentage of people believe sexual touching is sexually harassing. Yet, as described earlier, in some cases involving blatant sexual touching, the courts have granted summary judgment. Indeed, in their study of reported district court sexual harassment cases in the ten years since *Meritor*, Juliano and Schwab found that physical harassment of a sexual nature occurred in 41.8% of cases studied. Yet, the plaintiff won in only 59.4% of these cases.[94] Given that 64.9% of these cases involved pretrial motions on the substance of the claim, it is not unreasonable to assume that some physical harassment cases are being resolved in pretrial motions.[95] Even though it is difficult to ascertain how widespread the problem is, it certainly exists in the case law, as demonstrated in this chapter. Because of the common perceptions that sexualized touching (i.e., touching someone's breast, buttocks, and so on) is harassing, courts should let these cases go to the jury for "reasonable people" to make the final decision about context. Evidence about these perceptions could help both the judge and the jury make this assessment, giving a more accurate view of what reasonable people perceive.

Finally, there seems to be growing agreement even about more ambiguous behaviors. For example, the USMSPB shows many federal workers surveyed perceived that pressure for sexual favors and physical intimidation as sexually harassing. I described earlier cases involving both behaviors in which the court granted motions to dismiss or motions for summary judgment. In these cases, the jury did not even get a chance to hear the plaintiff's story. In addition, studies show that the repeated nature of the behavior has an impact on these perceptions. Yet, even in cases of repeated harassment, courts have been reluctant to allow these cases to go forward.

Not all cases must go to the jury. Certainly, the Supreme Court's position that every offhand comment does not equal harassment has some appeal. But the courts are dismissing some cases that are close under the supposition that the "reasonable person" would not deem the behaviors involved harassing. Social science, however, shows that the courts may have this common perception wrong. If the courts allow these cases to go to the jury, this will inform employers, employees, and the courts themselves about what sorts of behaviors are acceptable and not acceptable in the workplace. It also could lead to more consistency in judicial decision making on motions in these cases.

2. Another Approach Based on Effect

In addition to allowing cases involving these harassing behaviors to get to the jury, it may also help to focus the fact finder on the effect of the behavior on the target's ability to do his or her job rather than on some abstract notion of reasonableness. The legal standard under Title VII assumes a change in the conditions of the target's employment in order for the harassment to be actionable. Yet, few cases actually consider how the harasser's behaviors might alter the conditions of the target's employment.

Law professor Jane Dolkart has suggested a similar approach, which she calls an "individualized standard," that would include "evaluat[ing] the effect of the alleged harasser's conduct on the plaintiff's work environment."[96] Dolkart uses this along with a more contextually individualized approach to reasonableness that emphasizes the particular plaintiff's circumstances. Instead of a purely individualized approach, I am suggesting that the courts look to social science to develop what reasonable people perceive as harassing, leaving such cases to the jury when that information suggests that there is a dispute on this issue. Focusing the fact finders on the effects of the harassment might be particularly helpful for claims involving ambiguous forms of harassment because it directs them to the context in which the behavior occurs.

The legal standard requires that the harassment must be "sufficiently severe or pervasive 'to alter the conditions of [the target's] employment and create an abusive working environment.'"[97] From this perspective, the fundamental issue is whether the target is working under different conditions because of the harasser's or harassers' conduct. This approach allows the court to redirect its attention (in the case of a judge's decision on a motion or when the judge is the fact finder) or the jury's attention on what makes conduct actionable in the first place under Title VII: that it has an effect on a term, condition, or privilege of employment as set out in that statute. Relevant questions for the fact finder to consider become much more focused on the actions of the alleged harasser and the "objective" effects of the harasser's behavior using such a standard. For example, a juror would consider how the target's employment conditions were affected by the actions of the harasser. Would the target be reasonable in feeling differently about going to work each day? Do the actions of the harasser have implications for how the target performs his or her job? Such questions would direct fact finders to the effects of the behavior on actual working conditions.

This also should aid both jurors and courts in considering the context in which the behavior occurs. To determine whether a target's conditions of employment were altered, a jury necessarily would consider the context in which the behavior occurs. The conditions of a "reasonable person's" employment may not be affected by an offhand compliment from a coworker. On the other hand, they might well be affected by a proposition from one's direct supervisor. It also should help the courts deciding motions for summary judgment to avoid the trap of dividing up incidents so that the cumulative affect is not truly considered. Instead, the courts necessarily would evaluate how a target's employment was affected considering all the incidents of harassment. Although it is easy to consider each incident in a vacuum when the only determination is whether it is sufficiently severe or pervasive enough to meet some abstract standard (often seemingly contained uniquely within that judge's view of the working world), it is harder to disaggregate incidents when asked to consider whether a series of five incidents would alter the conditions of the target's employment the moment after the fifth incident. Perhaps this refocus on the effects on conditions of the target's employment along with social science perception data would better serve the courts as well as employers and employees in considering whether behaviors amount to actionable harassment.

2

The Reasonable
Woman Standard
Much Ado about Nothing?

Early studies regarding the common understanding of what constituted harassing behavior concentrated on dissimilar perceptions based on gender. Study after study showed that men and women differ in their perceptions of sexual harassment. Perhaps not surprisingly, many studies found that women believed more behaviors to be harassing than did men.[1] These studies were so compelling that they led to one of the first influences of social science on the legal standard in sexual harassment cases: the development and acceptance by some courts of the "reasonable woman" standard to assess sexual harassment of women.[2] Since the first court acknowledged this standard, debate has raged in both legal and social science circles about the efficacy of using such a standard to determine whether harassment is indeed sufficiently severe or pervasive to alter the conditions of employment.[3]

Use of the reasonable woman standard in the courts has facial appeal. Gender could have an impact on the assessment of what is harassment in several ways. For example, the gender of the target and harasser may have an impact on how people perceive harassment. Gender might also influence what behaviors are harassing to the target. However, the reasons for adoption of the reasonable woman standard revolve around perceptions of third parties. If assessments about whether behavior rises to the level of sexual harassment are to be made by third-party raters—in particular, either a judge or jurors—at least arguably the courts should acknowledge how the evaluator's gender plays a role in the assessments. In addition, because the "reasonable person" standard necessarily relies on the common perceptions of the average person, if women and men have differing perceptions, the legal standard should take this into account. Thus, studies involving differing perceptions of raters linked to gender are relevant to the objective component of the legal standard.

Although early studies showed a gap in perceptions between men and women concerning what is sexually harassing, questions remained even after the adoption of the reasonable woman standard by some courts of appeals. First, not all studies revealed a gender effect.[4] This led some to ask how big the "gender gap" is and whether it manifests itself for only some forms of sexual harassment. Further study revealed, for example, that the gender gap is more prevalent in cases of ambiguous behaviors.[5] Also, the size of the effect has become the focus of more recent study. If gender of rater accounts for only a small difference in the decision-making process of whether a behavior constitutes sexual harassment, should such an effect be given the status of a legal standard?

In this chapter, I begin by reviewing the reasoning that led some courts to adopt or ignore the reasonable woman standard. I then canvas social science data on differences in perception based on gender. Finally, I examine arguments for and against the reasonable woman standard in light of social science, including recent studies that attempt to ascertain whether the standard is working, i.e., studies that actually incorporate the "reasonable woman" standard as part of the assessment process. It may well be that the reasonable woman standard is doing more harm than good and that a different approach to the issue of "objective" reasonableness would provide better guidance.

A. The Legal Standard

The Supreme Court has yet to make a final pronouncement on the "reasonable woman" standard. Instead, the reasonable woman standard owes its genesis to the lower federal courts, although not all circuits have embraced it. This section begins by examining the courts' reasoning for adopting the standard and then addresses the reasons some courts have rejected it. Last, Supreme Court precedent is canvassed to see if it provides any clues to the Court's position on the standard.

The first courts recognizing target-specific standards provided little analysis for their decisions,[6] but this was not so for the Ninth Circuit. The court in *Ellison v. Brady* provided two main reasons for its adoption. First, it was concerned that using a reasonable person standard would "run the risk of reinforcing the prevailing level of discrimination";[7] harassers would continue their conduct because the particular behaviors were common (albeit discriminatory) in the workplace. The second reason was that this standard acknowledged differences in perspective between men and women. The court reasoned that women view sexual behavior differently than do men because they are the disproportionate targets of sexualized violence in this country. Thus, women find a wider range of behaviors disturbing than do men. While acknowledging that this would render some behaviors actionable where the harasser is unaware of the effects of his conduct, it explained that the reasonable woman standard would still protect employers from "idiosyncratic concerns of the rare hyper-sensitive employee."[8] As it concluded, "We adopt the perspective of a reasonable woman primarily because we believe that a sex-blind reasonable person standard tends to be male-biased and tends to systematically ignore the experiences of women."[9] The court contemplated that this might mean that employers will have to educate their employees on appropriate workplace behavior. Other circuits have adopted this standard (often relying on *Ellison*), but some have rejected it or remained on the fence as to its applicability.[10]

The Second Circuit explained its position in rejecting the perspective of the particular targeted group involved. In the context of racial harassment, in *Richardson v. New York State Department of Correctional Services*, the court instead adopted the perspective of a "'reasonable person who is the target of racially or ethnically oriented remarks.'"[11] The court reasoned:

> First, Title VII seeks to protect those that are the targets of such conduct, and it is their perspective, not that of bystanders or the speaker, that is pertinent. Second, this standard makes clear that triers of fact are not to determine whether some ethnic or gender groups are more thin-skinned than others. Such an inquiry would at best concern largely indeterminate and fluid matters varying according to location, time, and current events. It might also lead to evidence, argument, and deliberations regarding supposed group characteristics and to undesirable even ugly, jury and courtroom scenes.[12]

Although there may be some good reasons not to adopt the "reasonable woman" standard, the Second Circuit's reasoning seems faulty. First, the court misapprehends the nature of the inquiry. Focusing on the perspective of a person of the same gender, race, or ethnic background as the target does not incorporate the perspective of bystanders or the speaker. Instead, it refocuses the inquiry to the perspective of the person the *Richardson* court was most interested in: the target. Further, this is not a matter of determining whether one group is more thin-skinned than another. It is instead a way to acknowledge differences in perspective that are the result of differing life experiences. The court's concern that such a discussion could rely on "supposed characteristics" of groups is perhaps its best argument. After all, it is possible that people will default to stereotyped notions of harassment victims based on race, gender, or ethnicity, which would undermine equality. Indeed, it could well be that fact finders are doing this already.

Even though the lower federal courts have discussed the "reasonable woman" standard, the United States Supreme Court has avoided the issue. Some courts and commentators have argued that the Supreme Court in *Harris v. Forklift Sys., Inc.*, implicitly rejected the reasonable woman standard.[13] For example, the Eighth Circuit, which originally adopted the standard, subsequently retreated from it after *Harris*, stating that "[g]iven the Supreme Court's use of the 'reasonable person' standard [in *Harris*], we cannot find that the district court abused its discretion in using that standard in its jury instruction."[14] This may not be a fair reading of *Harris*. Although the *Harris* Court could have addressed the issue, it did not directly do so. Instead, the Court stated that to be actionable as a hostile environment, the workplace must be such that a "reasonable person would find [it] hostile or abusive."[15] This statement, made in the context of deciding whether harassment must "seriously affect [the employee's] psychological well-being" to be actionable, does not resolve the issue.

The Court's decision in *Oncale v. Sundowner*, a more recent Supreme Court pronouncement on sexual harassment law, is compatible with the reasonable woman standard. In that case, the Court explained that "the objective severity of harassment should be judged from the perspective of a reasonable person in the plaintiff's position, considering 'all the circumstances.'"[16] This decision is consistent with the use of the "reasonable woman" standard in that it expressly requires consideration of the "plaintiff's position," which at least arguably could include his or her gender. Therefore, it remains an open question at the Supreme Court level.

B. Social Science and the Reasonable Woman: The Impact of Gender on the Assessment of Harassment

1. Differences in Perceptions

Studies have shown a correlation between the gender of the perceiver and assessments of what behaviors are perceived as harassing. Early studies showed that men were more likely than women to enjoy some sexual interactions at work and have narrower definitions of what constitutes sexual harassment. As one group of researchers summed up:

> Men typically identify fewer behaviors as sexual harassment than do women. Sexual teasing, suggestive looks, sexual touching, and pressure for dates are all more likely to be called sexual harassment by women than by men. Although many men find sexual overtures at work to be flattering, most women find them to be insulting. Thus, a work environment that is offensive to women may seem acceptable to men.[17]

It appears, then, that men's perceptions differ from women's and that, in order to even the playing field, courts should account for women's perspectives in setting up the legal standard for sexual harassment directed at women. However, some data suggests the differences in perception may not be all that salient.

To begin with, not all studies have shown differences based on gender of rater.[18] In addition, there is consensus between men and women with respect to certain categories of behaviors. These categories are explored in detail in chapter 1, but a brief review here of several categories that have implications for differences in gender perception is useful in assessing the efficacy of the reasonable woman standard.

The most prominent area of agreement about what constitutes harassment is with respect to behaviors that are patently harassing. Studies do not find significant differences in male and female perceptions of more obvious forms of harassment, such as "sexual bribery, explicit propositions, and physical sexual advances."[19] Many of these studies were conducted using undergraduates, but the consensus appears in the latest United States Merit System Protection Board study as well.[20] There is consensus among men and women that such conduct constitutes harassment. Thus, the courts should have no problem sending these cases to the jury; at the very least the fact patterns are arguably sufficiently "severe or pervasive" to alter the conditions of employment and constitute action-able sexual harassment. In addition, both men and women perceive physical incidents of harassment as more harassing than nonphysical incidents of harassment.[21] Likewise, the courts should have little difficulty concluding such incidents are sexual harassment. Reasonable people—whether male or female—agree on this point.

However, early studies indicate differences between men and women in cases of more "ambiguous" behaviors. Frazier et al. explain:

> In general, male and female students were more likely to differ in their perceptions of more ambiguous or less severe behaviors, such as verbal harassment (e.g., coarse language, sexual remarks), sexual looks, flirting, and nonsexual touching. Although women were more likely than men to view these behaviors as harassing, the majority of both men and women did not define these behaviors as harassment.[22]

Some social science research supports the discrepancy between male and female perceptions of more ambiguous behavior but do so with a significant caveat: there are significant within-sex variations. Social science researchers explain that "[w]hen the harassment is mild or the event is ambiguous, neither sex exhibits any consensus. Some men and some women disagree, or they disagree in degree."[23] Other research supports the prevalence of within-sex variations.[24] Thus, it appears that in cases of ambiguous behaviors, most men and women would agree that there is no harassment, and there is some within-sex variation on this point. Usually, the types of ambiguous behaviors studied are not the types of behaviors held actionable by courts, at least standing alone or without frequent repetition.

In addition, even though studies have documented discrepancies between men and women in perceptions of harassment, there is some evidence that this is changing. For example, data from the USMSPB's 1987 study of sexual harassment in the federal workplace revealed that differences remained between men and women on the issue of whether "uninvited sexual teasing, jokes, remarks, or questions by a co-worker" "definitely" or "probably" constituted harassment. The difference was substantial: 64% of women versus 47% of men. Yet, that difference decreased by 1994. The USMSPB still found a difference then, but less of a difference: 77% of women considering it "definitely" or "probably" harassing and 64% of men as well.[25] And, the number of men and women who perceive such behaviors as harassing is increasing. Thus, there is reason to believe that consensus between men and women about even more ambiguous behaviors is growing. The same study revealed that this was the most prevalent form of harassing conduct.[26] The USMSPB study found that discrepancies between male and female respondents did not become palpable until more ambiguous behaviors were compared. Still, the majority of men and women believed that all six behaviors studied by the federal government would "probably" or "definitely" constitute sexual harassment if perpetrated by a coworker or supervisor.[27]

A recent set of five studies by Barbara Gutek and her colleagues also provides information about the gender gap in perceptions. These researchers sought to avoid some of the problems with earlier studies that did not provide detailed fact patterns. Using five sets of data (ranging from a short five-sentence description to a videotape of a mock trial), Gutek and her colleagues attempted to assess the effectiveness of using the "reasonable woman" standard in court. In all five studies, they "consistently found that [the] legal standard [i.e., reasonable woman or reasonable person] had very small effects on people's judgments of sexual harassment."[28] In addition, they examined gender effects. In three of the samples (the short scenario, the multimedia sample, and the adult scenario), gender was a predictor of the subject's assessment of hostile work environments. However, the effects were small. The greatest effect was generated by the student sample that read a short scenario. In that sample, sex accounted for 6% of the variance.[29] In all three samples, women's hostile environment ratings were higher than men's ratings.[30] Significantly, for some of the samples, there was apparently no gender effect. In particular, the videotrial study showed no gender effect in the assessment of whether there was a hostile environment.

Finally, two meta-analytic reviews of empirical research about gender differences merit discussion here. In the first, Jeremy Blumenthal gathered studies involving gender difference in perceptions of harassment in an attempt to determine whether the reasonable woman standard was justified. He was able to use 83 combined effect sizes from a total of 34,350 subjects.[31] He concluded that, "[b]ased on conventional interpretation of effect sizes[,] . . . [the effect of gender of the perceiver] can be characterized as slightly larger than a 'small' effect."[32] However, unlike the trend found in more recent USMSPB studies showing less gender differences, Blumenthal found a "tendency for more recent studies to yield larger gender differences."[33] He also considered the type of stimulus used to test the subject: mail or phone surveys, legal scenarios, laboratory studies, and videotapes. Interestingly, mail or phone surveys showed the least gender effect. Thus, Blumenthal opined that the increase in gender effect in more recent studies may be due to a methodological difference—fewer mail or phone surveys were used in those studies.[34] It is also noteworthy that the Blumenthal study included many studies of undergraduates. Thus, as mentioned in the introduction, it may well be that the results would be different if only working populations were studied.

In the second meta-analytic review, Rotundo and her colleagues looked at 62 studies that included 66 samples, with a total of 33,164 participants. The studies considered undoubtedly overlapped with studies considered by Blumenthal. Categorizing the behaviors studied into seven categories, ranging from impersonal derogatory attitudes to sexual coercion, Rotundo et al. found "that across a broad group of behaviors, the gender difference was small but in the predicted direction. The percentage of variance accounted for was small enough to suggest that other statistical artifacts or potential moderators were present."[35] Although gender differences were "larger for less extreme and more ambiguous behaviors" (such as derogatory attitudes and pressure for dates as opposed to sexual coercion), gender differences were small even for ambiguous categories (.33–.34 for derogatory attitudes and .28 for pressure for dates).[36] They concluded that there is "minimal support for the assumptions underlying the reasonable woman standard."[37]

Gutek and O'Connor believe other factors—aside from sex of rater— are more significant predictors of what behaviors people perceive as harassing. For example, they cite studies indicating that "[t]he severity of the incident, sex of the initiator, the age of the recipient, and the relative power of the initiator vis-à-vis the recipient have all been found to affect perceptions of sexual harassment."[38] They believe that the "perceptual gap" between men and women closes once certain circumstances are controlled, including "(1) the behavior in question, (2) the situation in which the behavior occurs, and (3) the characteristics of the study."[39] This led them to question the use of the reasonable woman standard in the courtroom.

Other researchers, likewise, have found factors other than biological sex to be better predictors of perceptions of sexual harassment. Hurt and her colleagues found in a study of undergraduates that the effects of gender in rating harassment dropped out once tolerance of rater to harassment was entered into the equation.[40] This led them to opine:

The current results indicating mediation of gender differences with tolerance levels are consistent with Gutek's findings and may help to explain them. If levels of tolerance are predicting perceptions of harassment, it seems reasonable to believe that not only are tolerance levels decreasing (i.e., we are becoming less tolerant of harassment), but also men and women are converging on attitudes toward harassment.[41]

Likewise, in a study of verbal messages, Solomon and Williams found the explicitness of the message accounted for 88% of the variance in perceptions of the message as harassing in a study of working students.[42] Although they found no main effect based on gender of rater, they did find an interaction between gender of rater and explicitness of message, which accounted for 8% of the variance in ratings. In particular, the women rated cases of highly explicit messages more sexually harassing than did the men.[43] When the explicitness was low, there was no significant effect based on gender.

A study by Baker and his colleagues supports this as well. Using both working and student populations, they found that "the sexual harassment perceptions of working women and working men were very similar. Both their relative ordering of the incidents' severity and their perceptions of each specific scenario indicated a high degree of agreement."[44] The authors of the study opine that their results may reflect a shift in societal understandings of sexual harassment, eventuating in more agreement between men and women.[45] Similarly, Henry and Meltzoff found no gender effects in perceptions of harassment in a study of 120 workers who were shown a videotape of relatively ambiguous coworker behavior.[46]

A recent study by Plater and Thomas suggests an interesting dichotomy in gender perceptions. In a study of university employees, they found no gender effects in the assessment of whether a supervisor had behaved inappropriately in an ambiguous scenario. However, they did find gender effects in the assessment of whether the hypothetical company should compensate the harassment target. Thus, many men may recognize harassment as improper but are reluctant to hold the company liable for such conduct. Plater and Thomas suggested that males in their sample may have identified more with the alleged harassing supervisor as well as the company and were therefore less likely to find compensation of the target appropriate.[47] However, men still agreed with women on the inappropriate nature of the behavior.

So what does all the data amount to? It indicates that the gap between men and women in perceptions and attitudes toward sexual harassment may be lessening. Perhaps there is increased understanding among men and women about what constitutes sexual harassment. It may well be that the media attention that both the Clarence Thomas/Anita Hill hearings and *Jones v. Clinton* received made more people aware of sexual harassment and increased understanding about this disturbing workplace phenomenon. There is some confusion in the studies about gender effects, but overall Gruber and his colleagues have summed up the findings well: "As a final note on the universality of sexual harassment, we would like to point out increasing evidence that suggests parallels between the experiences and perceptions of women *and* men. . . . [R]ecent studies have found that what men and women perceive as harassment, or as more or less severe harassment, is similar."[48] If perceptions of men and women are converging, the reasonable woman standard may be unnecessary or become so. In addition, it may well be that the standard is having little effect on the decision-making process even in courts in which it has been adopted.

2. The Effect of the Reasonable Woman Standard on Decision Making

Social scientists, at least at first, supported the use of the reasonable woman standard.[49] Psychology professor Richard Wiener details a great deal of such support. Aside from gender perception studies, Wiener explains that "[b]asic laboratory research has shown that men not only see women as more sexual but expect women to view men in a similar manner."[50] In addition, "[W]omen are more inclined to attribute the causes of sexual harassment to characteristics of the perpetrators and less to characteristics of the victim,"[51] whereas "men seem to be more likely than women to blame women for the harassment."[52] Wiener also explained that studies indicate that women use a broader definition of harassing behavior than do men.[53]

However, recent social science studies suggest that even in cases in which the reasonable woman standard is applied, it might not be causing a large or even measurable difference in outcomes. Although legal commentators have suggested that the reasonable woman standard should and does make a difference in case outcomes,[54] that assumption is not borne out by social science data. In a recent study of 1,904 individuals designed to assess the impact of the reasonable woman standard, Gutek et al. found that "[o]verall, the legal standard had very little impact on judgments, accounting for a maximum of 2% of the variance in respondents' assessment of hostile work environment sexual harassment."[55] The study included five substudies involving a variety of approaches to conveying the purported sexually harassing scenario. Using everything from a brief description of a sexual harassment scenario to an actual videotape of a fictional sexual harassment trial, the study's "findings suggest that people might not view a reasonable woman differently than a reasonable person, and thus the legal standard has little, if any, effect on judgments."[56] In particular, the legal standard had no effect on the assessment of the plaintiff's reasonableness: "Whether they were asked if plaintiff was a reasonable person or a reasonable woman, respondents considered her equally reasonable."[57]

The above assessment is consistent with the assessments in earlier, smaller studies on the impact of the legal standard. In their study of 199 undergraduate students, Wiener and his colleagues found that whether the "reasonable person" or "reasonable woman" standard was used in assessing the harassing incidents made no difference in that assessment. "Instead, [they] found . . . gender effects that were independent of legal standard, fact pattern (for the most part) and in-group identification."[58] Female students were simply more likely to find incidents harassing than were male students, regardless of the legal standard used. The scholars' research led them to question "the effectiveness of the reasonable woman standard to offset" the differences between perceptions of men and women.[59] This suggests that people, including jurors, will substitute their own subjective perceptions when faced with an ambiguous standard, such as reasonableness.

Likewise, Shoenfelt and her colleagues found no statistically significant differences when the standard was varied in a study of 162 undergraduates. As they put it, "[R]egardless of the standard, females made a determination of sexual harassment more frequently than males."[60] Theorizing that there might be a difference based on prior studies showing that women were better at taking the perspectives of others than men, they found no relationship between perspective taking and changing the decision on whether the scenario was sexual harassment.[61] Believing their study provides further support for the inefficacy of the reasonable woman standard, they argue that the debate on whether to use the standard or not is "moot."[62]

In addition, the Gutek et al. study found "modest" effects based on the gender of the assessor. Although "[c]ompared with men, women were more likely to find that the case constituted hostile work environment sexual harassment, to identify with the plaintiff, and to find her credible," there were no significant interactions between sex and the legal standard for these three outcomes.[63] The authors of the study are cautious in their conclusions; they believe it "premature to conclude that the reasonable woman standard does not or could not have an effect on sexual harassment determinations."[64]

Finally, the Juliano and Schwab study of reported sexual harassment cases suggests that the reasonable woman standard or, for that matter, the reasonable person standard, is not having much of an impact in the court system. In the cases they studied, only twenty-five had adopted the reasonable woman standard. Instead, they found that most district court cases—more than three-quarters—did not mention a reasonableness standard at all. Of the fewer than 25% that did, about 75% used the reasonable person standard.[65] Although they found "slightly higher" win rates for plaintiffs when the reasonable woman standard was used, the finding was not statistically significant because so few cases actually used it.[66]

C. Is the Reasonable Woman Standard Necessary?

The social science described above suggests that there is growing consensus between men and women about what behaviors constitute sexual harassment. To the extent that there are some differences in perception between men and women about some ambiguous behaviors, these differences may be decreasing. In addition, the gender of the perceiver appears to have a small effect on the decisions regarding whether a behavior is perceived as harassing. Gutek et al. found that gender accounted for, at most, 6% of the variance. Blumenthal likewise found that gender had slightly more than a "small effect."[67] Given the growing consensus between men and women, the small effect size, and its negligible effect on outcomes, it is time to reevaluate the efficacy of the standard. It is not my intent to rehash in detail the arguments for and against the standard. Indeed, whole books have been devoted to the subject.[68] Instead, I examine some of the common arguments for and against the standard and then look at what recent studies suggest about its usefulness.

The legal debate over the reasonable woman standard has involved several themes. One is typical of the double-edged sword encountered in establishing what often are characterized as "special" standards for women.[69] The argument is that if women truly have a different perspective, the legal system would be doing an injustice by continuing the "white male" status quo by using a "reasonable person" standard.[70] That standard will, necessarily, simply perpetuate male norms that do not speak to the experience of women in the workplace. On the other hand, a special standard smacks of paternalism, that women need special protection, reinforcing the stereotype that women are helpless or more fragile than men.[71] Others argue that it promotes essentialism, the existence of one prevailing female perspective.[72] This ignores the complexity of individual experiences, which can be influenced by not only gender but race, socioeconomic status, and so on. However, to give voice to the diversity of backgrounds that make up each individual in this context would lead to an entirely individualized standard that would be very difficult to predict.[73] Finally, still others have argued that the "reasonable woman" standard is a mere panacea and will do little, in the long run, to correct what it aims at: the dismantling of a system of male privilege that dominates the legal system and our society in general.[74]

Some commentators, while acknowledging the potential for paternalism, have been more pragmatic in their approach. To them, the reality is that women perceive situations differently. The law must reflect such differences when the target is a woman.[75] On the other hand, many commentators are concerned about how male judges and jurors will be able to assess situations from the perspective of this "reasonable woman."[76] How will male workers and employers know how to conform their behavior to what reasonable women believe is appropriate? What does this mean for jury selection?[77] How does this standard operate when a target has multiple perspectives, i.e., a black woman?[78]

Additional debate has centered on whether the "reasonable woman" standard has First Amendment implications. Does it chill speech in the workplace? The debate surrounding the First Amendment implications of sexual harassment law has taken on a life of its own[79]—a life that has not been particularly supported by the case law, which has almost uniformly ignored any purported First Amendment problems with the law.[80] In addition, studies show that the "pure" speech sexual harassment case is a rarity. In their study of reported sexual harassment cases from 1986 to 1996, Juliano and Schwab "found only three cases in which the plaintiff premised her entire complaint on sexual comments about women in general. They all lost."[81] Instead, the vast majority of cases (85%) involved at least some behavior directed at the plaintiff. In addition, Juliano and Schwab found allegations of posters or pinups (examples frequently used by those seeking to attack sexual harassment law using the First Amendment) in only 7% of the cases studied. Thus, scenarios that could even arguably be characterized as "pure speech" are few, and plaintiffs in these cases are generally unsuccessful on other grounds.

Psychologists at first supported the reasonable woman standard, but more recent studies have shown that it might not be all that effective, and therefore reasonably can be questioned. To the extent that differences persist in men's and women's perceptions with respect to what is sexual harassment, the reasonable woman standard does not appear to increase the sensitivity of men to women's position—at least without the help of an expert. The research to date suggests that the debate about the use of the reasonable woman standard is, in reality, much ado about nothing when it comes to outcomes.[82] Its value (or lack of thereof) as a symbol is another issue altogether.[83]

There is some evidence that male jurors in particular may benefit from expert testimony in these cases. Kovera and her colleagues did a study of mock jurors to determine whether expert testimony on gender stereotyping made a difference in jurors' perceptions of sexual harassment. Using 340 undergraduates and a scenario modeled after *Robinson v. Jacksonville Shipyards*, they found that using expert testimony significantly increased the number of men who found the defendant liable (from 31.3% of the sample without an expert to 60.3% for the sample with an expert). A similar effect was not found for women.[84] It also increased the number of men who rated the woman's workplace as hostile.[85] Gender effects were found as well, in that women were more likely to find the defendant liable than men. Thus, perhaps having an expert testify about gender stereotyping and related phenomena relevant to sexual harassment would be more effective than using the reasonable woman standard.

Symbolically, the reasonable woman standard is a double-edged sword. On the one hand, it acknowledges differences in perspective based on gender that persist (although perhaps are lessening). However, one should not ignore the downside—the potential that women will be essentialized as weaker, more sensitive, and more fragile than men in the workplace. Thus, it comes as no surprise that the judge who recognized the standard in *Ellison v. Brady* was a conservative Republican appointee.[86] The best result comes from changing the societal and workplace norms that render sexually harassing behavior acceptable workplace conduct. In this regard, studies show some hope of increased male sensitivity to and understanding of the issue and a converging of the attitudes of men and women. Increased public awareness through the Clarence Thomas/Anita Hill hearings and *Jones v. Clinton* may have been helpful in changing norms and raising awareness. Increased employer training (of the right sort) could be helpful as well.

Perhaps the real solution to the reasonableness debate is to not include reasonableness in the standard. Given that harassment must be sufficiently severe or pervasive to alter the conditions of employment, why must reasonableness come into play at all? The courts could use the perception data discussed in chapter 1 as the basis for these determinations instead. If the harassment meets the threshold levels set out in chapter 1, then the jury would be called upon to assess whether the behavior was actually sufficient to alter the conditions of the plaintiff's employment. This might be an easier determination for a jury to make than to try to envision what some abstract "reasonable person" might deem harassing. This would shift the focus back to the behavior of the perpetrator and how it altered the workplace environment and away from the reasonableness of the victim.[87] Although the justification for an objective reasonableness standard has been a desire to avoid employer liability to a "hypersensitive" employee, focus on perpetrator behavior will not result in liability if it does not reach the severe or pervasive level. Thus, minor comments or incidents will not be rendered actionable because they bother a hypersensitive employee.

Several courts have more or less taken this approach, with some good results. In *Davis v. United States Postal Service*, the Tenth Circuit, reviewing a trial court's decision to grant judgment as a matter of law after a jury's verdict in favor of the plaintiff, alluded to this focus. The defendant in that case argued that the plaintiff did not meet the objective and subjective components because she had remained on the job for a time subsequent to the harassment and performed well. In rejecting the suggestion that the plaintiff would have to quit her job to show that she found the environment hostile, the court explained, "'The criterion is not what a reasonable woman employee is capable of enduring, but whether the offensive acts alter the conditions of employment.'"[88] Thus, the court overturned the trial court's decision, holding that a reasonable jury could find for the plaintiff. In reaching this result, the court explained:

> Title VII does not presume that the reasonable employee is incapable of separating the deleterious effects of a hostile environment from the aspects of the job which she enjoys and finds fulfilling, and it is in part intended to provide her with means to put an end to the hostile or abusive behavior so she can continue in otherwise desirable employment.[89]

The Federal Circuit in *King v. Hillen* also emphasized the effects of the harasser's behavior on the conditions of the target's employment. In that case, the court was reviewing the termination of a federal employee accused of sexual harassment. In determining that the employee did commit acts that could constitute sexual harassment, the court emphasized both the context and the effects of the behavior on the target's working conditions. The court's emphasis on the effects of the behavior in its analysis resulted in its finding that the employee did commit acts of sexual harassment. The court explained, "It is the overall, composite effect on the terms, conditions, and privileges of employment that is the focus of the law, whose target is workplace discrimination."[90] This shift in focus was helpful to the fact finders in these cases, emphasizing the effect that the harasser's behavior had on the conditions of the target's employment. By lining up the fact finder's focus on the harassment's effect on the workplace environment as suggested in chapter 1, this might well provide the end to the reasonable woman debate.

3

The Conundrum
of "Unwelcome"
Sexual Harassment

When Anita Hill brought forward (reluctantly) her allegations of sexual harassment against then Supreme Court nominee Clarence Thomas, three questions were repeatedly asked by the public and by members of the Senate Judiciary Committee: (1) "Why did she not come forward earlier?"; (2) "How could she continue to work for him?"; and (3) "Why did she remain friendly with him?"[1] In other words, if Professor Hill was really disturbed by this behavior (or if it really happened at all), she would have done something more direct, more affirmative at the time the events took place. Underlying these questions is a presumption that Professor Hill must have done something to encourage this behavior or, at least, did not discourage it. She should have made clear to future Justice Thomas that his behavior was, as the Supreme Court has termed it, "unwelcome."[2]

A review of social science studies on women's responses to sexual harassment reveals that Professor Hill's reaction was typical of harassed women. But this common perception of the manner in which harassment targets *should* respond to such behavior reveals that there is an "idealized" victim out there, a chaste, demure woman who never engages in vulgar talk yet is strong enough to object (indeed, "resist") when confronted with acts of harassment. Legal commentators have noted (and derided) the similarity between unwelcomeness and long-abandoned concepts originating in rape law.[3] Some courts have bought into this myth of the perfect sexual harassment target, although others have understood it as at odds with the reality of working women's lives. Social science reveals that the latter courts have a more realistic view of the manner in which sexual harassment targets behave.

In its first case recognizing sexual harassment as a viable theory of discrimination under Title VII, the Supreme Court rejected the idea that if the plaintiff voluntarily—in that no one physically or otherwise forced her—engaged in a relationship with the harasser, the plaintiff could not proceed with her claim. The argument was that the target essentially had "consented" to the harassment. Apparently recognizing that relationships between, for example, a supervisor and his subordinate might appear (inaccurately) voluntary, the Supreme Court instead required that the plaintiff show only that the harassment was "unwelcome." Hence, whether she consented or not, the target could still bring a claim if the conduct was "unwelcome."[4]

Unsurprisingly, the unwelcomeness requirement has created controversy. On the one hand, those supporting the standard argue that it's often difficult to determine whether a person is encouraging or discouraging the behavior of the alleged harasser.[5] After all, don't many people meet future partners at work? On the other hand, the whole concept that sexual harassment could somehow be "welcome" is ludicrous.[6] Indeed, at least one court has acknowledged that "'welcome sexual harassment' is an oxymoron."[7] As discussed in chapter 1, given the level that harassment must reach in order to be actionable, the likelihood that any person would welcome such behavior seems slim. This has led critics to argue that the standard improperly focuses attention on the behavior of the target, rather than properly focusing on the harasser, who is the real wrongdoer.[8] The focus on the target discourages plaintiffs from bringing claims because in that way they avoid the intense and unfair scrutiny on their own behavior that such a lawsuit brings.[9]

Whatever the controversy looks like in theory, some lower courts have placed a significant burden on the harassment target not only to make clear harassment is unwelcome but also to report harassment. Although reporting harassment to the employer is relevant to whether the defendant can succeed in using the defense set out by the United States Supreme Court in the *Ellerth* and *Faragher* cases (discussed in more detail in chapter 5), courts also have found it relevant to unwelcomeness. In this context, courts question whether the target really felt the harassment unwelcome if she did not complain. Once again, social science studies can help inform both the debate surrounding this requirement as well as the standard itself. In spite of increased awareness of sexual harassment, there is little doubt that it is underreported.[10] In addition to being underreported, it appears that the most common response to harassing behavior is not for women to make clear to the harasser that the behavior is unwelcome but, instead, to ignore the behavior. Thus, this common response has implications for any standard that obligates targets to somehow show that the behavior is "unwelcome."

In this chapter, the current legal interpretations of the unwelcomeness standard at both the Supreme Court and lower federal court levels are examined. In addition, the unwelcomeness standard's interaction with the subjective component of the severe or pervasive standard set out in chapter 1 is discussed. From there, relevant social science research is detailed in an effort to determine the efficacy of current interpretations of the unwelcomeness standard. The implications of the findings of social science for the legal standard are explored. In the end, a solution to the conundrum of unwelcomeness is suggested that will make sexual harassment law more effective in preventing workplace harassment.

A. The Law of Unwelcomeness

The United States Supreme Court took the lead in establishing that, in order to be actionable, sexual harassment must be "unwelcome" to the target. In *Meritor Savings Bank v. Vinson*, the trial court held that the alleged voluntary nature of plaintiff Mechelle Vinson's relationship with her harasser negated any claim of discrimination. The Supreme Court disagreed, drawing a fine distinction: "[T]he fact that sex-related conduct was 'voluntary,' in the sense that the complainant was not forced to participate against her will, is not a defense to a sexual harassment suit brought under Title VII. The gravamen of any sexual harassment claim is that the alleged sexual advances were 'unwelcome.'"[11] This standard was developed in a case involving allegations of a consensual relationship; yet, the Court appears to have set a standard (as lower courts have assumed) that applies to all sexual harassment cases. While formulating the standard in this manner, the Court acknowledged that the issue of unwelcomeness "presents difficult problems of proof and turns largely on credibility determinations committed to the trier of fact."[12] Thus, unwelcomeness would not lend itself, for example, to summary disposition but instead would best be left to the fact finder.

The *Meritor* Court also explained that the unwelcomeness determination must be assessed by looking at the "totality of the circumstances." The court of appeals had held that "testimony about respondent's 'dress and personal fantasies' . . . 'had no place in the litigation.'"[13] The Supreme Court disagreed, stating that "[w]hile 'voluntariness' in the sense of consent is not a defense to such a claim, it does not follow that a complainant's sexually provocative speech or dress is irrelevant as a matter of law in determining whether he or she found particular sexual advances unwelcome."[14] Instead, the Court referred to the EEOC Guidelines to support its opinion that "the trier of fact must determine the existence of sexual harassment in light of 'the record as a whole' and 'the totality of circumstances, such as the nature of the sexual advances and the context in which the alleged incidents occurred.'"[15] Thus, although eschewing the voluntariness standard, the Court gave lower courts the green light to focus on the behavior of the target—her actions, her dress, and so on—in determining whether the harassment was unwelcome. In this respect, the analysis appears similar to that formerly used in rape cases, where the focus was on whether the target "asked for it."[16]

Since this case, the Federal Rules of Evidence have been amended to exclude some evidence that would arguably be admissible under *Meritor*.[17] Federal Rule of Evidence 412 extends rape shield laws to civil cases.[18] It establishes a presumption of inadmissability for evidence of a plaintiff's past sexual behavior or sexual predisposition.[19] An exception exists for civil cases if the evidence of "sexual behavior or sexual predisposition" is otherwise admissible under the rules and "its probative value substantially outweighs the danger of harm to any victim and of unfair prejudice to any party."[20] Thus, the presumption is that it is inadmissible. The advisory committee notes following the rule explicitly give as an example evidence of the target's "mode of dress, speech, or life-style" as being encompassed within the prohibition.[21] Accordingly, it appears that the drafters of this rule were aiming at the evidentiary portion of the Court's decision in *Meritor*.[22] The Supreme Court, however, has not discussed the interaction of Rule 412 with its statements in *Meritor*. This has left the lower courts in the position of making such determinations.

The advisory committee notes to Rule 412 suggest that the rule has applicability in discovery contexts as well. After mentioning that Rule 412 is an admissibility rule, the notes specifically state:

> In order not to undermine the rationale of Rule 412, however, courts should enter appropriate orders pursuant to Fed[eral] R[ule] [of] Civ[il] P[rocedure] 26(c) [governing discovery] to protect the victim against unwarranted inquiries and to ensure confidentiality. Courts

should presumptively issue protective orders barring discovery unless the party seeking discovery makes a showing that the evidence sought to be discovered would be relevant under the facts and theories of the particular case, and cannot be obtained through discovery. In an action for sexual harassment, for instance, some evidence of the alleged victim's sexual behavior and/or predisposition in the workplace may perhaps be relevant, non-work place [*sic*] conduct will usually be irrelevant.[23]

This has led lower courts to consider the policies underlying Rule 412 in resolving discovery disputes in sexual harassment cases.[24]

In addition to the unwelcomeness standard, the subjective component of the severe or pervasive element, as set out by the Court in *Harris v. Forklift Systems, Inc.*, forms another basis for courts' and litigants' exploration of the plaintiff's behavior. In *Harris* the Supreme Court explained that a plaintiff must show that she subjectively perceived the environment as hostile.[25] This element likewise focuses the fact finder on the target and at least arguably necessitates an inquiry into whether the plaintiff is the "type of person" who would find the behavior harassing. Because the subjective standard shares much of the same plaintiff focus as unwelcomeness, the lower courts sometimes have conflated the two inquiries for purposes of analysis.

1. Lower Court Interpretations of Unwelcomeness

The lower courts have addressed the issue of unwelcomeness in a variety of contexts, including in deciding discovery and evidentiary issues. In addition, the courts appear largely to have heeded the Supreme Court's statement that the issue of unwelcomeness is one best left to the trier of fact. Rather than leading to summary disposition, unwelcomeness more frequently appears to be raised after trial or as an evidentiary or discovery issue. However, occasionally a court will grant summary judgment because the plaintiff failed to show the conduct was unwelcome. In addition, permitting discovery on this issue might lead plaintiffs to drop or settle cases prematurely. Permitting evidence to be admitted at trial on this issue can prejudice and humiliate plaintiffs. It also can provide a basis for jurors to invoke the stereotype that women who are targets of gender-related aggression and hostility in the workplace somehow "ask for it."

If unwelcomeness poses such problems for plaintiffs, the underlying justification for it should be examined. The court in *Delaria v. American General Finance, Inc.*, explained, "[T]he rule that the sexual or sex-based behavior at work is unwelcome ensures consensual work place sex does not provide the basis for a civil action."[26] Certainly it is no accident that the *Meritor* Court developed the unwelcomeness standard in a case in which the plaintiff allegedly had sexual intercourse with her boss forty to fifty times. Although the *Meritor* Court eschewed voluntariness as the standard, the idea that consensual conduct will lead to a lawsuit remains salient and appears rooted in the stereotype of the "scorned woman" who retaliates against her former workplace paramour by alleging that their consensual relationship was not truly consensual but, instead, harassment. This does not describe the typical sexual harassment case, and therefore is a strange way to develop a rule that applies to all cases. The problem this standard has caused is evident in some of the decisions described below.

Thematically, cases involving issues of unwelcomeness fall into several general categories. First, there are cases in which evidence of unwelcomeness becomes confused (and the standards thereby conflated) with the subjective component of the "severe or pervasive" standard.[27] In other words, behavior of the target is seen as relevant to whether she subjectively found the behavior harassing (even though the behavior might meet the objective standard). Second, there are cases in which the courts find (either after trial or on a motion for summary judgment), that the plaintiff did not show that the behavior was unwelcome because she, too, engaged in purportedly similar behavior. Third, there are cases in which courts are critical of arguments that the plaintiff's actions provide evidence of her "welcoming" the harassment, and instead find that there is a significant difference between the plaintiff's behavior and that of her harasser(s). In these cases, the courts often emphasize the context in which the behaviors take place and are able to distinguish the plaintiff's behavior from that of her harasser(s). Fourth, there are cases in which targets respond more passively, by ignoring the behavior or otherwise not being obvious that it is unwelcome. Fifth, there are cases in which unwelcomeness is raised in discovery or as an evidentiary matter. Finally, there are the cases that the rule was created for: a seemingly consensual relationship that the plaintiff asserts was not welcome. Interestingly, quid pro quo cases, where this fact pattern is likely to occur, are the least frequently brought cases.[28]

A. INTERACTION BETWEEN UNWELCOMENESS AND THE SUBJECTIVE COMPONENT

It is understandable why courts would confuse unwelcomeness with the subjective component of the severe or pervasive standard. Determining whether the target subjectively believed the behavior was harassing can involve the same sorts of evidence as proving that the behavior was unwelcome. For example, any behavior or words of the target at the time of the harassing incidents might be indicative of her both finding (or not finding) the behavior subjectively harassing as well as providing indications that she found it unwelcome (or welcome). As the court in *Balletti v. Sun-Sentinel Co.* explained, "Whether a plaintiff subjectively perceived her work environment as abusive is closely related to another element of her claim—whether she welcomed the conduct."[29] In *Balletti*, the court actually considered both elements together. Like the subjective standard of severity, the unwelcomeness inquiry also is highly subjective and depends largely on the actions and intentions of the plaintiff.[30] Given the overlap between these two standards, perhaps the unwelcomeness requirement is unnecessary on this basis alone. However, the subjective component also may suffer from the same problem as unwelcomeness: encouraging stereotypical thinking (e.g., that the target "asked for it") on the part of the fact finder.

Van Jelgerhuis v. Mercury Finance Co. provides an example of a court's intermingling the two issues. In this case, the court analyzed unwelcomeness and the subjective component of the severe or pervasive standard in addressing the defendant's argument that the plaintiffs' "participation in bawdy office talk evidence[d] that they were not as subjectively offended by their environment as they now claim."[31] The court in that case rejected the defendant's proffered explanation of the plaintiffs' behavior, concluding that the harassment complained of, being from a supervisor, could reasonably be considered different—and be deemed more threatening—by the targets than interactions with coworkers. In this case the plaintiffs' on-the-job behavior did not cost them their lawsuit, but other courts view such behavior otherwise.

B. THE CASE OF THE ALLEGEDLY VULGAR PLAINTIFF

Case law examining unwelcomeness is replete with examples of courts using the female targets' behavior—for example, using vulgar language at work—as indicative of welcoming sexual harassment.[32] In effect, these courts seem to be ruling that certain plaintiffs do not deserve the courts' protection. Such plaintiffs are essentially, to the courts, unharassable. *Hocevar v. Purdue Frederick Co.*, a split decision by the Court of Appeals for the Eighth Circuit, provides a telling and recent example of the split in the courts' views on the unwelcomeness requirement. In this case, a majority of the court upheld the trial court's granting of summary judgment. Judge Beam, one of the judges who upheld summary judgment, explained that the plaintiff's use of vulgar language indicated that she did not find the language and behavior in her workplace "unwelcome."[33]

A bit of context is helpful in assessing the judges' decisions and reasoning in this case. According to dissenting (in part) Judge Lay, the plaintiff's supervisor

> distributed sexually explicit material at business meetings; he made threats of violence towards female staff members, he *constantly* referred to women as "bitches," "fucking bitches," and "fat fucking bitches," he told stories of animal violence . . . ; he told jokes at meetings that were derogatory towards women and contained profanity; he introduced a new employee as the "fucking new guy;" and claimed that new pharmaceutical products were so exciting a physician would be "creaming his jeans" to get them. Hocevar [the plaintiff] also testified that Amundsen exhausted a portion of a staff meeting by playing an audiotape of the Jerky Boys which contained obscene, vulgar, and sexually explicit "prank" phone calls to businesses on topics such as genital warts.[34]

The plaintiff also testified to other acts of harassment by other employees, including a regional manager's making sexual advances toward her, which entailed full-body contact with the plaintiff.[35] Thus, the case involved both verbal and physical harassment.

A majority of the court upheld granting summary judgment in the employer's favor. One of these judges, Judge Beam, rested his decision in part on the plaintiff's own use of the words "bitch" and "fuck" in the workplace. He remarked that:

> Hocevar's own testimony indicates that Amundsen's use of offensive language was not unwelcome because she used the offensive language herself. Hocevar admitted that she also called the new co-worker the "fucking new guy" at the business meeting. She further admitted that she used the words "bitch" and "fuck" around both Amundsen and other Purdue

employees. I find that these actions on the part of Hocevar vitiate her contention that the mere use of these words was unwelcome.[36]

Judge Beam appeared to misunderstand or, perhaps, was inappropriately selective in assessing the conduct involved in plaintiff's claim, which included more than "mere words." The plaintiff also testified to specific acts of harassment directed at her, as well as to the derogatory and gendered nature of the negative environment directed specifically at the women working for Purdue. He also ignored the context in which the statements were made and the pervasiveness of the harassment.

In disagreeing with Judge Beam's analysis in this regard, Judge Lay distinguished the behavior of the plaintiff from those of her supervisors and emphasized the context in which the words were used:

There is a world of difference between the use of the infrequent swear word in the workplace, not actionable when not directed to a specific gender, and direct words demeaning to women in general. While Hocevar's infrequent use of foul language may indeed, when presented to a jury, diminish her claim that the behavior of Amundsen and others was "unwelcome," it in no way bars her claim as a matter of law. I am unaware of any case that precludes a plaintiff from arguing that the employer's constant use of sexually charged language and off-color jokes is unwelcome merely because the plaintiff at times engaged in swearing. Such a reading is inconsistent with the mandate that courts consider the totality of the circumstances of a case. . . . Further, Judge Beam's analysis utterly fails to address Amundsen's threats of violence, his dissemination of sexually explicit material at meetings, his condonation of sexually graphic behavior at meetings, and the behavior of other Purdue managers, all apparently because Hocevar admitted to the infrequent use of foul language. The record further shows that Hocevar's swearing was not directed as a demeaning word of harassment at any person or group of people. It is one thing that an employee use vulgarity in his or her general communication; it is quite another when the vulgarity is directed at a specific social group who reasonably could find it to be demeaning to their own self-being.[37]

Thus, the context in which the language and behavior occurs was extremely important to Judge Lay. He pointed out that the plaintiff's reaction to the harassment also supported her assertion that it was unwelcome.

Likewise, there are court decisions, sometimes after trial, that turn on the unwelcome nature of the harassment and result in a victory for the defendant on that issue much in the manner of Judge Beam's in *Hocevar*. Often imbued with issues of socioeconomic status and notions of appropriate female behavior, these cases present problems for the federal courts.

In *Balletti v. Sun-Sentinel Co.*, the plaintiff endured a significant amount of harassing conduct, including having her male coworkers pretend to spit and/or urinate on her, drop cups of water on her, leave a dead cockroach at her work station, and leave a tube of vaginal cream at her work station. One coworker even exposed his genitals in her presence. In addition, she was called names, including "fucking cunt," "fucking bitch," and "diesel dike."[38] Finally, there were also sexually explicit cartoons, stories, and photographs posted on the company bulletin boards. One of these was altered to depict the plaintiff. Like other courts that have discussed unwelcomeness, the court acknowledged that the issue was "closely related" to the subjective component of the claim, and ultimately considered them together.[39] The plaintiff complained about some of the incidents, although she apparently did not want an investigation pursued. Eventually, the plaintiff was fired for refusing to take a drug test after a coworker allegedly observed her smoking marijuana in a restroom.[40]

The case became difficult for the court because of some conduct on the part of the plaintiff. The plaintiff referred to coworkers in vulgar terms; altered clippings and placed them on bulletin boards (apparently in a similar manner as those depicting her); attempted to pull down a coworker's pants; talked about using her vibrator; and "bragged to her male coworkers that she 'ate more pussy' than they did, and touted the pleasures of 'fist fucking.'"[41] The court noted that the plaintiff was a lesbian, although it is unclear how this factored into its decision. After trial, a United States magistrate held for the defendant, reasoning:

Against this backdrop, Balletti [the plaintiff] cannot be characterized as the victim of a sexually hostile environment. Her belated complaint about the harassment, her disapproval of the investigation, and her reported enjoyment of her job are not consistent with the conclusions she urges upon the Court. Moreover, she was among the most prevalent and graphic contributors to the pressroom environment. Her crude and vulgar behavior far exceeded any matters of which she complained. Her behavior here is fatal to her claims. These are not the actions of an employee who subjectively perceives her work environment to be abusive or of one who seeks to convey to her co-workers that their behaviors are unwelcome.[42]

In so reasoning, the court noted that the holding does not mean that a plaintiff's "mere participation" in some vulgar acts will bar her claim. However, it did note that the plaintiff must at some point make clear to her coworkers that the conduct is unwelcome.[43]

Interestingly, however, Kim Balletti did complain about the vulgar behavior directed at her. In particular, the vaginal cream incident (a tube of vaginal cream was left at her work station with a note on it stating that it was "Kim's kunt kreme") crossed a line for Balletti, and she mentioned it to a supervisor. However, the court dismissed this incident because Balletti told the supervisor that she did not want the complaint investigated and would not cooperate with the investigation. Although this might provide a defense for the employer in terms of imputing liability for the harassment under *Ellerth* and *Faragher*, it is hard to understand how Balletti's complaint did not evidence that she found the behavior—or at least this incident—unwelcome and subjectively harassing.

Other courts have held similarly when confronted with a plaintiff who actively participated in sexual banter and acts in the workplace. In most of these cases, the courts held for the defendant only after considering all the evidence during a bench trial.[44] In addition, several courts noted that the plaintiff's use of vulgar language or engaging in crude behavior would not have barred her claim if she had made it known at some point that the behavior was unwelcome.[45] Further, the work environments generally were permeated by sexual conduct and banter from many employees, including the plaintiff.[46] Thus, the harassing environment scenarios discussed in chapter 4 often form the backdrop for these cases. The split between the courts that consider such behavior dispositive of a plaintiff's sexual harassment claim and those that do not often turns on whether the court can understand the context in which the behavior occurs.

C. CONTEXTUAL COURTS AND PLAINTIFFS WHO PREVAIL

Some courts have considered the context in which the female target acted, as Judge Lay emphasized in *Hocevar*. In doing so, the courts have listened carefully to the targets' explanations for their actions. In addition, these courts have been skeptical about the nature of the gender dynamic in these workplaces as portrayed by the employer. *Carr v. Allison Gas Turbine Div., Gen. Motors Corp.* provides an example. In this case, the Seventh Circuit distinguished between foul language generally and conduct that was directed at the plaintiff. The plaintiff was the first woman to work at the particular shop at the General Motors plant involved in the case, and her male coworkers were unhappy about her presence. The harassment she endured included referring to her "on a daily basis" as a cunt, whore, and so on. Her coworkers played a variety of sex-related "pranks" on her, including one coworker's showing her his penis on two occasions.[47] In spite of the nature of the conduct, the trial judge found for the defendant employer because he viewed the harassing conduct as "invited."[48] The trial judge relied on the plaintiff's conduct, for example, that she used the "f word" and told dirty jokes. Likewise, a female welder who worked in close proximity to the plaintiff had assessed the plaintiff as vulgar and unladylike—"a tramp."[49]

The Seventh Circuit, via Judge Posner, assessed the situation differently:

Even if we ignore the question of why "unladylike" behavior should provoke not a vulgar response but a hostile, harassing response, and even if Carr's testimony that she talked and acted as she did in an effort to be "one of the boys" is (despite its plausibility) discounted, her words and conduct cannot be compared to those of the men and used to justify their conduct and exonerate their employer. . . . The asymmetry of positions must be considered. She was one woman; they were many men. Her use of terms like "fuck head" could not be deeply threatening, or her placing a hand on the thigh of one of her macho coworkers intimidating; and it was not she who brought the pornographic picture to the "anatomy lesson." We have trouble *imagining* a situation in which male factory workers sexually harass a lone woman *in self-defense* as it were; yet that at root is General Motors' characterization of what happened here. It is incredible on the admitted facts.[50]

Judge Posner emphasized the context in which the behavior occurred: a single woman, the first amidst all men in a traditional male occupation. The court also considered the nature of the harassment in reaching this conclusion. This was not a case of only foul language in the workplace; this involved a series of acts and language directed at the plaintiff. As Judge Posner put it, "Of course it was unwelcome."[51] The court in this case appears to imply that there is a certain level of behavior that no woman could possibly welcome. Thus, the few vulgar statements and actions of the plaintiff could not be viewed as somehow "welcoming" the harassment.

The court in *Swentek v. USAir, Inc.*, took a slightly different approach, although the outcome on this issue was similar. The plaintiff in this case also used foul language and engaged in sexually oriented pranks. The court distinguished between the defendant's arguments that the plaintiff was not the "type of person" who would find the behavior unwelcome and the plaintiff's actual response to the harasser's acts in determining whether the conduct was unwelcome. The court explained:

> It [the trial court] held that Swentek's own past conduct and use of foul language meant that Ludlam's comments were "not unwelcome" even though she told Ludlam to leave her alone. In his oral opinion, the judge determined, not that Swentek welcomed Ludlam's comments in particular, but that she was the kind of person who could not be offended by such comments and therefore welcomed them generally. We think this was error. Plaintiff's use of foul language or sexual innuendo in a consensual setting does not waive "her legal protections against unwelcome harassment." . . . The trial judge must determine whether plaintiff welcomed the particular conduct in question from the alleged harasser.[52]

The trial court in this case appeared to have conflated the unwelcomeness inquiry with the subjective standard for severe or pervasive harassment. In addition, the trial court stereotyped the plaintiff as an "unharassable woman" because she occasionally used vulgar language in other contexts in the workplace. Yet, the plaintiff told her harasser that his actions were unwelcome. The court of appeals looked at the difference in context between the plaintiff's voluntary statements and the circumstances under which she experienced the harassment. In addition, the conduct of the plaintiff in question was unknown to the harasser, so its relevance to unwelcomeness was questionable at best.

D. THE PASSIVE PLAINTIFF

Aside from courts that look at the vulgar words or behavior of the plaintiff in an effort to determine whether the particular behavior was welcome, there is an occasional court that assesses whether passive responses can signal unwelcomeness. For example, how does a court assess the inaction of a plaintiff in the face of harassment? Initially some courts held against passive plaintiffs,[53] but many courts show an understanding of the difficulties that sexual harassment poses for its targets. Complaining may be troublesome when the harassment comes from a supervisor or coworker who could make the target's job more difficult. Perhaps courts are more understanding of passive responses because such responses are consistent with stereotypes of appropriate female behavior. Unlike plaintiffs who fight back or attempt to fit in, these women are acting in a "more feminine" or demure fashion. However, even though courts are understanding in these cases, passive responses can hurt women's claims under the *Ellerth/Faragher* affirmative defense, which is discussed in more detail in chapter 5.

Chamberlin v. 101 Realty, Inc. provides an example. In this case, the plaintiff never verbally rejected the advances by her supervisor. Instead, the plaintiff withdrew her hands from the harasser's grasp, changed the subject, or left his presence. The court found this sufficient evidence of the unwelcome nature of the advances, especially given that they came from a supervisor. The court explained:

> [T]he perspective of the factfinder evaluating the welcomeness of sexual overtures in these circumstances must take account of the fact that the employee may reasonably perceive that her recourse to more emphatic means of communicating the unwelcomeness of the supervisor's sexual advances, as by registering a complaint, though normally advisable, may prompt the termination of her employment, especially when the sexual overtures are made by the owner of the firm. Thus, Chamberlin [the plaintiff] was confronted with an employment dilemma not unlike that in *Meritor*, where sexual advances were made by the employee's supervisor and company procedure mandated that employees bring their grievances to the attention of a supervisor.[54]

The plaintiff's more passive responses were sufficient, from the court's perspective, to support the trial court's judgment in the plaintiff's favor.

Other courts have held similarly when the plaintiff responded passively.[55] In *Wilburn v. Fleet Financial Group, Inc.*, the defendant moved for summary judgment, arguing that the conduct of the alleged harasser (once again, a supervisor) was welcome. The defendant's argument in this case was based largely on what the plaintiff did not do:

> (1) she never told [the harasser] to stop touching her; (2) she never told him to stop sending the voicemail messages; (3) she never told him to stop sending explicit e-mails; (4) she never complained about [the harasser] to any supervisor, manager, or Human Resources representative at Fleet [the defendant]; and (5) she herself had used sexually explicit language in conversations with co-workers at Fleet and outside of the office.[56]

Essentially, the defendant argued that the plaintiff needed to be more explicit that the behavior was unwelcome. In addition, during the plaintiff's psychological evaluation, she apparently admitted that she had had a dream that she and her supervisor were intimate and "innocently shared" that dream with him.[57] Plaintiff testified that she laughed off many of the alleged harasser's inappropriate comments and refused to answer his sexually explicit questions. She also told him that she was not interested in him. Plaintiff's coworkers heard her complain about the harasser's conduct.[58] There was no disagreement that the behavior directed at the plaintiff reached the severe or pervasive level.[59] Given the disagreement between the plaintiff's and defendant's versions of the facts, the court held an issue of fact existed as to unwelcomeness.[60]

The defendant also sought to rely on plaintiff's "consensual sexually explicit exchanges" with other people that came from her personal computer as evidence that she welcomed the alleged harasser's conduct. Thus, the defendant argued that she was not the "type of woman" who could be harassed. The court disagreed, explaining that "the fact that a plaintiff engages in sexualized conduct outside work cannot mean that uninvited sexual advances of her employer were not offensive as a matter of law."[61] Where a plaintiff responds passively, courts are not leaping to the conclusion that the plaintiff welcomed the harassment.

E. UNWELCOMENESS IN DISCOVERY
AND EVIDENTIARY CONTEXTS

Unwelcomeness also plays a part in cases during the discovery process as well as as an evidentiary matter either before (via a motion in limine)[62] or during trial. In many ways, this may be the area in which the unwelcomeness standard is most problematic. In the discovery context, defendants can use unwelcomeness to pry into the plaintiff's other relationships, conversations, and consensual sexual behavior. This practice can be invasive as well as embarrassing and can discourage plaintiffs from pursuing otherwise meritorious claims. Similarly, in the context of trial, a decision to admit such evidence could not only embarrass the plaintiff publicly but also skew the fact finder's opinion against her and her claim. Courts' approaches to these issues have varied greatly. Some have relied on Federal Rule of Evidence 412 to limit both discovery and admission of such evidence; others have permitted discovery and found ways around Rule 412.

The discovery issue sometimes turns on from whose perspective unwelcomeness is judged. So, for example, if the judge believes that the unwelcomeness inquiry is based on how the perpetrator was interpreting the target's behavior, only actions by the target that the perpetrator knew of are relevant to whether the harasser believed the target welcomed the behavior. The United States magistrate in *Howard v. Historic Tours of America* (a case brought under the District of Columbia Human Rights Act) took such a position, concluding that information about the plaintiffs' relationships with other employees was irrelevant to unwelcomeness because the perpetrator knew nothing of such relationships.[63] Thus, wholesale questioning of the plaintiffs about past relationships with coworkers was not permitted.

The reasoning of the court in the *Howard* case bears further examination. The defendants in that case argued that such information was relevant to whether or not the plaintiffs welcomed the actions of the harassers. The court made clear that it was not reasonable for a coworker to believe that a woman would welcome sexually harassing conduct from him because she engaged in a consensual relationship with another coworker:

[T]hat perception would be reasonable only if it fairly could be said that a man who learns of a woman's affair is justified in believing that she will be as willing to have a sexual relationship with him as she was to have one with her lover. While such a perception might have been justified, in men's minds, in Victorian England and Wharton's "Age of Innocence" in America, when men discriminated between the women they married and the women they slept with, it has nothing to do with America in 1997. While religious and other leaders condemn it, sexual behavior, outside of married life, between consenting adults is so common and so commonly accepted by the society, that it is absurd to think that any man in 1997 can be justified in believing that a woman who engaged in it is so degraded morally that she will welcome his sexual advances without protest.[64]

Thus, reasoned the court, the only argument such a man could make is that "because a woman took one co-worker as a lover he is justified in his belief that she will accept him and welcome his sexual advances. That, in all but his imagination, is *non sequitur*. That a woman has a relationship with one co-worker hardly justifies his conclusion that she will welcome all of his advances seeking the same kind of relationship."[65] In this decision, the court eschewed the "prim and proper" myth of the "perfect" sexual harassment victim. The court looked at the reality of the modern workplace and current sexual mores to conclude that the defendants' position on unwelcomeness was outdated.

The *Howard* court also emphasized the nature of the behaviors involved. It is one thing for a woman to welcome, for example, being asked out on a date. However, the behavior involved in *Howard* was

coarse, brutish and assaultive to the point of a violation of the criminal law. Defendants cannot seriously be contending that a woman who voluntarily has a sexual relationship with a co-worker thereby welcomes the kind of behavior to which these women claim to be subject. . . . [U]nless one is ready to concede the illogical—that a woman who engages in voluntary sexual behavior with one co-worker welcomes the sexual behavior of other co-workers no matter how reprehensible and gross it is.[66]

The court suggests that there is a certain level of behavior that no women could possibly welcome.

In addition, some courts have refused to admit evidence about the target's past sexual behavior or conversations under Rule 412 because of the possibility of prejudice to the plaintiff resulting from introduction of that evidence. In *B.K.B. v. Maui Police Dept.*, the court upheld sanctions against the defendant's attorney and declared a mistrial based on the introduction of evidence of discussions the target had with a coworker about her sexual fantasies. The court explained, "[C]ourts have held in similar cases that the probative value of evidence of a target's sexual sophistication or private sexual behavior with regard to the welcomeness of harassing behavior in the workplace does not substantially outweigh the prejudice to her."[67] The court in *Jaros v. Lodgenet Entertainment Corp.* refused to admit a variety of evidence under Rule 412, including the plaintiff's use of vulgar language, a comment by the plaintiff to a coworker about picking up men in a local bar, and descriptions of the plaintiff's allegedly provocative clothing. The court used a variety of arguments in reaching the decision that this evidence was inadmissible. It concluded that the vulgar language was inadmissible "because there was nothing to suggest that her obscene language invited sexual harassment."[68] The comment about picking up men at a local bar was inadmissible because the harasser knew nothing about that comment.[69] The court concluded that the evidence on the plaintiff's "tight fitting" clothes "if admitted at trial, would have carried the attendant danger that jurors would base their verdicts on their opinions about Jaros's [the plaintiff's] morality and not the law of sexual harassment."[70] Thus, the court ruled that all this evidence was inadmissible.

That these cases ultimately held the evidence inadmissible is of little comfort to plaintiffs who had to endure discovery on such sensitive and personal subjects as well as to plaintiffs who did not encounter such sympathetic courts and actually endured the admission of such information into evidence. In *Rodriguez-Hernandez v. Miranda-Velez*, the plaintiff was fired after complaining about sexual overtures from a representative of her employer's largest customer. Throughout the lawsuit, the defendant attempted to malign the plaintiff's character. The court explained, "Defendants continually sought to make an issue of plaintiff's sexual history. In the course of this litigation, defendants attempted to paint the plaintiff as sexually insatiable, as engaging in multiple affairs with married men, as a lesbian, and as suffering from a sexually transmitted disease."[71] Indeed, at one point during discovery, the defendant requested that the plaintiff submit to an AIDS test. The court denied the request and refused to admit much of the evidence, but the plaintiff nonetheless had to endure a significant amount of unnecessary harassment during the discovery process itself.[72]

Other plaintiffs have had information that is not only humiliating but also prejudicial admitted at trial with very little showing of relevancy. In *Fedio v. Circuit City Stores, Inc.*, the court admitted evidence of plaintiff's past "sexual" behavior at work, including that she said she would wear a certain ring until she "got laid" (and later she stopped wearing it); a statement she made about keeping a delivery person waiting at her door while she had sex; and her statements that she had been the victim of date rape prior to working with the defendant.[73] The court found the information "highly probative of how little Plaintiff would be offended by Lancer's alleged sexual innuendos when she in fact felt comfortable publicizing information regarding her sex life."[74] Here, the court held the information relevant to the subjective component of the severe or pervasive standard. Even as to this element, there is, as other courts have acknowledged, a significant difference between a plaintiff's statements to her friends in a consensual context and the statements and actions of supervisory employees. The court did not consider the context in which these statements were made in evaluating their relevance to the underlying claim.

The court in *Fedio* relied on one policy behind Federal Rule of Evidence 412—"shelter[ing] alleged victims" from embarrassment—yet ignored another policy behind the rule. The rule also was designed to avoid application of gender stereotypes that admittance of this evidence induces. The court stated that "[t]o allow an alleged victim to publicly flaunt her sexual behaviors and yet remain protected by Rule 412 would be tantamount to a complete disregard of the rule's purpose."[75] A court's allowing in evidence like this when it is not even clear the harassers were aware of it runs the very real risk of prejudicing the plaintiff's claim and branding her as the "type of woman" who is essentially unharassable.

The plaintiff in *Sanchez v. Zabihi* was required to answer an interrogatory that asked whether she had made any "personal, romantic, or sexual advances towards any co-worker"; had been the subject of any such advances; or had had a "personal, romantic, or sexual relationship" with a coworker.[76] Although the United States magistrate limited the discovery from a ten-year period as requested by the defendant to a three-year period, the plaintiff still endured intrusive discovery about personal information. The defendant's theory—that the plaintiff "was in fact the sexual aggressor"—could have been supported with evidence from the harasser and anyone who observed their interactions. To allow sweeping discovery into the plaintiff's consensual relationships is both embarrassing and feeds the stereotype of the "scorned woman" who alleges sexual harassment after a failed relationship (or failed attempts at a relationship) to retaliate against her purported paramour. It also suggests that because a woman welcomes a relationship with one coworker, she would welcome harassing behavior from others.

Thus, plaintiffs are not always able to avoid discovery and admission of private and often personal information during the course of a lawsuit. Some courts are more sympathetic to the plaintiffs' arguments than are others. However, instances in which plaintiffs are forced to submit to intrusive discovery as well as to endure such evidence aired in the public forum of the courtroom provide a basis to reconsider the use of this evidence as well as the efficacy of the unwelcomeness standard itself.

B. Social Science and Unwelcomeness

Social science findings are helpful to understanding the problem with the unwelcomeness requirement. To begin with, sexual harassment is an underreported workplace phenomenon. Social scientists have posited a variety of reasons for this that fall into two main categories: (1) sometimes targets fail to realize or comprehend their situations as involving sexual harassment, and (2) when they do identify an incident as harassment, the most common response is not to report it but to ignore it. The implications for an unwelcomeness standard are clear. If women do not identify a situation as sexually harassing, they may not respond to it in a manner that would signify its unwelcomeness. In addition, even in cases in which they do identify it as such, their strategies for coping with it do not most commonly involve confronting the harasser or taking some other overt and obvious action to signify that the behavior is unwelcome. This could lead fact finders (including judges) to misapprehend that the conduct was not offensive or was not unwelcome.

In addition, social scientists have posited that differences in perceptions of social cues between men and women may play a role in sexual harassment. I discussed in more detail the differences in perceptions of harassment based on gender of perceiver in chapter 2, but one aspect of this difference is particularly relevant to the unwelcomeness standard. There is some evidence that men and women interpret sociosexual interactions differently. Thus, a man may interpret a smile directed at him by a woman as inviting more intimate contact, whereas a woman meant her behavior to be only friendly.[77] Potentially, the alleged harasser may view behavior as welcomed when that was not the putative target's intent. A review of social science on miscues in the workplace helps in understanding whether sexual harassment results from simple misunderstandings between men and women.

When it comes to passive responses, it seems that most courts are ruling consistently with social science. However, once vulgar workplaces and more aggressive responses are added to the equation, the courts lack an understanding of how these workplaces operate. Often women in blue-collar environments do not behave in a stereotypical "ladylike" manner. This has led to confusion in some courts in making sense of the target's behavior. This is not all that surprising, given that relatively few federal judges have had any experience in such workplaces.

1. Responses to Harassment

Most studies indicate that women use a variety of passive responses to harassment. For example, the 1994 U.S. Merit Systems Protection Board study of federal employees reveals that the most frequent response of those who are harassed—44%—is to ignore it.[78] A substantial number did report more active approaches, including asking the harasser to stop (35%) and threatening to tell or actually telling others (10%). However, most used passive strategies, such as ignoring it (44%), avoiding the harasser (28%), making a joke of it (15%), or going along with the behavior (7%).[79] It's also noteworthy that although ignoring the behavior is the most frequent response according to this survey, there was a wide variety of responses to harassment. There does not appear to be a "one size fits all" response to harassment. In addition, some of these responses might not signify that the harassment was "unwelcome." For example, making a joke of it or going along with it could be viewed as "welcoming" the harassment, even though the target was sufficiently offended by the behavior to identify it as harassment. Indeed, making a joke of it or going along with harassment may well be an attempt by the target to fit in and downplay the effects of the harassment.

These responses are consistent with what social scientists have found about responses to harassment as well as the ramifications of those responses.[80] In his 1989 review of studies assessing women's responses to sexual harassment, James Gruber noted that avoidance responses to harassment were the most frequent responses, whereas confrontational strategies, such as confronting the harasser or reporting him, were the least frequent responses.[81] Gruber does note some difficulties with these studies.[82] Many targets tend to use coping strategies rather than being overt in expressing that they do not welcome the behavior. This may be a fairly wise strategy in many instances. It allows women and men seemingly to minimize the impact of harassment by ignoring it.[83] If some form of retaliation is possible—and studies do show that job loss and transfer to a different job are potential outcomes for employees sexually harassed[84]—the choice to simply ignore the behavior may well be a reasonable one.[85] However, even ignoring harassment or avoiding harassers has implications for the target of harassment. Avoiding harassers can interfere with and disrupt the target's job performance as the target rearranges his or her job duties to avoid the harasser.[86]

In addition, the severity of the harassment also may influence whether the target will make the behavior's unwelcomeness obvious. The U.S. Merit Systems Protection Board survey supports what other researchers have found regarding the severity of the harassment and the target's response. Generally, the more severe the harassment, the more assertive the target's response.[87] The USMSPB study shows that many do not report harassment because they do not think it serious enough.[88] This likewise suggests that the severity of harassment has an effect on reporting. Baker and his colleagues found in a study of student subjects that the severity of the harassment "had a relatively strong effect on the individuals' reactions."[89] Other studies suggest that a variety of variables, such as frequency of the offensive behavior, perceived offensiveness, and feminist ideology of the target, affect whether women will report harassment.[90]

A target's being overtly negative toward the harasser when he directs behavior toward her may help her show the behavior was unwelcome, but being more assertive may not help the target of harassment. In her analysis of data from the 1988 USMSPB study, Margaret Stockdale, while noting that the effects were "small," found that "the use of confrontive coping strategies tended to exacerbate negative consequences, especially for men."[91] She suggests that other strategies be developed to help targets of harassment both cope with and address harassment in the workplace.

2. Responding in Kind

There is less empirical social science evidence focusing specifically on targets responding defensively or in an effort to fit in, but there is evidence that some targets employ these strategies. As noted earlier, the USMSPB found that 35% of those who were harassed asked the perpetrator to stop.[92] Some women respond more emphatically than simply asking the harasser to stop, including using vulgar language or sometimes even threatening their harassers. Anecdotal evidence from both historians and sociologists suggests that this occurs specifically in blue-collar environments, although there are examples from white-collar environments as well.[93] These defensive strategies have confused the courts that envision women behaving and working in a "ladylike" fashion, and not responding to sexist behavior in kind. There has been little systematic attempt to study this type of response, but preliminary study suggests courts misapprehend what's happening in these cases.

Descriptions of sexual harassment in blue-collar work environments reveal the persistence of this problem in these workplaces.[94] Indeed, in an early study of 138 women autoworkers, Gruber and Bjorn found that 36% of the women reported experiencing sexual harassment, although other studies have suggested the incidence of harassment of women in nontraditional jobs is as high as 75%.[95] The most common responses included ignoring or responding mildly to harassment; however, 14.9% verbally attacked the harasser, and 6.9% physically attacked the harasser.[96]

Some sources likewise document instances in which sexually harassed women fought back. Yet, the case law suggests that such efforts would have cost them in the courtroom had they sued. For example, Eisenberg details an account of three women who were eating lunch in one of their cars when a male coworker urinated on the car. When they went to their supervisor to complain, the coworker denied that he did it. When one of the woman responded, "Oh, bullshit, you did this," the supervisor responded, "If you talk like that, you don't deserve to be treated like a lady."[97] When it became clear that the supervisor would not help, the woman who complained ultimately took out a Swiss army knife and threatened to slash the coworker's car tires if he did not apologize. He apologized, and she carried her point. The woman who detailed the story found the message clear: "Talk like a lady if you expect to be treated like one."[98] It is interesting how the attitude of the supervisor parallels that of some courts. In addition, the woman's reliance on self-help in the face of supervisor inaction may provide one of the answers as to why women engage in similar acts in response to harassment.

In a study of women miners, sociologist Suzanne Tallichet recounted the response of one woman to a rumor her foreman started that she had performed oral sex on him. She confronted the foreman in front of her male coworkers, stating, "'When did I suck your goddamned dick down the jackline?'"[99] When he responded that he did not know what she was speaking about, she responded, "'You're a goddamned liar. You told everyone of them and you didn't think that they'd find out.'"[100] The female miner's relationship with her coworkers had suffered because of the rumor, leading her to the confrontation.

Another interesting facet of Tallichet's study was the women miners' recognition that they crossed certain gender-related behavior lines at their own peril. One of those lines was using conduct or vulgar language similar to that of the men. "[T]hey'll treat you how they see you act," was the comment of one woman miner.[101] Both Tallichet and Yount, who also studied female miners, found that some women checked both their language and behavior.[102] The women believed that they had a moral obligation to themselves and to other women miners to avoid promiscuous behavior. Women who went further, making it clear that they were there to work and would not engage in romances with coworkers, were questioned about their sexual orientation and stereotyped as lesbians. Although some women miners appeared to try to curb their own banter, Yount's study of coal miners indicated that banter was used by male miners to fit in.[103]

Other accounts of confrontational strategies by women in blue-collar positions reflect that such efforts would often backfire on women, leading to more harassment, including cold-shoulder treatment.[104] Other women flirted to fit in, to obtain help on the job, or to receive easier assignments, although in the long run flirting ended up being an ineffective strategy that often led to more harassment and fewer work opportunities.[105] From Yount's account, one of the more successful strategies used by women miners was acting like "tomboys." These women attempted to fit in by emphasizing their interest and enthusiasm for the work. They also joined in pranks and practical jokes, including participating in witty comebacks. In addition, these women avoided behaviors associated with women, including wearing makeup and styling their hair.[106] In effect, these women came close to becoming "one of the boys."[107] This, however, was not without its risks as well. As Yount explained, if a tomboy met the level of vulgarity that her male coworkers used, she ran a greater risk of encountering sexual harassment that distressed her. Instead of evaluating these women as coal miners, they were once again evaluated as women.[108]

Similarly, sociologist Mary Lindenstein Walshok described a situation in which a woman physically hit a man who grabbed her breasts in a blue-collar workplace.[109] She theorized about why sexual harassment occurs in these workplaces and, in particular, the role that common backgrounds and understandings played in the dynamic that led to harassment. She opined that the lack of "common signs or anchors" resulted in invocations of "conventional sexual scripts"—essentially stereotypes—to govern male-female interactions.[110] She also contemplated how this might work in a blue-collar setting in particular:

> Given that most men, and blue-collar men in particular, have had much less opportunity to see and define women in multidimensional or varied roles, women who can define themselves or present themselves in terms that are familiar to the men help take the pressure off. This does not mean the women have to come across masculine. It does mean that the interests, values, and experiences that provide a common basis for interaction between blue-collar men have to be shared in some way by the new women. In order to cut it, you have to go with the norms of the dominant group.[111]

Under Walshok's theory, women who attempt to fit in—to find that common ground, whether it be by using the same language or ignoring or laughing off blatantly vulgar conduct—would have a better chance of success in these workplaces. Women who made no effort to find a common ground with their male coworkers would be more likely to become targets of harassment. There is, however, a downside to trying to fit in, as Walshok explains: "The down side of the more verbally and physically aggressive character of the blue-collar milieu is the stereotypic assumption that women who 'talk dirty' probably are more open to sexual overtures; such women are not put on pedestals."[112] The use of this "stereotypic assumption" is evident not only in the responses of coworkers to the words and sometimes actions of these women but also in many courts' treatment of the "vulgar" plaintiff. Yet, as a coping mechanism designed to help women fit in, this may well be a wise strategy.

3. Misreading Social Cues

Social scientists have identified differences in interpretation of sociosexual cues between men and women. As a general matter, social science findings suggest that men interpret social interactions differently than women.[113] For example, men are more likely to interpret behaviors that are intended to be friendly as being sexually motivated. Antonia Abbey conducted several studies of undergraduate students to see if male and female students interpret behaviors differently in dating and social scenarios.[114] One can envision how differing interpretations might cause problems in the workplace. A male supervisor might notice that one of his female employees smiles at him when they speak to each other. The supervisor might read this as an invitation for some sort of relationship, whereas the employee simply might be trying to be friendly to the boss, upon whom her economic well-being rests. Although at first this data may seem consistent with differing perceptions based on gender of what is sexually harassing, miscue findings are of more limited applicability to sexual harassment law for a number of reason explained below.

A study by Johnson and her colleagues evaluated miscues in the context of evaluating a professor/student sexual harassment scenario. Using 187 female and 165 male undergraduate students, they played a five-minute videotape showing a professor and student interacting about an extension on a due date. They varied the actions of the professor between three levels: not at all harassing, mildly harassing, and moderately harassing. They also varied the student's response to the harassment between a positive response and a negative one. Male subjects rated the female student's behavior as more seductive, sexy, and promiscuous than did the female subjects. Interestingly, there was no effect based on the response of the student. The response, either "Yes, I guess that's alright" or "No, I don't think so," would likely be key to a finding of unwelcomeness.[115] Yet, there was no effect on the ratings—sexy, seductive, promiscuous, flirtatious, and so on—based on the student's response. This led the authors to conclude that subjects did not view mild refusals and reluctant acceptances differently. Still, they note the limitations of their study. They could not conclude that those who misperceive a woman's friendliness are more likely to engage in acts of sexual harassment.[116]

Although the above studies do not involve workplace scenarios, psychology professor Margaret Stockdale has noted the potential for miscues to play a role in workplace sexual harassment. For example, she posits that men who score higher on the likelihood to sexually harass scale might be more likely to misperceive women's cues at work as well as in social settings. As she explains, "Preliminary data suggest that the tendency to sexually misperceive is associated with traditional sex-role attitudes, tolerance for sexually harassing activities, and nonacceptance of feminists' views about sexual harassment (e.g., sexual harassment is related to power)."[117] In addition, the tendency of men to misperceive is related to other measures of sexually aggressive belief systems. Thus, it appeared that miscue data did have potential application to sexual harassment.

Studies of miscues in workplace settings, however, paint a different picture. Current research suggests that the role misperceptions play in workplace sexual harassment is equivocal at best. In his 1996 article canvassing research on misperceptions as they relate to sexual harassment, Professor Frank E. Saal concluded that "[c]onsidered all together, these studies failed to yield any notable support for" the hypothesis that "some of the less egregious examples of sexual harassment of women in organizational environments are attributable to men's misperceptions of women's friendly, outgoing behaviors as signals of sexual interest or availability, and to those males' subsequent responses . . . based on their misperceptions."[118] Professor Saal was limited in generalizing somewhat because of the few studies that had attempted to find this phenomenon in the context of sexual harassment at work, yet he still concluded that the most likely alternative potential explanation for harassment was power—that men sexually harassed women because women are less powerful in the workplace. Thus, it is unlikely that miscues play a significant role in workplace sexual harassment, where the norms of behavior are very different from dating scenarios.

C. What to Do about Unwelcomeness

There are several implications for courts' interpretations of unwelcomeness based on social science. Although commentators have argued that courts should abandon unwelcomeness on policy grounds,[119] once the various scenarios involving unwelcomeness are parsed, unwelcomeness seems unnecessary or irrelevant in most cases. Indeed, there are only two situations in which a court arguably might be justified in examining unwelcomeness. The first is the situation that the standard appears to be designed for: the potential for a failed consensual relationship to turn into a sexual harassment suit. The second is the situation in which the harassed employee engages in vulgar speech or behavior, sometimes in defense, but sometimes as an apparent instigator of sexually harassing conduct. In most other situations (and there are many well represented in reported cases) unwelcomeness should play no part in the evaluation of the plaintiff's case. Given the relatively few cases in which unwelcomeness may be legitimately an issue, perhaps the standard should be entirely eliminated. I begin by discussing whether unwelcomeness is relevant at all in the context of sexual harassment law. From there, I discuss cases in which it is at least arguably relevant. By considering the cases in which unwelcomeness plays a role, I hope to suggest a different way for courts to resolve the conundrum of unwelcomeness.

1. Unwelcomeness Is Irrelevant in Most Cases

In a large number of sexual harassment cases, the unwelcomeness requirement can lead to investigation and public display of information that bears little to no relevance to the issue of whether or not the target was sexually harassed. In these cases, an inquiry into unwelcomeness serves only to embarrass and humiliate the plaintiff. There are two main types of cases in which this happens. First, cases in which the plaintiff responds passively to harassment. Second, cases in which the harasser's behavior is so vulgar that it is untenable that anyone would welcome the behavior. Some courts have acknowledged that there are such cases and have ruled accordingly. Yet, this has not stopped defendants from raising the issue.

First, in cases involving passive responses, many courts seem to understand that a plaintiff need not say "stop that" in order to show that the behavior is unwelcome. Given the prevalence of avoidance responses, the courts interpreting passive responses as signaling unwelcomeness have done so consistently with social science accounts. However, that does not mean that courts have been consistent in the interpretation of passive responses or that an inquiry into unwelcomeness will not occur in these cases.

Passive responses to harassment are likely to increase as more women coming off public assistance enter the workforce. Welfare reform in particular has placed lower-income women in the difficult position of needing a job (or, sometimes, two or three jobs) to support their families.[120] As the safety net formerly provided by public assistance erodes, these women will be desperate to keep their jobs. The result is that lower-income women will be particularly vulnerable to harassment and will be in the worst position to complain. Retaliation could mean financial disaster for them and their families. Thus, they are very likely to passively respond or give in to harassment, such as requests for dates and the like. It is increasingly important that courts continue to assume that passive responses (such as ignoring the harassment, walking away, or going along with the behavior) do not signal welcomeness. Any courts that have read passive behaviors as welcoming harassment need to rethink their positions. Until all courts and defendants understand passive responses, the plaintiff's behavior may be subject to unnecessary and inappropriate scrutiny.

Aside from passive responses, it is difficult to envision under what circumstances harassment that reaches an actionable level could be deemed "welcome." Given that workplace conduct is not actionable until it reaches a level that makes it sufficiently severe or pervasive to alter a term, condition, or privilege of employment, it seems unfathomable that harassment that reaches this degree of seriousness could somehow be considered "welcome."[121] Some cases discussed above focused on the harasser's behavior, essentially taking the position that no person would welcome the behavior involved in the case. In cases of ambiguous talk or behavior, the severe or pervasive standard should curtail cases involving overheard conversations about the latest rather raunchy episode of "Friends." Such conversations will not be sufficiently severe or pervasive enough to alter the conditions of employment. However, most sexual harassment cases do not involve such conversations but, instead, involve gross, disgusting, and often physical behavior. Indeed, as Judge Posner put it, "[W]elcome sexual harassment is an oxymoron."[122]

2. Other Problems Caused by Unwelcomeness

Although unwelcomeness may have resulted in fewer cases being thrown out of court summarily than have the three other elements of a sexual harassment claim, this does not mean that the inquiry into unwelcomeness does not have deleterious effects on the plaintiff and her claim. First, the imposition of personal and often embarrassing discovery might discourage a plaintiff from pursuing her claim. For example, the Eighth Circuit's Gender Fairness Task Force reported that 52.5% of plaintiff's lawyers agreed that discovery in sex discrimination cases was "inappropriately intrusive" into personal lives of parties and witnesses sometimes, often, or many times.[123] Such intrusive discovery could lead a plaintiff to abandon her claim or settle for less. Second, unwelcomeness inquiries may result in some claims never being taken to court because lawyers are making the assessment that the plaintiff cannot show that the conduct was unwelcome. The prevalence of this phenomenon is much more difficult to assess. It is documented that sexual harassment plaintiffs (and employment discrimination plaintiffs generally) have difficulty in gaining access to the court system because lawyers are often reluctant to take these cases.[124] To the extent that unwelcomeness exacerbates this problem, this is another reason to limit its use.

The unwelcomeness element is all the more suspect because of the manner in which some courts have applied it in cases involving facts that bear little resemblance to the consensual relationship scenario for which it apparently was originally designed. The unwelcomeness standard has caused all sorts of problems in cases involving a variety of fact patterns. For example, as was detailed earlier in this chapter during the discussion of the case law, it has led to inquiry into the plaintiff's past sexual habits, her discussions with coworkers, and any other types of behavior that might show she is "the type of woman" who would welcome the often disturbing behavior of her harasser. In addition, Federal Rule of Evidence 412 has not kept some of this information from being discovered and eventually admitted as evidence in some sexual harassment cases.

Commentators have parsed the problems that unwelcomeness has fraught at the discovery and trial phases. In particular, plaintiffs' lawyers have argued that defense lawyers use unwelcomeness to open up the plaintiff's past sexual history to public view in an effort to force a low settlement or a plaintiff to abandon the lawsuit. On the other hand, defense attorneys argue that they are simply seeking to develop their clients' cases based on issues such as unwelcomeness and damages.[125] Unwelcomeness is not the only culprit in this regard; damages requests for emotional distress can also open up the plaintiff's past to scrutiny.[126] While defense attorneys are acting to further their clients' position, the harassment target is being revictimized by abusive discovery tactics. A plaintiff's consensual behavior with coworker friends or in a consensual relationship with a coworker, as the court in *Howard* pointed out, is at best of questionable relevance. Instead, courts should focus on the actual interactions between the plaintiff and the harasser. The presumption that a woman who engages in a consensual relationship with one coworker would welcome often vulgar and offensive conduct from a supervisor is, as one court put it, a non sequitur.[127]

3. Failed Relationships

Shifting to the situation that spawned the unwelcomeness requirement—the purported failed consensual relationship—the United States Supreme Court's basing a legal standard on what appears to be an unusual case does not seem sensible, especially given the problems that unwelcomeness has caused. In the context of a consensual relationship, it is doubtful that a plaintiff would sue if she truly welcomed the conduct. Courts have suggested that unwelcomeness performs a notice function. In other words, a target's words or conduct indicating unwelcomeness should tell the potential harasser to back off. Underlying this is a concern for spurious allegations—the stereotypic notion of the "scorned" woman. This woman reacts to a relationship breakup by alleging that her supervisor or coworker sexually harassed her; in reality they had engaged in a consensual relationship. To the extent that unwelcomeness is helpful for putting potential harassers on notice that their behaviors are problematic, the *Ellerth/Faragher* defense and notice standard for coworker harassment (an entirely separate element of the claim) performs this function. As is explained in chapter 5, harassment by a coworker is not actionable unless the employer knew or should have known of the harassment and failed to remedy it. Liability, in effect, is not triggered without employer knowledge, generally as a result of an employee complaint. Thus, an additional notice requirement is superfluous.

The occasional commentator has assumed that failed-relationship sexual harassment cases are common,[128] but there is little evidence to suggest that women or men frequently or even commonly use sexual harassment allegations in this seemingly vindictive manner. Given the statistics on how often harassment occurs and how infrequently targets actually complain about it, let alone how few claims actually result in a lawsuit, the possibility of someone's bringing a claim of this sort seems doubtful at best. Couple this with the real psychological demands of litigation (e.g., the effects on the plaintiff, her family, her work relationships), and the possibility that someone would bring a claim based on spite seems absurd.[129] The more likely scenario coming out of a failed consensual relationship is that the male is in a position to make the woman's work life more difficult, and the woman is harassed as result of the breakup. Although this does not mean a vindictive lawsuit is never filed, legal standards that are applied to all cases should not be based on an obscure, aberrant case, especially when application of that standard leads to other more serious problems. Instead, the standard should be set by the vast majority of cases, which rarely involve this sort of situation, especially when other elements of the claim might cover it.

Logically, it does not seem that there would be many cases based on a vindictive former paramour, but ascertaining how frequently this occurs is difficult. Commentators have assumed that it is a common phenomenon. One commentator has cited a study that dates back to 1988, which purports to show that 27% of sexual harassment disputes "have roots in soured romances."[130] The statistic purportedly comes from a study by *Working Woman* magazine. However, nowhere in that study are there any statistics about failed relationships. The closest the study comes to that issue is asking how many sexual harassment complaints related to "pressure for dates."[131] "Pressure for dates," however, does not equate with a failed consensual relationship. A woman might be pressured for dates after dissolving a consensual relationship, but there is no way to know how many cases in this category are based on that fact pattern versus a woman's simply being pressured for dates by someone in whom she has no romantic interest. Put simply, this statistic says nothing meaningful about the frequency with which plaintiffs vindictively assert sexual harassment claims as a result of failed relationships.

In a more recent survey of human resources professionals, 24% of those responding indicated that sexual harassment claims had resulted from a workplace romance.[132] However, this does not include how many resulted in actual lawsuits or the nature of those complaints. It could well be that the woman broke off the relationship and was harassed in response. Most research on workplace romances has been done separately from sexual harassment research. Recently, Pierce and Aguinis have suggested a framework that attempts to explain the link between workplace romances and sexual harassment. While acknowledging that this research is in its "infancy," they posit that, based on the type of romance involved, certain types of sexual harassment conduct may or may not be more likely.[133] However, there is little research to support exactly how this link operates or how frequently romances result in sexual harassment suits.[134]

Those who support arguments for reform of sexual harassment law based on the failed consensual relationship scenario have a difficult time pointing to reported cases that actually involve this fact pattern. Michael Frank and Richard Epstein have alluded to this purported phenomenon, but their support for its being common is thin. Frank cited several cases for the proposition. However, in the cases cited, the plaintiff is far more sympathetic than the soured romance scenario suggests. For example, one case involved a quid pro quo claim in which vindictive behavior was directed by the harasser at his former paramour rather than a jilted woman retaliating against her former paramour by filing a sexual harassment case.[135] Further, in many cases cited the plaintiff lost because the courts reasoned that the discrimination was not based on her gender but, instead, on a failed relationship, a situation discussed in more detail in chapter 4.[136] In the rare case cited by commentators that involved a woman who sued at least arguably because she was "jilted," the plaintiff lost.[137] Thus, it is not unreasonable to assume that lawyers will be reluctant to take such cases and that very few such cases will make it into the court system.

4. The Role of Miscues

Another possible justification for the unwelcomeness element is that the courts are envisioning situations in which the putative harasser believes that the target is interested in him only to find out that she is offended when he repeatedly asks her out for a date. Essentially, the harasser is misreading the social cues that the target is allegedly providing about her level of interest in him. This scenario is unrealistic for two reasons. First, a coworker asking another coworker out on a date likely will never result in actionable harassment because it does not reach the severe or pervasive level. The only way such conduct could become actionable is if the badgering becomes so great that it amounts to pervasive harassment or the harasser begins to treat the target badly for refusing his request(s). In either scenario, being told "no" or "I'm busy" should signal unwelcomeness.

In addition, the cases described above did not involve these situations. Instead, they involved vulgar behavior that appears designed to humiliate the target and/or gratify the harasser in some way. Rarely does a case involve a smile from a woman that leads to her being grabbed, fondled, or otherwise abused. A smile might lead to a request for a date, but a woman's saying no to such a request evidences the unwelcomeness of the request. Grabbing a woman's breast or calling someone a "cunt" is, at best, an extremely unlikely means to bring about a consensual relationship. Clearly, harassers in such cases are not interested in a consensual relationship. Unwelcomeness simply should not be a factor in these cases.

Finally, the latest social science evidence suggests that miscues do not play a significant role in workplace sexual harassment. Far from justifying a standard that places a burden on the plaintiff that amounts to a presumption of welcomeness, social science suggests the opposite. If anything, the burden to show that the plaintiff welcomed the behavior should be on the defendant and be available only in limited types of cases.[138] This is sensible in that the harasser is in the best position to explain what he was thinking when he directed the behavior at the plaintiff.

5. Vulgar Plaintiffs

Once sexual harassment enters a blue-collar environment or the targets' responses meet a certain level of vulgarity, the courts have difficulty understanding and interpreting what is happening in the workplace. In these cases the courts often misinterpret the behavior of the target as welcoming the behavior. This is indeed a problem if the target simply is responding in kind either to try to "fit in" or to act defensively to protect herself. Social science as well as the history of working women provides a better understanding of what is going on in these workplaces and suggests how the courts have missed the mark.

In the vulgar plaintiff cases, unwelcomeness often appears to perform a notice-like function.[139] If the plaintiff engages in similar behavior, courts suggest that she must let the employer know that the behavior is unwelcome. However, the element for imputing liability to the employer requires that the employer "knew or should have known" about the harassment (in the case of coworker harassment) in order to be held liable. In addition, in cases of supervisor harassment, aside from quid pro quo cases, the plaintiff generally must report the behavior to the employer under an employer's sexual harassment policy in order for it to be actionable. So, unwelcomeness is redundant; the *Ellerth/Faragher* affirmative defense provides a notice function already.[140]

Instead, courts that rule in this manner often give life to the stereotype of the "unharassable" woman. This unharassable woman occasionally uses vulgar language (perhaps in an effort to fit in or be "one of the boys"), might make an obscene gesture, would defend herself from sexually harassing conduct (by, perhaps, calling her harasser an equally vulgar name), and does not behave in a manner that the judge would like her to conduct herself. These women should not be protected, according to some courts, because they simply are not "ladylike." This standard of "ladylike" behavior is permeated with socioeconomic class connotations as well as with stereotypes about what is and is not appropriate female conduct. What the unwelcomeness standard allows courts to do is put the behavior of these women under a microscope throughout the litigation. It begins in the discovery process, during which plaintiffs are asked such questions as with whom they have engaged in relationships at the workplace. It continues through summary judgment and trial, during which the plaintiff's behavior is assessed to determine whether she somehow "asked for" this form of harassment. The parallel to the treatment of rape victims is obvious, and one that Rule 412 was intended to stem. However, it has not stopped some courts from assessing certain women as somehow undeserving of protection from discrimination at work. They are, in effect, unworthy of the courts' concern.

Courts need to engage in a more contextual analysis of the facts of these cases. These plaintiffs should be permitted to present their stories to the fact finder, the jury, who is in a better position to understand the problems of working people, including the need to protect one's job as a primary source of income. In most cases, the plaintiff's explanation will reveal that unwelcomeness was not the issue but, instead, an attempt by the plaintiff to either fit in or defend herself. The burden of showing that the behavior is unwelcome should not be on the plaintiff in these cases, but instead on the defendant.

4

Conceptualizing Sexual Harassment as "Because of Sex"

Why sexual harassment occurs has not been the focus of court cases. This is not all that surprising. Courts are not in the business of describing and studying human interactions; they are, however, very much involved in human interactions when they rise to the level of recognized actionable wrongs. Thus, they make decisions that necessarily involve human interactions and motivations. That does not mean that the underlying theory of why a particular legally cognizable wrong happens does not enter into courts' opinions; it just means that the courts usually wait for some other discipline—such as chemistry, biology, or social science—to bring the relevant theory to the courts' attention. It is often up to lawyers, then, through legal argument and sometimes expert witnesses to explain how the science behind human conduct should interact with the legal standard.

This chapter examines one of the most fundamental elements of the sexual harassment claim—that the harassment is because of sex. It does so by examining current social science models on why workplace sexual harassment occurs. Harassment is actionable under Title VII only because courts have characterized it as discrimination based on "sex," the term used in that statute. How and why the behavior occurs may help in understanding how it can be characterized as discrimination because of sex. I begin this chapter by examining the courts' growing consideration of the because of sex element of the claim. Since the Supreme Court's decision in *Oncale v. Sundowner*, the lower courts increasingly have focused on this element of the claim. In addition, it has caused them some difficulty in certain types of cases, which I describe below.

It is important to note that the term "sex" as used in Title VII does not appear to refer to sexuality or sexual conduct. Although there is a dearth of legislative history underlying the use of the term in the statute,[1] it does appear settled that Congress meant at least to include the simple distinction between males and females in using this term. Those in Congress who argued in favor of including "sex" as a protected class acknowledged that women lacked the same employment opportunities as men.[2] On the other hand, commentators often use the term "sex" to refer to biological sex—either male or female. The term "gender" is used to refer to how people express their maleness or femaleness as well as how society conceives of these statuses. Thus, "gender" encompasses societal expectations and constructs of what it means to be male or female. The courts use the terms interchangeably and not very precisely.[3]

As with their use in the courts, these terms are not used in a wholly uniform manner in this chapter. The cases reveal situations in which it is difficult to use these terms precisely. For example, the term "sexual harassment" is sometimes used to connote behaviors motivated by sexual interest; yet sometimes sexually oriented behavior is used as a means of gender harassment. Thus, sexual behavior is used to force compliance with societal norms of "appropriate" male and female behavior. Instead of devising universal definitions that will fit the various ways that these terms are used in this chapter, I have attempted to be clear about how I am using the terms in the particular context in which I am discussing them. Much like sexual harassment itself, the terms are difficult to apply absent context, and the context often suggests that these terms are insufficient to describe the various ways both sexual and nonsexual behavior can be sexually harassing. I am hopeful that it will be clear throughout the chapter how the terms "sex," "sexual," and "gender" are being used.

I begin this chapter by trying to understand how the courts conceive of "because of . . . sex" in the context of sexual harassment, with an emphasis on cases in which the courts have had difficulty in characterizing the behavior as "because of sex." In addition, I canvass social science theory on why sexual harassment happens. I then compare the formulations and applications of the terms by the courts to how social science conceives of sexual harassment. It is to be hoped that a more thorough understanding of the conditions under which sexual harassment happens will help the courts understand why it is a form of sex discrimination, even in cases that are currently giving the courts conceptual difficulties.

A. Legal Interpretations of Because of Sex

1. Supreme Court Precedent

In its first case recognizing sexual harassment as a cause of action under Title VII, *Meritor Savings Bank v. Vinson*, the Supreme Court linked the claim to the language of the statute. Acknowledging that there was little legislative history to guide it, the Court still concluded based on lower court precedent and the EEOC Guidelines, that harassment based on sex was actionable. The defendant in the case argued that Title VII was limited to employer practices that had an economic impact. The Court disagreed, quoting from lower court cases that emphasized that "'[t]he phrase "terms, conditions, or privileges of employment" in [Title VII] is an expansive concept.'"[4] Analogizing to the growing body of case law on racial harassment, Justice Rehnquist concluded:

> Sexual harassment which creates a hostile or offensive environment for members of one sex is every bit the arbitrary barrier to sexual equality at the workplace that racial harassment is to racial equality. Surely, a requirement that a man or woman run a gauntlet of sexual abuse in return for the privilege of being allowed to work and make a living can be as demeaning and disconcerting as the harshest of racial epithets.[5]

Although the Court recognized the claim as being based on sex, precisely what this encompassed was left largely to lower court interpretations and later Court pronouncements.

That the Court has found the meaning of the terms "because of . . . sex" in Title VII somewhat problematic becomes obvious from its decision in a case involving a discriminatory promotion. In *Price Waterhouse v. Hopkins*, the Court split over the meaning of "because of . . . sex." Although much of the dispute in the case was resolved by Congress in the Civil Rights Act of 1991, the case is interesting because of the role gender stereotypes played in various justices' analyses. In particular, Justice Brennan's plurality opinion acknowledged the impact of stereotypical thinking that went into Price Waterhouse's refusal to elevate Ann Hopkins to partnership at the firm. Several partners who participated in the decision used stereotypes of appropriate female behavior (and Hopkins's failure to conform to them) in assessing her candidacy. For example, Hopkins was told to walk more femininely, talk more femininely, and wear makeup. In response to the defendant's argument that these statements were irrelevant, Justice Brennan explained:

> As for the legal relevance of sex stereotyping, we are beyond the day when an employer could evaluate employees by assuming or insisting that they matched the stereotype associated with their group, for "[i]n forbidding employers to discriminate against individuals because of their sex, Congress intended to strike at the entire spectrum of disparate treatment of men and women resulting from sex stereotypes." . . . An employer who objects to aggressiveness in women but whose positions require this trait places women in an intolerable and impermissible catch 22: out of a job if they behave aggressively and out of a job if they do not. Title VII lifts women out of this bind.[6]

Justice Brennan likewise approved of expert testimony on stereotyping that was used at the trial court level. Dr. Susan Fiske, whose work on stereotyping is discussed later in this chapter, played a significant role as an expert at trial. Justice O'Connor, in a separate opinion, also approved of the stereotyping analysis used to rule in favor of Hopkins, with a resulting majority of the Court on this issue.[7] As is explained in the next section, some lower courts have extended this stereotyping analysis to sexual harassment cases.

The Supreme Court's most extensive discussion of what is meant by "because of . . . sex" in the sexual harassment context comes from *Oncale v. Sundowner Offshore Services, Inc.*, a case in which the Court held that same-sexual harassment was actionable under Title VII. In that case, the Court provided three examples of ways that a plaintiff could show that the harassment was because of the victim's sex. First, where the harassment involved propositions for sexual favors, the Court reasoned that it's reasonable to believe that the harassment would not have occurred but for the victim's sex. Thus, cases in which the harasser is gay and harasses persons of the same sex could satisfy the because of sex requirement. This fits within the sexuality paradigm that the courts often use.[8] However, the Court also acknowledged that non-sexually oriented forms of harassment could likewise be actionable. This second category includes situations in which the harasser uses such sex-specific derogatory terms that it becomes clear that the harassment is motivated by dislike of persons of that sex. This form of harassment fits within the concept of gender harassment discussed earlier in the introduction. Finally, the victim can offer evidence that compares treatment of women to the treatment of men, for example, showing that women were treated poorly compared to men. The Court used these three "evidentiary routes" as examples and did not indicate that these were the only means a plaintiff could use to prove discrimination based on sex.[9] Instead, the Court pointed out that, whatever manner the plaintiff chose to prove her case, "she must always prove that the conduct at issue was not merely tinged with offensive sexual connotations, but actually constituted 'discrimina[tion] . . . because of . . . sex.'"[10]

Although *Oncale* seems to broaden the concept of sexual harassment, some commentators have noted that the three scenarios given in dicta are limiting. These scenarios are based on a traditional heterosexual male norm that results, as law professor David Schwartz put it, in the Court's "attempting to resolve the same-sex issue in a manner consistent with formal equality principles while at the same time trying to avoid extending Title VII protection to gender nonconformists."[11] Some of the lower court cases that attempt to characterize harassment as "because of sex" suggest that Professor Schwartz's description may well be correct.

2. Lower Court Analysis of "Because of . . . Sex"

Following *Oncale*, lower courts have struggled to fit particular fact patterns into the Supreme Court's categories of actionable sexual harassment to satisfy the because of sex element. Several types of cases have generated problems. First, there are cases involving same-sexual harassment. Even after *Oncale*, the courts have struggled with whether the harassment was based on sex or sexual orientation, a status not covered by Title VII. They also have struggled to distinguish between situations in which male-on-male heterosexual harassment amounts to discrimination because of sex as opposed to situations that can be dismissed as nonactionable "male horseplay." This has led to some dubious inferences of homosexuality in cases so that courts could characterize the harassment as because of sex based on sexual interest. Second, courts have difficulties assessing cases in which the harasser harasses both men and women. These "equal opportunity harasser" cases rarely come up in the context of a bisexual harasser, and more often involve a supervisor or coworkers who engage in vulgar behavior directed at men and women. Finally, there are the failed relationship cases, as discussed briefly in chapter 3, in which courts sometimes hold that the harassment was based not on sex but, instead, on the failed relationship. In this section, some typical opinions by courts discussing whether the harassment in question is based on sex are considered.

A. SAME-SEXUAL HARASSMENT CASES

In spite of the Supreme Court's decision in *Oncale* that same-sexual harassment is actionable under Title VII, lower courts continue to struggle with cases that do not fit the heterosexual norm. Some have assumed that the three means of proving that harassment was based on sex given in *Oncale* were not an exhaustive list, but were merely examples.[12] Some courts have avoided the problem by extending the stereotyping analysis of *Price Waterhouse* to cases of gay or effeminate men who are harassed by other men. Other courts have become confounded with how to characterize sexual aggression among heterosexual men. Still other courts have stretched to find evidence suggesting the harasser was gay, and therefore the harassment could be actionable based on the traditional sexual interest approach.

The en banc Ninth Circuit decision in *Rene v. MGM Grand Hotel, Inc.* provides an example of the type of case that the courts find problematic. Plaintiff Rene was targeted by his coworkers for sexual harassment because he was gay. I write "because he was gay" rather guardedly. A plurality of the Ninth Circuit went to great pains to explain that sexual orientation was "irrelevant" to Rene's claim of sexual harassment. Indeed, the trial court granted summary judgment in the employer's favor, reasoning that Rene was harassed not because of his sex but because of his sexual orientation. However, the nature of the conduct suggested to a majority of the court that it was based on sex. Rene was touched and grabbed in a sexual manner (including sticking fingers through his clothes to his anus) by his coworkers. Thus, the plurality reasoned that "[t]he physical attacks to which Rene was subjected, which targeted body parts clearly linked to his sexuality, were 'because of . . . sex.' Whatever else those attacks may, or may not, have been 'because of' has no legal consequence."[13] What motivated the harassers—sexual interest, misogyny, personal dislike, inappropriate humor, boredom—made no difference to the plurality. It was the sexual nature of the actions that rendered the harassment "because of sex."

Another group of three judges, which gave Rene a majority on appeal, saw this case differently. To them, it was not the sexual nature of the activity here, but the fact that it was motivated by stereotypes of appropriate male conduct that made it because of sex. Relying on *Price Water-house* and *Nichols v. Azteca Restaurant Enterprises, Inc.*, a Ninth Circuit case that likewise held gender stereotyping harassment actionable as sexual harassment under Title VII, this group argued that Rene was essentially treated as if he were a woman. As the court described plaintiff's testimony during his deposition,

> his co-workers teased him about the way he walked and whistled at him "[l]ike a man does to a woman." Rene also testified that his co-workers would "caress my butt, caress my shoulders" and blow kisses at him "the way . . . a man would treat a woman," hugged him from behind "like a man hugs a woman," and would "touch my body like they would to a woman, touch my face." Rene further testified that his co-workers called him "sweetheart" and "muñeca" ("doll"), "a word that Spanish men will say to Spanish women." This occurred "many times."[14]

Thus, the three judges reasoned that Rene was harassed because he was a male who did not conform to male stereotypes. In a sense, his sexual orientation resulted in his coworkers treating him as though he were not "male enough."

Four judges disagreed with both characterizations and dissented. They saw this as a case of discrimination based on sexual orientation—a status not protected under Title VII. Suggesting that Congress should amend Title VII if it wished to extend its protections to sexual orientation, the dissenters also were unimpressed with Judge Pregerson's argument that this was improper gender-based stereotyping harassment. They distinguished *Nichols v. Azteca Restaurant Enterprises, Inc.*, arguing that Rene did not behave in a feminine manner on the job. In fact, Rene himself stated that he was "masculine."[15] Thus, reasoned the dissenters, this was not a case of stereotyping.

The three opinions described from this case reflect three common approaches taken by lower courts when confronted with same-sexual harassment of a gay male. Some courts will hold for the plaintiff and others will not, depending on the fact pattern and the court's general approach to harassment that involves the plaintiff's sexual orientation.

Nichols v. Azteca Restaurant Enterprises, Inc. provides another example of the stereotyping approach to same-sexual harassment. In that case, plaintiff's coworkers subjected him to "a relentless campaign of insults, name-calling, and vulgarities."[16] They constantly referred to him as "'she'" and "'her.'" He was called "'faggot'" and "'fucking female whore.'" They told him that he carried his tray "'like a woman.'" Relying on *Price Waterhouse*, the court concluded:

> At its essence, the systematic abuse directed at Sanchez [the plaintiff] reflected a belief that Sanchez did not act as a man should act. Sanchez was attacked for walking and carrying his tray "like a woman"—i.e., for having feminine mannerisms. Sanchez was derided for not having sexual intercourse with a waitress who was his friend. Sanchez's male co-workers and one of his supervisors repeatedly reminded Sanchez that he did not conform to their gender-based stereotypes, referring to him as "she" and "her." And, the most vulgar name-calling directed at Sanchez was cast in female terms. We conclude that the verbal abuse was closely linked to gender.[17]

Thus, even though much of the discrimination apparently related to the plaintiff's sexual orientation, the court fashioned a theory that fit within the settled law under Title VII. Gay plaintiffs who have framed their allegations in terms of stereotypes have withstood motions to dismiss as well as motions for summary judgment.[18]

Plaintiffs who have not framed their claims in terms of stereotypes have not been so successful. The court in *Bibby v. Philadelphia Coca Cola Bottling Co.* held against a plaintiff who had not framed his allegations in terms of improper stereotyping. The plaintiff, who was gay, was assaulted by a coworker. He was told that "everybody knows you're gay as a three dollar bill," as well as "everybody knows you take it up the ass," and called a "sissy."[19] He also was harassed by supervisors, who yelled at him, enforced rules differently against him, and did not address problems he was having with machinery. Graffiti that featured his name was left up for longer than usual.[20] The court in this case recognized a theory of sexual harassment based on improper stereotyping, but it did not believe that this was such a case. Instead, this case amounted to discrimination based on sexual orientation—a status not protected by Title VII.

The matter becomes further complicated when the target is heterosexual. In these situations, courts take several approaches. Sometimes they dismiss the harassment as based on personal animosity or as "horseplay," even though the harassment has a significant sexual component. Sometimes they find the sexual nature of the harassment sufficient. Finally, some courts engage in speculation about whether the harasser is in fact gay and ask whether there is sufficient evidence to support it. The cases then present a typical sexual harassment scenario—the harasser was sexually attracted to the victim—one of the fact patterns suggested as actionable in *Oncale*.

For example, in *Johnson v. Hondo, Inc.*, the plaintiff, a heterosexual male, worked in an all-male environment at a Coca Cola bottling plant. A coworker frequently stated to the plaintiff that he would make the plaintiff "suck my dick," sometimes while grabbing his own crotch. This coworker also would brush against the plaintiff. The harasser likewise made derogatory comments to plaintiff about the plaintiff's girlfriend. In response, the plaintiff called his harasser names: SOB, fag, and faggot.[21] The trial court granted summary judgment for the employer, holding that this behavior was based on a personal grudge—not gender. The Court of Appeals agreed, noting that "[b]esides the sexual content of Hicks' remarks there is absolutely nothing in this record that supports a reasonable inference that the remarks were directed at Johnson on account of his gender."[22] Instead, the actions of the harasser were dismissed as "simply expressions of animosity or juvenile provocation."[23] Other courts have held similarly.[24] As the court in *EEOC v. Harbert-Yeargin, Inc.* callously put it in the context of two heterosexual male plaintiffs who were touched, poked, and prodded in their genital areas:

> Georgie Porgie pudding and pie
> Goosed the men and made them cry
> Upon the women he laid no hand
> So it cost his employer 300 grand[25]

In spite of characterizing the behavior involved as "gross, vulgar, male horseplay," two judges on the panel upheld the trial court's decision to set aside the jury's verdict in the plaintiffs' favor.[26]

Some cases involve what can initially be characterized as personal animosity that later takes a turn toward sexual conduct. For example, in *Davis v. Coastal International Security, Inc.*, the plaintiff, a supervisor, reprimanded the harassers for job-related misconduct. From that point forward, these two employees harassed the plaintiff, including slashing his car's tires repeatedly. Eventually the harassment evolved into sexually oriented behavior—they would grab their own crotches, make kissing gestures, and use a phrase referring to oral sex. Upholding the trial court's grant of summary judgment, the court concluded that the behavior was not motivated by gender but, instead, by a "personal grudge." Although the plaintiff tried to argue that some of the actions amounted to sexual propositions, the plaintiff's own testimony that neither he nor his harassers were gay undermined such arguments. Further, plaintiff's attempt to assert that the harassers treated men differently as a group than women was met with skepticism by the court because plaintiff provided no evidence that other men were targeted similarly.[27] Instead, he was the sole target of the harassers' indignities.

Plaintiffs have fared better when there was some evidence suggesting that the harasser is gay. In *LaDay v. Catalyst Technology, Inc.*, plaintiff's supervisor made comments about seeing the plaintiff with his girlfriend, remarking, "'I see you got a girl. You know I'm jealous.'"[28] Another day, this supervisor came up behind the plaintiff and fondled his anus. When the plaintiff objected, the supervisor laughed and walked away. Later, the supervisor spit tobacco on the plaintiff's hard hat and shirt, saying, "'[T]his is what I think of you.'"[29] The plaintiff refused to return to work because the harasser was his supervisor that day. Once the plaintiff filed his complaint, it came to light that two other former employees had made similar complaints about the same supervisor. When the plaintiff returned to work under another supervisor, employees insulted him and made working difficult for him because of his complaints about the harasser.[30]

Contrasting this case to *Rene v. MGM*, the court argued that there was significantly more evidence of homosexual interest in this case. There was also a dearth of other explanations for the supervisor's behavior—the plaintiff was not gay and there appeared to be no other reason for animosity. As the court explained, "To the contrary, Craft [the harasser] seems to have been angered by La Day's apparent *heterosexuality*, as evidenced by his comment that he was 'jealous' of La Day's girlfriend."[31] Thus, there was enough evidence suggesting that the supervisor was gay and was making sexual advances to overcome a motion for summary judgment.[32]

B. THE "EQUAL OPPORTUNITY" HARASSER AND HARASSING ENVIRONMENTS

Another fact pattern that has perplexed lower courts is that in which men and women both apparently are harassed. In what sense, these courts ponder, can the harassment be because of sex? These cases come in two varieties. The first involves "equal opportunity harassers": harassers who direct crude and vulgar behavior (and the occasional sexual overture) to members of both genders. The second involves situations in which generally crude conduct pervades a (usually) predominantly male workplace. Women entering the workplace complain about the crude and vulgar behavior. As I explain below, some courts have adopted a "coming to the nuisance" or "assumption of risk" approach in these harassing environments.

Ocheltree v. Scollon Productions, Inc. is an example involving both. Although this case ultimately was affirmed in part and reversed in part by an en banc Fourth Circuit,[33] the various approaches of the judges on the panel provide insight into the courts' problems with these cases. Plaintiff Lisa Ocheltree worked in the production shop at an employer whose workforce was predominantly male. Her coworkers had explicit conversations about sex, commented upon other coworkers' sexual habits, used vulgar language, and told sexual jokes. In addition, three sets of incidents were directly aimed at her. Her coworkers pretended to perform oral sex on a mannequin on a routine basis apparently to see her reaction. In another incident, she was shown a picture of a man with pierced genitalia and asked her opinion. Finally, a coworker sang her a song with vulgar lyrics. A male coworker corroborated parts of her testimony. The jury found for Ocheltree, and the employer appealed the denial of its motion for judgment as a matter of law.[34]

The Fourth Circuit initially reversed, holding that the conduct was not based on her sex. The court reasoned that Ocheltree would have been exposed to the vast majority of the incidents had she been male; therefore, the actions were not based on her sex. The court evaluated only three behaviors as being directed at her: the mannequin incidents, the lewd song, and the body-piercing magazine. Every other incident was seen or overheard by the entire workforce. In addition, much of the behavior had been occurring before she joined the workforce. In this way, the court dismissed a large chunk of her case, explaining that "[t]he discussions certainly were sexually explicit, including the discussion regarding the body-piercing magazine, and while they were generally degrading, humiliating, and even insulting, they were not aimed solely at females in any way."[35] As further support for its position, the court noted that two of her male coworkers also had complained about the behavior. Although there was some testimony that the behavior worsened after Ocheltree complained, there was no evidence that linked this to her directly. Instead, it worsened for everyone—both men and women.[36] With so much behavior out of the way, the court concluded that the three incidents directed at Ocheltree were insufficiently severe or pervasive to meet the legal standard for harassment.

Judge Michael dissented in part in the case, arguing that the behavior involved here could be viewed as "because of sex" in two ways: (1) because it made Ocheltree uncomfortable and self-conscious as the only woman working in her area, and (2) because some of the graphic descriptions of sex portrayed women as sexually subordinate to men. Relying on *Jacksonville Shipyards*, Judge Michael argued that even behavior that is not directed at women can create a hostile environment. Analogizing to race, he argued that under the majority's reasoning an African American worker entering an all-white workplace where racial slurs were the norm would not have a claim for racial harassment because the slurs were not directed at him (because the slurs had been ongoing before he arrived) and the white employees were exposed to the same slurs. Just as his hypothetical workplace is more hostile to the African American employee because he is black, so too is the workplace at Scollon hostile to Ocheltree because she is a woman.[37] Judge Michael looked carefully at the nature of the statements made before Ocheltree in this case; comments like "she gave good head" and "she swallows," he reasoned, portray women as sexually subordinate to men. Thus, "they express and reinforce gender hierarchy in the workplace" and provide sufficient evidence that the harassment was "based on sex" to withstand a motion for judgment as a matter of law.[38]

Ultimately, the en banc Fourth Circuit agreed with Judge Michael, upholding that a reasonable jury could find the conduct based on the plaintiff's sex. Picking up on some of Judge Michael's analysis, the court reasoned that the behavior directed at Ocheltree was intended to draw a reaction from her and make her feel uncomfortable. In addition, much of the talk was specifically offensive to women because it portrayed them as subordinate. There was no evidence that employees directed similar behavior at men in an effort to embarrass them.[39]

Holman v. State of Indiana presents the alleged "bisexual" harasser scenario. A husband and wife were both harassed by the same individual. Their harasser, a male shop foreman, requested sexual favors from both, although the harassment of the woman appears more severe and pervasive. The harasser touched her, stood very close to her while asking her to sleep with him, and also made sexist comments on the job. Her husband alleged that the same foreman had grabbed his head while requesting sexual favors. Both alleged that the foreman retaliated against the husband as well for rebuffing his advances.[40] The appellate panel upheld the trial court's motion to dismiss because plaintiffs did not allege discrimination based on sex—both a male and female plaintiff were harassed by the same person. The panel explained, "Title VII does not cover the 'equal opportunity' or 'bisexual' harasser, then, because such a person is not *discriminating* on the basis of sex. He is not treating one sex better (or worse) than the other; he is treating both sexes the same (albeit badly)."[41] The plaintiffs argued that this just encourages harassers to direct their actions at both sexes, even though they are really interested in only one of the genders. Harassment directed at both males and females essentially then provides employers with a free pass on such discrimination. The court was unimpressed with this argument, stating that it seemed "unrealistic" and that "[i]t is hard to imagine that would-be harassers will know the intricacies of sexual harassment law and will manufacture additional harassments to attempt to avoid Title VII liability, particularly when doing so will increase their risk of being fired, sued under state law, and ostracized."[42]

Brown v. Henderson presents a situation similar to *Holman*. The plaintiff worked for the postal service. She was harassed along with a male coworker for having a purported romance. However, there was evidence that the harassment was not because of the relationship but because of a hotly contested union election that the plaintiff lost. Some of the evidence she provided did not appear to have any obvious genesis in that election. She alleged that there was frequent vulgar talk on the job that she necessarily overheard, although it was not directed at her. In addition, there was some behavior directed at her and her purported boyfriend because of their alleged relationship. In particular, a vulgar picture of a naked obese woman was posted near her alleged paramour's mail route with a caption indicating it was the plaintiff. Another picture of two elephants mating was placed in the same spot with a caption indicating that it was plaintiff and her purported paramour.[43]

In its analysis, the court emphasized the individual nature of the discrimination analysis. As the court explained, "In other words, what matters in the end is not how the employer treated *other* employees, if any, of a different sex, but how the employer *would have* treated *the plaintiff* had she been of a different sex."[44] However, if both male and female employees are treated similarly, this gives "rise to an inference that their mistreatment shared a common cause that was unrelated to their sex."[45] That the harassment involved sexually oriented behavior was insufficient to vitiate the presumption. Here the court concluded that the harassment was based on the dispute over the union election. To this end, the plaintiff's own testimony suggested that this was the case. Thus, the court upheld the trial court's grant of summary judgment.

Other courts have been more sympathetic to plaintiffs, at least in situations in which there is an argument that one sex was harassed in a different manner than the other. In *Beard v. Flying J, Inc.*, the employer argued that the harasser, a supervisor, harassed men and women alike. The court looked at the nature of the harassment, concluding that women were harassed differently. The plaintiff alleged that the supervisor frequently brushed against her breasts and once rubbed a pair of cooking tongs across her breasts as well as flicked a pen across her nipples. All of this occurred during a three-week period. Apparently, the supervisor also gave men what were termed "titty twisters," whereby he would grab and twist their nipples.[46] He also spoke to the men in sexual terms. Even though both men and women experienced forms of harassment, the court still held that a jury could find that the discrimination was because of sex:

> We observe, first of all, that this conduct is not the same as what occurred to Ms. Beard [the plaintiff], partly because it is probably not sexual, and in any case it carries an entirely different cultural and contextual message. A plaintiff in this kind of case need not show, moreover, that only women were subjected to harassment, so long as she shows that women were the primary target of such harassment.[47]

Similarly, in *EEOC v. R&R Ventures*, the court held that the conduct could be characterized as based on sex when the manager of a Taco Bell directed sexual comments at young women who worked for him. The employer argued that the manager treated male and female employees badly, but the depositions of the plaintiffs and a male coworker indicated that only the women had complained about the manager's behavior, which suggested that it was different for men and women.[48]

A variation on the theme of the equal opportunity harasser is the equally harassing workplace, or the "coming to the nuisance" approach to sexual harassment. These cases involve situations in which the workplace is permeated with vulgar talk and behavior. Typically, they are all-male or predominantly male workplaces. Once women enter these workplaces, the behavior becomes objectionable to the newly arrived female segment of the workforce. In this situation, some courts have held that the harassment has nothing to do with the women's presence. Instead, it predated their presence and therefore cannot be "because of sex" in the sense used under Title VII. Women who enter these workplaces—many of which are blue-collar—have assumed the risk or have come to the nuisance. Therefore, the employer cannot be liable, the argument goes, if the women are offended by some of the conduct that occurs there.

An example of a case in which the court took this approach is *Gross v. Burggraf Construction Co.* In *Gross*, the plaintiff drove a water truck for a construction company. She alleged that her supervisor harassed her, including referring to her as a "cunt"; stating to another employee with reference to the plaintiff that "sometimes, don't you just want to smash a woman in the face?"; and yelling at her by saying, "What the hell are you doing? Get your ass back in the truck and don't you get out of it until I tell you."[49] He also called her dumb and used profanity with reference to her. There were other allegations, as well, about her supervisor's general dislike of having women in the workplace. The court essentially held that this type of vulgar language was part and parcel of life on a construction site:

> In the real world of construction work, profanity and vulgarity are not perceived as hostile or abusive. Indelicate forms of expression are accepted or endured as normal human behavior. . . . Accordingly, we must evaluate Gross' claim of gender discrimination in the context of a blue collar environment where crude language is commonly used by male and female employees. Speech that might be offensive or unacceptable in a prep school faculty meeting, or on the floor of Congress, is tolerated in other work environments.[50]

With this backdrop, the court proceeded to go through each allegation by the plaintiff and dismiss it as a reflection of the nature of construction work sites—not sex discrimination. Thus, summary judgment was appropriate in the case.

Contrast that case to one of the most famous sexual harassment cases, *Robinson v. Jacksonville Shipyards, Inc.* Although this plaintiff ultimately prevailed, the case has been a source of controversy on a number of grounds, including its First Amendment implications. Plaintiff Lois Robinson was a welder at a shipyard for more than ten years. In this predominantly male workplace, she was subjected to a variety of forms of sexual harassment—some directed at her specifically and some that simply pervaded the workplace environment. There were many pin-ups, often pornographic, of nude women posted throughout the work-place. Some were specifically placed in areas that Robinson was known to frequent. Comments of a sexual nature were often made in her pres-ence—some specifically directed at her. She was also harassed by certain men. Some of this harassment reflected hostility to women in the work-place and some had more of a sexual quality.

The court's opinion includes page after page of findings of fact as to specific and general instances of sexual harassment at the shipyard.[51] In ruling in favor of Robinson, the court found that three types of harassing incidents occurred during her tenure at the shipyard. First, there were in-stances of harassment that reflected a general dislike of women in the workplace. Second, sexual behavior was directed at her that easily raises an inference that the harassment is based on sex. Finally, the court in-cluded incidents that were not directed at a particular person but are more offensive to members of one sex than the other. The court ex-plained:

> This third category describes behavior that creates a barrier to the progress of women in the workplace because it conveys the message that they do not belong, that they are welcome in the workplace only if they will subvert their identities to the sexual stereotypes prevalent in that en-vironment. That Title VII outlaws such conduct is beyond peradven-ture.[52]

To the court, its detailed findings of fact supported the existence of all three types of harassment at the shipyard. As we see from the *Gross* case, not all courts would agree with this assessment.[53]

3. Harassment Following a Failed Consensual Relationship

Courts also have held that harassment following a failed consensual rela-tionship was not "because of sex" but, instead, because of the resulting personal animosity that often accompanies such failed relationships. Some cases involving consensual relationships are discussed in chapter 3. However, some cases consider these fact patterns in terms of whether the harassment that ensues can be characterized as "because of sex."

Succar v. Dade County School Board presents an example of a case in which the court held that the harassment following a failed consensual relationship is not based on sex but, instead, on personal animosity. In that case, a male plaintiff had a relationship with a colleague that lasted one year. After it ended, the female teacher started threatening her former paramour's wife and son. She also verbally and physically harassed the plaintiff himself, apparently seeking to embarrass him in front of his colleagues and students. The trial court granted the employer's motion for summary judgment.[54] The court concluded that Title VII "'is not a shield against harsh treatment in the workplace. Personal animosity is not the equivalent of discrimination. . . . The plaintiff cannot turn a personal feud into a sex discrimination case.'"[55] The court concluded that the harassment was not based on the plaintiff's sex, being male, but instead on his former paramour's anger with him after their failed relationship. As the court explained, the plaintiff's "gender was merely coincidental."[56] Since *Succar*, the Eleventh Circuit has extended this rationale to quid pro quo sexual harassment cases.[57]

Courts have engaged in other strange analyses to avoid characterizing harassment following a failed consensual relationship as based on sex. In *Galloway v. General Motors Service Parts Operations*,[58] the Seventh Circuit held that the term "sick bitch" when directed by a male employee to a female employee was not a "gendered" term. The plaintiff had engaged in a consensual romantic relationship with one of her coworkers. After that relationship ended and for a period of approximately four years until the plaintiff quit, the alleged harasser repeatedly called plaintiff a "sick bitch," or simply "sick."[59] Apparently, the plaintiff had been hospitalized at one time for psychiatric problems. The alleged harasser also made several more explicit statements. On one occasion, he said, "If you don't want me, bitch, you won't have a damn thing." On another occasion he made an obscene gesture at her and said, "Suck this, bitch."[60]

The court held that "bitch" and "sick bitch" in this context were gender-neutral terms, stating, "[w]e find greater merit in the district judge's third ground [for summary judgment], that 'sick bitch'—and, we add, the other verbal abuse, and the obscene gesture, that Bullock [the alleged harasser] directed toward Galloway [the plaintiff]—was, in context, not a sex- or gender-related term."[61] The court reasoned that, although "bitch" is "rarely" directed at heterosexual men, the term did not emphasize female traits that "might be thought to be inferior to men in the workplace, or unworthy of equal dignity and respect. In its normal usage, it is simply a pejorative term for 'woman.'"[62] In this context, where the coworker is making these statements to a former girlfriend, it is hard to imagine how these statements could be considered somehow "ungendered." Indeed, if the context is key to Judge Posner's decision, it seems more reasonable to allow the plaintiff the opportunity to develop that context before a jury instead of granting summary judgment.

Other courts have been more sympathetic to plaintiffs harassed as a result of a former consensual relationship. For example, in *Green v. Administrators of Tulane Educational Fund*, the court evaluated a situation in which a secretary/office manager sued when a doctor harassed her after she refused to continue a consensual relationship. The harassment was not of a sexual nature but, instead, took the form of gender harassment. The former paramour allegedly made the plaintiff's work difficult. For example, he had the locks on her desk broken and her drawers searched. The trial judge entered judgment in the plaintiff's favor after a jury verdict in her favor. Relying on *Oncale*, the Court of Appeals upheld the jury's verdict, finding sufficient evidence in the record to support that the former paramour's harassment was "causally related to" the plaintiff's gender. The court held that a jury could reasonably infer from the timing of the harassment that it occurred because she refused to continue that relationship.[63]

These cases reflect some of the fact patterns in which the courts have struggled to decide whether or not the harassment was because of sex. Perhaps social science can provide the conceptual insight necessary to understand whether these fact patterns do amount to discrimination because of sex.

B. Social Science Models of Sexual Harassment

Early in the study of sexual harassment, social scientists (and legal scholars as well)[64] argued that sexual harassment was not about sex but about power.[65] Indeed, in certain situations and for certain individuals, the link between sex and power seems to increase the likelihood that sexual harassment will occur.[66] The power model is not the only theory that attempts to explain why sexual harassment occurs. A related theory, the organizational model, posits that sexual harassment is a result of power and hierarchy in organizational structure. In addition, psychologists have theorized that stereotypes about sex roles, known as sex-role spillover theory, play a part in why sexual harassment occurs. More recently, legal and management scholars have reasserted a natural/biological model to explain why sexual harassment occurs. In the following sections, I describe these models and the research testing them.

1. The Sociocultural or Power Model

One of the earliest advocates of the power model of sexual harassment was Catharine MacKinnon, one of the foremost political/legal theorists in this area of the law. Under this model, sexual harassment results from imbalances in power between men and women. Because men are the power holders in American society, they are in a position to exert that power over women in the form of sexual harassment. Sexual harassment, under one understanding of this model, is used to perpetuate patriarchy, the main way in which men continue to dominate in American society.[67] This model, for example, might explain gender differences in perceptions of sexual harassment that arise from and are perpetuated by patriarchy.[68] Another understanding of this model is that sexual harassment reflects the overall structure of heterosexism in American society.

Tangri et al. summarized the basic premises behind this model well:

> According to this model, male dominance is maintained by cultural patterns of male-female interaction as well as by economic and political superordinacy. Society rewards males for aggressive and domineering sexual behaviors and females for passivity and acquiescence. Members of each sex are socialized to play their respective and complementary roles. Because women, more than men, are taught to seek their self-worth in the evaluation of others, particularly of men . . . they are predisposed to try to interpret male attention as flattery, making them less likely to define unwanted attention as harassment. Their training to be sexually attractive, to be social facilitators, and avoid conflict, to not trust their own judgment about what happens to them, and to feel responsible for their own victimization, contributes to their vulnerability to sexual harassment. According to this model, the function of sexual harassment is to manage ongoing male-female interactions according to accepted sex status norms, and to maintain male dominance occupationally and therefore economically, by intimidating, discouraging, or precipitating removal of women from work.[69]

From this description, this model could be used to explain the low reporting rates of women who are harassed as well as any self-blame women direct at themselves as a result of experiencing harassment.

The little research directly testing this model has lent it some support. For example, Tangri et al. found some support for the power model of sexual harassment in their analysis of U.S. Merit System Protection Board data. In particular, they opined that the finding that the more educated a woman was, the more likely she would be sexually harassed supported this model. The effects of the gender makeup of the work group likewise supported this model (sexual harassment was more likely in a work group in which the opposite sex predominated). Finally, women's expectations about the outcomes of sexual harassment incidents (predictions of negative job outcomes if sexual overtures were turned down), they asserted, supported this model.[70] A recent study by sociologist Stacy DeCoster and her colleagues supported the power model as well. They found, in a study of employees of a national company in the telephone industry, that the most common targets of sexual harassment were powerful women (a descriptor based on level of education and longevity with the company). They opined that harassment is used against such women because they threaten male dominance.[71] Psychologist Margaret Stockdale has argued that this model is helpful in understanding how sexual harassment works at a macrolevel—how it furthers patriarchy, which is a societywide social phenomenon. She suggests that micromodels are needed to help explain how sexual harassment operates in particular workplaces.[72]

Recent research on sexual harassment of men likewise has suggested a link between harassment of men and power, but from a slightly different perspective. In a study of workers of a public utilities company, Berdahl and her colleagues found that comments from working male subjects regarding what constituted sexual harassment supportive of the influence of power in these cases. They summed up well how power might work differently for men than for women: "[S]exual harassment can be interpreted as one aspect of the negotiation and renegotiation of gender roles that act as forms of social control. According to this framework, men will experience as sexually harassing phenomena that threaten their high status, and women will experience as sexually harassing phenomena that reinforce their low status."[73] Their study found that men perceived gender harassment the least bothersome form of behavior and sexual coercion the most bothersome.[74] One could argue that men find the latter behavior far more threatening to their roles as dominant males.

More recently, Margaret Stockdale has picked up on law professor Katherine Franke's concept that same-sexual harassment is used to "enforce or perpetuate gender norms and stereotypes,"[75] and has sought to frame a theory that incorporates current social science on the harassment of men. Stockdale theorizes that men's harassment falls within two broad categories: approach-based harassment, where the intent is sexual interest, and rejection-based harassment, where the intention is "humiliation or debasement."[76] Reviewing studies of sexual harassment of men, she found that men experiencing same-sexual harassment report rejection-based harassment more often. She argues that such rejection-based harassment "is conducted to enforce preferred heterosexist, hypermasculine gender-role behavior."[77] Men who are hypermasculine possess rigid male sex role identities, including "calloused sex attitudes toward women, a conception of violence as manly, and a view of danger as exciting."[78] Heterosexism is an ideology that denigrates nonheterosexual behaviors. People exhibiting these ideologies use related behavior to improve their image among others. Thus, rejection-based same-sexual harassment performs two functions: it denigrates the perceived "deviant" while bolstering the masculine ethos of the harasser.[79] Stockdale sees this form of harassment as parallel to gender harassment.[80] This theory is supported by a study by Miller involving traditional masculine occupations. He found that men in such occupations not only engaged in gender harassment to discourage women from entering their workforce but also used it against men who did not conform to gender roles.[81] Thus, just as they harass women, men harass other men to enforce male dominance.

Stockdale's theory is further supported by a recent study she and her colleagues conducted. Using two samples (343 students and 246 working and nonworking adults), they sought to study differences in perceptions of approach-based and rejection-based harassment. Using well-developed scenarios similar to real cases, they found support for their hypothesis that a man who is a "target of same-sex, rejection-based harassment is viewed, especially by sexists, rather disparagingly and that his claim of sexual harassment is not very credible."[82] Other research on male-on-male sexual harassment also suggests that men use harassment to enforce gender roles.[83]

2. The Organizational Model

A close relative of the power model, the organizational model emphasizes how organizations create hierarchical power structures that may result in sexual harassment. However, unlike the traditional power model, the focus under this theory is power imbalance—not gender. Thus, it is organizational power and its imbalances that create situations in which harassment may occur. Under this model, a woman in a supervisory position is as likely to harass a subordinate as a male supervisor. However, because women tend to have less organizational power, they are disproportionately represented in the group that is harassed.

The organizational model is particularly helpful in accounting for quid pro quo harassment. And, indeed, some studies have found partial support for this model.[84] However, psychologist Margaret Stockdale has opined that it may not provide a very accurate explanation for all types of harassment.[85] More recent studies about power imbalances have suggested that this model may not be the best. It is unclear to what extent the organizational status of a harasser affects various aspects of sexual harassment, including perceptions of harassment.[86] Thus, the efficacy of this model as a complete explanation can reasonably be questioned. Still, there is reason to believe that organizational position may help explain some aspects of harassment; it just does not appear to do the whole job.

3. Sex-Role Spillover Model

While some social scientists have been focusing on power, other social scientists have examined the link between sexual harassment and gender stereotypes.[87] In particular, Barbara Gutek and Bruce Morasch developed what they call the "sex-role spillover" theory of sexual harassment. Sex-role spillover is "the carryover into the workplace of gender-based expectations for behavior."[88] Gutek and Morasch posit this model as an explanation alternative to the "power" model of harassment, arguing that differences in power between men and women do not explain coworker harassment.[89] They distinguish sex roles from work roles, which they define as "a set of expectations associated with the tasks to be accomplished in a job."[90] They also believe that the sex ratio, i.e., the percentage of males and females on the job, has an effect on spillover. For example, women in male-dominated jobs should experience more sex-role spillover than those in more gender-integrated workplaces. The former are seen as "deviating" from normal sex roles and are therefore more likely to experience harassment on the job.[91] In addition, this can lead to women in nontraditional fields taking longer to label their experiences as "sexual harassment."[92] In the case of women in predominantly female jobs, their work roles become associated with more feminine attributes because women dominate in these jobs. In such contexts, women are less likely to perceive harassment because it is more likely to be deemed "part of the job."[93] This model has the advantage of being more heavily tested than some of the other models.

Social scientists who have researched stereotypes posit that stereotypic thinking by men regarding the manner in which women behave can play a part in the type of harassment women will encounter as well as how often they will be harassed.[94] Women, under this theory, fall into a variety of subtypes. Psychology professor Kay Deaux has summed up the impact of subtypes on harassment:

> [G]eneral stereotypic beliefs about women and men are supplemented by more specific images of certain kinds of women and, to a lesser extent, men. Some of these stereotypic subtypes are organized around images of sexuality. To the extent that this subtype is endorsed or believed to be common, a person may have a propensity to apply the belief to an individual woman who is thought to fit the stereotype. The "fit" may be fictitious, but the ramifications of the belief may nonetheless be carried out in actions that could constitute sexual harassment in a work environment.[95]

Psychology professors Susan Fiske and Peter Glick have identified three basic subtypes of women in the workplace: (1) the sexy women (i.e., "vamp"); (2) the nontraditional women (i.e., "feminist"); and (3) the traditional woman (i.e., wife, mother, and the like).[96] According to Fiske and Glick, "The fit between stereotyped images of women and jobs promotes not only potential discrimination . . . but also sexual harassment specifically."[97] For example, women who engage in nontraditional occupations (i.e., those traditionally occupied by men) are "seen as disrupting the "masculine camaraderie" that infuses the culture of the occupation."[98] These women threaten gender-related self-esteem and therefore are more likely to be harassed.[99] This may mean that more traditional women are not as often harassed because they are viewed as "mother," "little sister," or "daughter," but this "protection comes at the cost of assuming unprofessional and permanently subordinate work roles."[100] Indeed, as Gutek and Morasch argue, it may well mean that these women are so indoctrinated into a gender-related work role that they do not recognize the forms of sexual harassment they experience at work on a daily basis.[101]

People are most likely to employ stereotypes when faced with ambiguous situations. In their article evaluating the use and misuse of stereotype information in the courtroom, Borgida and his colleagues reviewed social science data and identified situations in which women are more likely to be harassed:

> For example, the experimental and nonexperimental data that provide the basis for such testimony suggest that gender stereotyping is more likely when (1) the target person is isolated or only one of a few individuals in an otherwise homogeneous environment, (2) members of a previously excluded group move into an occupation that is nontraditional for their group, (3) the workplace is a sexualized environment (e.g., when pornographic posters, graffiti, and sexual remarks are tolerated), and (4) individuating information about target individuals or the evaluative criterion is ambiguous.[102]

The lack of individuating information—information about the particular worker—leads coworkers and supervisors to default to stereotypes in assessing that worker. In this manner, the stereotypes help supervisors and coworkers derive meaning from ambiguous and/or incomplete information.

In addition, Susan Fiske has linked stereotyping to power. Her theory is that people who are in positions of power employ stereotypes in dealing with their subordinates because they do not need to attend to individuating differences between workers. Using *Jacksonville Shipyards* and *Price Waterhouse* as examples, she opined, "Stereotypes reinforce one group's or individual's power over another by limiting the options of the stereotyped group, so in this way stereotypes maintain power. . . . Power is control, the stereotypes are one way to exert control, both social and personal."[103]

Preliminary research on male-on-male sexual harassment shows that a traditional male gender role—a stereotype—might well play a part in the sexual harassment of men.[104] According to this research, men who do not fit the traditional norms of masculinity are more likely to be sexually harassed. Social scientists have posited that sexual harassment is sex discrimination when it is used to "enforce or perpetuate 'hypergender' norms and stereotypes," including hypermasculinity, which is linked to heterosexist standards.[105] As psychologist Margaret Stockdale and her colleagues theorize,

> [B]isexual and equal-opportunity harassment constitutes sex discrimination even though members of both genders are harassed because such an act can directly subordinate women by conditioning employment benefits on sexual cooperation or creating a hostile work environment for women, and it can indirectly subordinate women by harassing men in order to maintain male dominance through hypermasculine ideology.[106]

In particular, sex-role spillover would explain why men who deviate from traditional masculine gender roles would be harassed. Such men defy traditional gender expectations and are harassed for this reason. Like sex-role spillover for women, this is likely to occur in male-dominated environments. Stockdale and her colleagues opine that this might be the result of less concern by the employer about sexual harassment in these environments because there are few to no women to harass (the traditional paradigm of a harassment case); men who have a tendency to harass will use male substitutes (e.g., weak men, gay men, or men who do not otherwise fit masculine norms); and/or it may serve as an initiation rite of sorts.[107] These explanations are consistent with the fact patterns described earlier in this chapter. These researchers acknowledge that more research needs to be done to flesh out the experience of male-on-male sexual harassment. In particular, preliminary studies show that men who have experienced this form of harassment are more likely to experience gender harassment than men who are harassed by women. In addition, men experiencing same-sexual harassment are more likely to work in male-dominated workplaces and to have a male supervisor than men who have experienced no harassment or harassment by a woman.[108] Thus, stereotypes provide an explanation for some same-sexual harassment.

4. The Natural/Biological Model

One of the enduring explanations for sexual harassment is found in a natural or biological model. There are several strains of this model. Initially, theorists argued that sexual harassment is a result of natural sexual attraction between men and women. More recently, legal and management academics have suggested a more nuanced approach to this model based on evolutionary psychology or biology.

The current evolutionary psychology/biology model is premised on the idea that men and women evolved differently as a biological matter, which resulted in differing strategies in sexual relationships. In particular, males have evolved to maximize reproductive sex; females have evolved to find mates who will help care for their children, for females are disproportionately (due to biology) burdened with the care of young children. Although this might cause some males to seek out mates for longer-term commitments (for example, to guarantee paternity), it also may cause some males to seek low-commitment sexual relationships, which would be of a lower cost to the males. Females, on the other hand, are interested in males who can make longer-term commitments to provide for their dependent children.[109]

Management professors Michael Studd and Urs Gattiker proposed a far-reaching potential for this explanation to aid in understanding why and how sexual harassment occurs. Everything from why younger women tend to be disproportionately objects of sexual harassment (due to their increased reproductive capacity) to why women are more likely to feel harassed by lower-status men (due to their lower potential to provide support for children) is explained using evolutionary theory. However, Studd and Gattiker are unable to account for all the data surrounding sexual harassment. Indeed, they concede that "evolutionary theory does not predict that all men in all situations will sexually harass women in the workplace. It is more likely that there is a threshold for coercive male sexual behavior which depends on such factors as specific features of the social environment and individual or development differences in personality."[110]

More recently, law professor Kingsley R. Browne has used evolutionary biology to explain much of the sex inequality that persists in American workplaces. In particular, Browne uses a biological model to explain why sexual harassment may be a result of miscommunication. Disclaiming that sexual harassment is about power, he argues that evolutionary biology suggests that sexual harassment is about sex.[111] Power is used only to increase males' reproductive capacity, so the operative feature of sexual harassment is sex. If Browne is correct, other social scientists as well as legal scholars have underestimated the biological underpinnings of sexual harassment, including in areas that cause courts difficulties, such as same-sexual harassment.

Browne argues that sexual harassment often is based on misperceptions and that this renders the "reasonable woman" standard improper. Relying on studies by Antonia Abbey and her colleagues, mentioned earlier in chapter 3, he argues that men interpret women's behavior as sexual in the workplace when women are simply trying to be friendly. This miscommunication or misperception leads to women's believing they are being sexually harassed when men are simply acting on biology.[112] Even though the studies of student communication in dating and other social settings by Abbey et al. suggest this explanation, other studies suggest that the social context of work creates a different dynamic. Indeed, although the former showed that misperceptions did occur in dating and other social situations, they also found that men and women were able to clear up misunderstandings by making their intentions known.[113] Matters that are cleared up informally by men and women should rarely lead to allegations of sexual harassment.

Browne's position is inconsistent with studies evaluating the role of misperceptions of workplace sexual harassment specifically. As discussed in chapter 3, there is little support for miscues playing a significant role in workplace sexual harassment. Thus, social science undermines such biologically based arguments. This is consistent with many of the cases described in chapter 1 as well as earlier in this chapter. These cases do not appear to involve fact patterns in which men are likely to get a date or begin a courtship. Many of the behaviors involved in sexual harassment cases are degrading and demeaning behavior and do not have courtship as an obvious objective.

Browne also has used biology to explain same-sexual harassment. Rather than focusing on the cases with which the courts have trouble (harassment of gay men or heterosexual same-sexual harassment), his primary concern is with heterosexual men who are harassed by gay men. Browne argues that men who are objects of the desire of gay men may lose their status in male hierarchies, resulting in less reproductive success. Thus, men may respond negatively to romantic overtures by gay men. He argues that men who are harassed by gay men should have a cause of action because reasonable men would find this behavior harassing.[114] Some social science literature suggests men find male sexual behaviors directed at them more harmful than female behaviors.[115] Browne does cite one case that held against plaintiffs who were uncomfortable because of homosexual references by coworkers and supervisors; this case predates *Oncale*.[116] After *Oncale*, expressions of sexual interest from members of the same sex that reach the severe or pervasive level should be actionable. Indeed, it does not appear that fact patterns of this sort are proving all that problematic for the courts; they are comfortable in concluding that same-sexual harassment is "because of sex" when the harassment is based on sexual interest.[117]

The cases in which the courts seem to have difficulties with same-sexual harassment tend to arise in a different context. It is not the heterosexual men who are complaining of harassment by gay men but, instead, the gay man who is harassed by heterosexual coworkers or heterosexual men harassing heterosexual men. Browne does not examine these fact patterns using evolutionary biology, although I suppose he might argue that men react negatively to gay men because they undermine the status hierarchy of men generally and therefore their reproductive potential as well. In addition, although it does appear that harassment of gay men is a form of policing gender norms by more dominant men, it is unclear why the law should favor this form of human behavior (natural or not) at the expense of gay or heterosexual men who have difficulties on the job or are forced out of jobs due to harassment. Indeed, this form of harassment, linked to status hierarchies, could easily fit within the power model or be linked to stereotypes of appropriate male behavior and thus be explained by sex-role spillover theory.

There are also other problems with using evolutionary biology or psychology to set sexual harassment standards. One concern in that regard is problems with the underlying evolutionary biology.[118] In addition, even evolutionary biologists agree that environment has a great effect on human behavior.[119] It does not explain why many men do not sexually harass or under what circumstances they refrain from harassing. It does not explain much of the sexual harassment described in the case law, i.e., behavior that does not appear designed to gain any sort of sexual relationship.

Finally, at best saying that sexual harassment has some roots in biology provides only a descriptive account of evolutionary tendencies; it makes no normative assertions. It does not mean that sexual harassment is inevitable. As biologist Owen Jones put it, "'[I]s' does not imply 'ought,' and a proffered explanation should never be assumed to be coextensive with a justification."[120] It is called the "naturalist fallacy" by biologists, who realize that simply because something is a biological tendency does not make the behavior involved "right."[121] With work being so fundamental to the ability of people to eat, clothe, and house themselves, work is central to most people's ability to survive in American society. To the extent sexual harassment drives some people out of the workplace, regardless of any purported biological basis, it makes sense to try to curb it. Given the acknowledged effects of environment on biological tendencies, there is reason to believe that it is possible to end or at least lessen harassment by using environmental factors. Indeed, in the next section of this chapter, environments in which sexual harassment is likely to occur are described. Social scientists have studied a variety of environmental factors and their relationship to sexual harassment.

As an explanation that could be used in court, biology has other troubling ramifications. Explaining complex human interactions and behaviors as "natural" or "biological" leads courts to be less critical in examining and accepting such behaviors. Arguments from biology are very powerful in court. Litigants have successfully used biology or "human nature" to justify underlying gender stereotypes. Similar arguments have been used to justify everything from prohibiting women from practicing law to denying citizenship to children of American fathers.[122] Science is special to the courts; it justifies positions that are politically unpalatable. After all, it's not the court's "fault" if the biological makeup of human beings dictates the result. Thus, one should be critical in accepting such explanations of human behavior because they have the "force" of science behind them—a force that courts sometimes find hard to resist. Yet, science is often just another form of argument. This is especially true about claims of evolutionary biology or psychology, which provide plenty of room for speculation and have little to no empirical support. Further, even if such arguments offer some explanation of some human behavior, legal standards need to be able to handle the variants in human behavior. As I noted above, if sexual harassment is in the interest of males for propagating the species, why don't all men sexually harass? The dynamic is more complex than this simple biological explanation suggests.

5. Synthesizing the Models and Data

Aside from the natural/biological explanation, the models discussed above do not take into account the characteristics of harassers. In addition, although they suggest something about the general workplace culture in which harassment might occur (sex-role spillover theory is especially helpful in this regard), a review of some of the studies on sexual harassment suggests that no one model explains all sexual harassment cases.

Rather, sexual harassment seems to entail a combination of workplace environment and individual characteristics of the harasser.[123] In this section, I review data on workplaces in which sexual harassment thrives as well as data developed to help understand what type of men sexually harass. It is my hope that an overall model will emerge that will be helpful to the courts.

A. ENVIRONMENTAL FACTORS

Social science research suggests that an important factor in whether a woman is likely to be harassed in her workplace is its environment. There is increasing evidence suggesting that the workplace environment is a significant factor in lessening and even ending harassment in the workplace. As professors Jackie Krasas Rogers and Kevin Hanson stated, "[G]endered work behavior (even that which results in sexual harassment) should be understood as constructed within and by gendered workplaces."[124] In particular, the general atmosphere on the job, the attitudes of supervisors, the diversity of the workforce, as well as what behavior is or is not tolerated all appear to have a relationship to the amount of harassment that occurs.

To begin with, if a work environment is free of demeaning images, talk, and behavior, it is less likely that workers will be harassed there. This may seem obvious because some of these behaviors, in and of themselves if repeated, would contribute to a sexually harassing work environment, but social science studies show a pronounced relationship between less serious forms of conduct and sexual harassment. For example, studies show a correlation between the presence of pornography in the workplace and the incidence of harassment. Studies suggest that "interpersonal forms of sexual harassment such as uninvited sexual attention are more common in offices where the presence of pinups and other more impersonal sexual behaviors are part of the general sexual ambience."[125] Pryor and his colleagues could not show a direct cause and effect relationship, but they did note a high correlation between instances of harassment and these other environmental factors.[126]

These studies are supported by others in which men were "primed" with sexual images. Such men are more likely to respond to women in a sexual manner. Deaux explains:

> Extending the analysis of situational influences to the work setting, we
> can predict that the presence of explicitly sexual material will prime im-

ages of women that emphasize sexual rather than professional qualities. Photographs from *Playboy* or *Hustler* magazine do little to evoke images of professional competence or traits of intelligence, knowledgeability, and career motivation. Rather, the sexual subtype takes precedence over other possible images of women and thus creates an atmosphere in which sexual harassment is likely to flourish.[127]

Pornography in particular "targets women and reduces them to their sexual characteristics" in the workplace.[128] In their study of the influence of sexist priming on subsequent behavior, Rudman and Borgida showed male subjects television commercials that portrayed women as sex objects. They then asked the subjects to interview and evaluate a female candidate for a managerial position using a preselected set of fourteen questions. The subjects were asked to pick seven questions from the set of fourteen—seven of which were sexist and seven of which were neutral. The researchers found that test subjects primed with sexist images "asked significantly more sexist questions than did controls."[129] In addition, subjects who were told that they had the power to make the decision on the applicant asked more sexist questions, and men scoring high on the likelihood to sexually harass scale (LSH) asked more sexist questions. Further, at the end of the interview, they asked subjects to write "whatever came to mind" about the interview. Primed men wrote more words on physical attributes and the clothing of the interviewee and fewer words regarding qualifications for the job than did control subjects.[130]

In their study of sixty student subjects, some of whom were shown a pornographic video and some of whom were shown a control video, McKenzie-Mohr and Zanna found that "[f]or gender schematic males, exposure to nonviolent pornography seems to influence the way they view and act toward a woman in a task-oriented (or 'professional') situation."[131] After viewing pornography, these men were interviewed about their transition to college life by a female subject. Gender schematic males were those who were classified as masculine sex-types after taking the Bem Sex Role Inventory to determine whether the subjects self-identified as masculine or feminine. The behavioral differences included acting more sexually motivated, moving closer to the female subject, and having faster and greater recall on the female subjects' appearance. They also remembered less about what the female subject asked them. This led McKenzie-Mohr and Zanna to surmise, "Intuitively, the implications appear grave. If a male manager views a female employee as a sexual object, information that is relevant to her work performance, her continuation in the position, or her promotion may be overlooked."[132]

In addition, harassment is more likely to occur in workplaces where it appears to be permissible. For example, if harassment is tolerated or is not properly remedied, employees will receive the message that it is acceptable behavior.[133] The corresponding message to victims of harassment is that they might as well not complain; nothing will be done about it. In addition, if harassment is perpetrated by supervisors or other company higher-ups, lower-level employees will believe it is permissible for them as well.[134] One particularly interesting study showed that men with a predisposition to harass are more likely to do so when given a "harassing role model," i.e., when they have observed a man doing the job they were assigned to do engaged in harassing behavior.[135]

This role model behavior fits in with the establishment of what social scientists call "local norms." Social scientists and others have conducted a variety of studies in an attempt to assess how local norms of behavior factor into the perceptions of harassment in the workplace. Some have explicitly identified what are known as "sexualized work environments."[136] In these environments, "sexual jokes, comments, innuendos, and sexual or seductive dress are tolerated, condoned, or encouraged."[137] Because of the nature of the environment, supervisors themselves may become "desensitized" to harassing situations.[138]

The above is supported by a study by the United States Department of Defense. In it, a higher percentage of harassing incidents occurred in workplaces in which the commanding officer was deemed to encourage harassment. Researchers ran a multiple regression analysis that revealed that the "more men at a location [who] saw the CO [commanding officer] as indifferent or neutral with regard to sexual harassment, the more women at that location were harassed."[139] Additionally, in a study conducted of a large organization in 1991, psychologists found that women who had been sexually harassed in the previous two years were more likely to view managers as negatively responding to allegations of harassment and less likely to believe management made a positive response to their complaints. The researchers also conducted a multiple regression analysis and discovered that the more men who agreed that "[t]he management has discouraged employees from complaining about sexual harassment," "the more women in that office were sexually harassed."[140]

In the second survey, employees also were asked about incidents of sexually explicit pictures or written materials, sexually oriented incidents at office parties, sexually explicit graffiti, sexually explicit software on company computers, and gender-segregated work-related parties. The researchers theorized that such incidents also would affect local social norms and lead to a higher incidence of sexual harassment. They concluded that "*inter*personal forms of sexual harassment such as uninvited sexual attention are more common in offices where the presence of pinups and other more *im*personal sexual behaviors are part of the general sexual ambience."[141] Interestingly, they reached this conclusion by comparing the number of these sex-related behaviors reported by men in the offices with the response of women having experience with uninvited sexual attention in the same office. They found the two items significantly correlated.

Diversity in the workforce appears to help lessen harassment. At least one survey has shown "that women working in male-dominated settings more often reported experiencing a highly stereotyped workplace, with higher levels of unwelcome sexual overtures, than [did] women working in settings with more equal numbers of women and men."[142] Gruber found that routine contact with men on the job increases sexually harassing behavior. Indeed, social science evidence suggests that once a "critical mass" of nontraditional employees are present at a workplace, incidents of harassing behavior directed at nontraditional employees will decrease and the character of the workplace will change to incorporate the newcomers as part of the local norm.[143] Likewise, in its extensive study of federal employees, the USMSPB found that "[v]ictims [of sexual harassment] are more likely than nonvictims to work exclusively or mostly with individuals of the opposite sex."[144]

B. INTERACTION WITH THE HIGH LSH MAN

At the beginning of this section, I mentioned that sexual harassment is a function of both person and situation. The research discussed above focuses on the situation. Social scientists also have identified characteristics of men likely to sexually harass. To this end, John Pryor has developed a self-report measure of men likely to sexually harass (LSH).[145] This measure was developed to test the likelihood that a person will engage in acts of quid pro quo sexual harassment. The methodology developed to assess this is "conceptually similar" to that developed to study rapists.[146] Indeed, studies of high LSH men tend to show that, as do rapists, these men link sexuality with power and dominance.[147] The connection between LSH and other forms of sex-related indicators has been studied as well.

Several patterns emerge. First, correlations between other types of sexual aggression scales reveal a relationship between LSH and other behaviors. This tends to suggest that sexual harassment is yet another point in the continuum of "male-aggressive/female-passive patterns of interaction."[148] Second, "the profile [of the LSH man] that emerges from these findings is that LSH is related to an identification with a stereotypic view of masculinity. High LSH men tend to view themselves as hypermasculine."[149] In addition, "One thing apparently unrelated to the sexual motives characteristic of the high LSH man is any sense of seeking sex as a means to an emotional relationship with a woman."[150] Given this, it is not surprising that one study has indicated that "high LSH men link thoughts about sexuality with thoughts about social dominance."[151] Research by Pryor et al.,[152] Bargh and Raymond,[153] Barak and Kaplan,[154] and others[155] supports this theory.

High LSH men also may be aware of situational constraints on their behavior. In her study comparing the reactions of high and low LSH men to harassing acts of a role model, LaVite found that 89% of high LSH men touched the confederate they were training, compared to only 36% of low LSH men.[156] This suggests that creating local norms by providing nonharassing role models may help reduce workplace harassment even in high LSH men.[157] The study conducted by Rudman and Borgida, however, suggests that even low LSH men will be more likely to harass if primed, i.e., if they are shown suggestive pictures of women or witness others engaging in harassing behavior.[158] Thus, the behavior of both high and low LSH men may well be affected by the environment in which they work.

C. MORE MODELS BASED ON THE DATA

More recently, psychologists have tried to synthesize the models and the data in an effort to provide a fuller and more inclusive account of how sexual harassment operates in the workplace. Louise Fitzgerald and her colleagues proposed a model that provides two basic causes of sexual harassment: "organizational climate and job gender context."[159] By organizational climate, they mean aspects of the organization that signal tolerance of sexual harassment in the workplace. By job gender context, they mean the sex composition of the work group as well as the nature of the job duties, i.e, whether they are traditionally considered male or female. They hypothesized that these two elements largely determine the prevalence of sexual harassment in the workplace.

Fitzgerald et al. tested the model using a sample of 357 women employed at a large utility company. To assess job gender context, they asked participants whether they were the first member of their sex in the particular job; whether their immediate supervisor was male or female; and to estimate the gender makeup of their work group on a five-point scale (1 being almost all men, and 5 being almost all women). They used the Organizational Tolerance for Sexual Harassment Inventory (OTSHI) to assess the organizational environment. Finally, they asked participants about sexually harassing incidents that they had experienced over the past two years. For this assessment, they used the revised SEQ, which includes the three main types of sexual harassment: gender harassment, unwanted sexual attention, and sexual coercion. They also assessed the psychological, health, and job impact of the harassment on those who experienced it.[160]

Fitzgerald et al.'s data supported the hypothesis that organizational tolerance of sexual harassment was a significant factor affecting whether women were sexually harassed. The gender makeup of the workplace played a role as well. However, it was not a skewed gender makeup per se that led to increased harassment but, instead, the combination of the presence of large numbers of male workers along with job tasks that are traditionally considered male that seemed to cause the effect. Although the researchers noted limitations in their research design, this outcome does suggest that they are headed in a productive direction. One of the potential areas they designated for further examination was the role of individual factors related to the harasser. They suggested that characteristics of the individual harasser may have more impact in quid pro quo cases, whereas workplace environment may have more impact in hostile environment cases.[161] This has intuitive appeal, given what Pryor has found with respect to men who score high on the LSH inventory. Accordingly, the factors that lead to harassment likely vary depending on a combination of the workplace context (including the two factors developed by Fitzgerald) and individual characteristics of the harasser.

Another possible factor that may have an impact is the vulnerability of the target. Hesson-McInnis and Fitzgerald analyzed data from the 1988 USMPSB study to test a model of sexual harassment that incorporated this factor. To test the relationship between target vulnerability and harassment, they looked at the age, educational level, and marital status of the target.[162] Interestingly, they found that the "occurrence and intensity of harassment were well predicted by victim vulnerability, a male-dominated job context, and an organizational context that was relatively tolerant of harassing behavior."[163] However, target characteristics were not predictive of forms of gender harassment studied by the USMPSB. These forms of harassment were predicted solely by organizational variables, leading these researchers to call into doubt models, such as the biological model, that do not take a multidimensional approach to sexual harassment.[164] Each of these models provides helpful information. The task becomes how to incorporate them into legal doctrine.

C. *Rethinking the Concept of Because of Sex*

The question remains as to whether the courts' interpretation of the standard "because of sex" needs reformulation, given the current theory on how sexual harassment operates. A review of the models in light of the data suggests that all of them provide some information about the conditions under which harassment occurs. In addition, they all suggest that sex plays a role. Thus, the models provide a basis for the courts to rule that the harassment was because of sex. Particular models may be more helpful to explain and understand harassment in specific contexts. In this part of the chapter, I begin by looking to social science to see if the types of cases that cause the courts problems can be conceptualized as because of sex. Then, I create a legal standard that will help courts identify situations in which the harassment is likely sex based. This standard will be practical and, I hope, therefore useful to the courts, lawyers, and litigants.

I do not discuss all forms of sexual harassment here. What I am particularly concerned with are the three scenarios identified earlier in this chapter that have caused the courts problems in conceptualizing the behaviors involved as because of sex: (1) same-sexual harassment; (2) the equal-opportunity harasser and harassing environment; and (3) the failed consensual relationship. Looking at these specific cases does not necessarily lead to a grand theory of sexual harassment; however, looking at these cases in addition to other cases described in this book does suggest a multifactored approach that has its roots in discrimination because of sex.

Before considering the three specific scenarios, it's worth noting that there have been several recent and compelling attempts to reconceptualize sexual harassment law. Law professors Vicki Schultz, Kathryn

Abrams, and Katherine Franke, among others, have all attempted to re-formulate sexual harassment law.[165] Others already have parsed their theories, so I do not do so in detail here.[166] Their efforts are somewhat different from mine in that they are designed to envision an overall theory, partly in an effort to encompass same-sexual harassment (or, at least, certain forms of it) within the theory of sex discrimination. My effort is more of what I call "law on the ground": I want to give litigants, lawyers, and courts something they can use in the court system to help them understand, argue, and rule in these cases. Although the difficulty of conceptualizing various forms of sexual harassment as discrimination because of sex has led several commentators to resort to tort law as a solution,[167] I resist this temptation. Instead, I place sexual harassment where I think it belongs: as a form of sex discrimination under Title VII. Looking at the text of the statute in light of social science leads to a practical solution.[168]

1. Conceptualizing Problematic Cases as "Because of Sex"

A. SAME-SEXUAL HARASSMENT

Understanding how same-sexual harassment works is very important to the employment opportunities of men. Preliminary studies suggest that men are more likely to be harassed by other men than by women (or, at the least, that men are more likely to be harassed by persons of the same sex than are women who are harassed).[169] Thus, if same-sexual harassment can be characterized as sex discrimination under Title VII, men will have a tool to eliminate this form of harassment. The power model (including Stockdale's rejection-based theory), sex-role spillover theory, as well as Fitzgerald's integrated approach all are helpful in understanding why same-sexual harassment is discrimination because of sex. The cases examined earlier in this chapter involved two types of scenarios: (1) men who deviated from gender norms, either because they were gay, appeared to be gay, or did not play along with "macho" male behavior in the workplace, and (2) heterosexual men who were singled out by other heterosexual men for harassment that involved sexual conduct.

The first category of cases involves men who defy gender stereotypes of appropriate male behavior or challenge male-driven workplace norms. In this way, they threaten the hierarchy inherent in patriarchy. Harassment of these men by heterosexual men is not about sexuality but, as Stockdale points out, about rejection as a means of enforcing gender conformity, while boosting the ethos of the harasser.[170] Even though the harassment might have a sexual component, sexuality is used to show the dominance (or power) of the harassing man vis-à-vis his target. This is likewise consistent with Fitzgerald's focus on job context. These men are usually in all-male workplaces and are essentially treated like a woman in the context of being the first woman or one of few women in a predominantly male workplace. Their lack of macho characteristics sets them apart from other men. In the case of gay male targets, their failure to have sexual relations with women additionally sets them apart from other men.

It is easy to see how this form of harassment is "because of sex," and, indeed, some courts and judges (as explained earlier in this chapter), have characterized it as such. These men are singled out for their nonconformity with prevailing gender norms. This does not mean that all male-on-male horseplay will be considered sexual harassment. Instead, the particular context in which the harassment takes place needs to be analyzed. A careful look at the gender makeup of the work group, the tasks assigned the target, and the nature of the harassing incidents should help fact finders decide whether the harassment was because of sex. It should also be noted that such harassment will still have to reach a certain level to be actionable. Preliminary studies of male-on-male harassment indicate that most of it is verbal in nature and that men do not find this type of harassment all that upsetting.[171] Arguments regarding whether the harassment was because of sex or sexual orientation, under this analysis, become semantic. Because the sexual orientation of the target often triggers stereotypes regarding the appropriate behavior of men, it fits well within the stereotyping model of sexual harassment.

Law professor Linda Hamilton Krieger has linked stereotypes to discrimination based on sex in the context of "ordinary" sex discrimination cases:

> Expressions of gender-based normative stereotypes do indeed indicate that an employee's gender is entering into decisionmaking; it is logical to infer from such statements that males and females are being subjected to differing role expectations and behavioral standards because of gender. If one understands stereotypes in this way, it is reasonable to conclude that statements reflecting stereotypes, made in connection with a particular employment decision, indicate the presence of conscious discriminatory intent.[172]

Krieger's approach is applicable to same-sexual harassment cases involving effeminate or gay men. The discrimination, instead of being an adverse employment decision, is in the form of harassment, which often reflects what behavior is or is not deemed appropriate—stereotypically—for males. Rather than involving a particular employment decision, it is reflected in the nature and content of the harassment itself.

Instead of being conceptualized as "because of sexual orientation," cases involving male-on-male heterosexual harassment often fail because courts conclude they are based on personal animosity. Yet, even in these cases, careful attention to the context helps in understanding whether the harassment was because of sex. First, the cases being brought (at least those reported) do not tend to involve men goofing around at work, e.g., joking around and the like. The cases in which men complain usually involve sexual conduct.

Law professor David Schwartz has argued that many feminist legal scholars have essentially thrown out the baby with the bath water in attempting to reformulate sexual harassment law. Some courts have been willing to assume behavior is because of sex if it involves sexual conduct. Schwartz calls this the sex per se rule. He argues that feminist attempts to reconceptualize sexual harassment have undermined this rule and thereby the efficacy of sexual harassment law generally.[173] I am somewhat sympathetic to Schwartz's position (because courts and jurors will likely have an easier time with such a bright-line rule), but I believe that the feminists he critiques have a legitimate concern that the emphasis on sexual conduct distracts courts from other forms of sex discrimination. Yet, assuming all sexual conduct—even when perpetrated between heterosexual males—is because of sex without a theory to explain how it is sex discrimination, while pragmatic, is not wholly satisfying.

Fortunately, there is a way to conceptualize male-on-male heterosexual conduct that should be helpful in separating mere horseplay from sex discrimination. Using as an example a case described earlier in this chapter—*Johnson v. Hondo, Inc.*—helps explain how these cases can be understood as sex discrimination. In *Johnson*, a heterosexual male was harassed by a male coworker in an all-male environment. The coworker threatened to make his target perform oral sex (while he grabbed his own crotch) and made derogatory comments about the target's girlfriend. The target responded by calling his harasser names: SOB, fag, and faggot.[174] The court concluded that the case involved nothing more than personal animosity.

Using the power model, it becomes easy to understand this harassment as sex discrimination. Identification as a heterosexual is fundamental to the identity of many males. Indeed, power theory links heterosexism to patriarchy. References to sexual conduct renders the plaintiff in this case the equivalent of a woman. The harasser threatened to make the plaintiff perform oral sex—a sexual act identified with subservient females. Kingsley Browne might argue that this undermined the target's stature in the patriarchy. Therefore, recognizing such a claim has the potential to reinforce patriarchy. However, it is really the harasser who is trying to use patriarchy in order to assert power over his target. It is no accident that he uses sexual conduct to do this. As explained above, sexual conduct renders the target like a woman—a lower-statused gendered person. Thus, recognizing such a claim might well undermine patriarchy by punishing those who use of one of its key tools—sexuality—to harass people in the workplace.

Although Vicki Schultz has argued recently that sexual harassment law has gone too far, resulting in employers prohibiting and disciplining "relatively harmless sexual behavior,"[175] the behavior in *Johnson* was not (and likely was not intended to be) harmless. It undermined the victim's identity as a man. Law professors Hilary Axam and Deborah Zalesne summed up the interrelationship between heterosexual male sexual harassment and male-on-female sexual harassment well: "Upon examination of the conduct at issue in each type of case, it becomes apparent that opposite-sex and same-sexual harassment both frequently serve to devalue femininity, discipline divergence from prescribed gender roles, and assert dominance of the masculine over the feminine through scenarios of sexual objectification, domination, and abuse."[176] As Mary Anne Case points out, "[W]hatever is gendered feminine is seen as less valuable than what is gendered masculine."[177] If courts recognize that these fact patterns involve sexual harassment, this has potential to help women because such recognition undermines patriarchy.

This still does not answer the question of where the line is between actionable conduct and "mere" horseplay. Certainly, there are instances in which some men engage in physical behavior, boasting, and other conduct that is either designed to place them on the top of the status hierarchy or, more benevolently, simply to have fun or relieve stress. Increasingly, feminists have become concerned that employers are trying to eliminate all sexuality from the workplace.[178] This is of concern because sexuality is part of who people are. It cannot simply be checked at the door of the workplace.[179] Yet, it is one thing to joke around, and quite another thing to use sexuality to undermine a worker's ability to stay on the job. That's what Title VII is aimed at: keeping people working regardless of the protected characteristic. Scenarios that involve harmless fun do not seem to result in sexual harassment cases. In addition, many will not reach the actionable "severe or pervasive" level. The line seems to be drawn for many men at sexual conduct. Even though the behavior may begin, for example, as a personal grudge, once again, it takes a turn to sexual conduct for a reason. The harassers' particular behaviors—grabbing their own crotches, making kissing gestures at the target, and referring to oral sex—were designed to undermine the target as a man. In this sense, it is discrimination because of sex. Thus, actions with sexual connotations can be considered because of sex in these contexts.

B. EQUAL OPPORTUNITY HARASSERS AND HARASSING ENVIRONMENTS

Equal opportunity harasser cases likewise present a difficult problem for the courts. The models presented above suggest that equal opportunity harasser situations may involve men high in LSH—men who link sex with power. Thus, harassment is used in these contexts to establish the harasser's dominance over both men and women. In this way the harasser acts to reify the power hierarchy inherent in patriarchy. In addition, sometimes women experience harassment that is different in kind (and clearly sex-specific) than men experience.

In some of the cases referred to earlier in this chapter, the court parsed the nature of the harassment directed at women and men and found that the harassment directed at women was different. Such harassment took on certain characteristics because of the target's sex. Thus, it became possible to conclude that the harassment directed at women was because of their sex due to the nature of the harassment itself. Due to the differences in treatment, these cases fit well within the concept of discrimination because of sex.

The cases involving harassing environments are explainable as discrimination because of sex, based on data on workplaces where harassment occurs as well as Fitzgerald's integrated model of harassment. The dynamics of workplaces in which there is one or few women lend themselves to sexual harassment. In addition, employers that tend to condone harassment also have increased rates of harassment. Finally, the cases described involved conduct directed specifically at women and/or the harassment was perpetrated in such a sex-specific way that the harassment clearly involved the target's sex. The women in these contexts were not harassed as coworkers but as women coworkers.

Gross v. Burggraf provides an example. In that case, the court essentially held that construction workplaces are vulgar, and women who enter them should expect the behavior to be commonplace. In coming to this conclusion, the court ignored that some incidents of harassment were directed at the plaintiff—some of which included gender-specific references. For example, the supervisor's reference to "smashing" a woman in the face is sex-specific and was made with reference to the plaintiff. The court likewise ignored the workplace demographics, which included few women. Finally, the court was unwilling to consider that the same behavior might be experienced differently by women in such a context than by a man. A supervisor's yelling at a woman in a demeaning manner in a context in which she is one of few women should make the court consider whether the yelling was truly due to a mistake by the worker or was a result of a mistake by a woman worker.

Similarly, in *Brown v. Henderson*, one must wonder whether the harassment was due to a dispute over a union election between two candidates or between a woman candidate and her male counterpart. In other words, the court needs to critically examine, especially given the sex-specific and sexual nature of the harassment in that case, whether the harassment was not directed at the target because she was a *woman* who ran for a union position.[180] The courts should be skeptical when the harassment takes a sexual turn in such a context. Sexuality can be used to objectify and demean women in the workplace, making it much more likely that the harassment was "because of sex." Judge Michael, dissenting in part, in *Ocheltree v. Scollon Productions, Inc.*, acknowledged that actions and words that demean women reinforce hierarchy in a manner that makes the harassment "because of sex."[181] The social science suggests he is correct.

C. FAILED CONSENSUAL RELATIONSHIPS

Looking at the few cases reported that involved failed consensual relationships, power theory, sex-role spillover, and Pryor's LSH model, all provide helpful insight into the dynamics of these fact patterns. Many of these cases involve higher-status males and lower-status females (although the *Succar* case involved a female coworker who harassed a male target). Some cases involve coworkers. Depending on the context and nature of the harassment, most cases easily are classified as "because of sex."

Cases involving higher-status males are most easily explained as because of sex. Although the initial consensual nature of the relationship may be explainable by use of a biological model, the resulting harassment appears to be more a result of the exercise of power by the harasser. For example, in *Green v. Administrators of Tulane Educational Fund*, a doctor harassed his secretary/office administrator allegedly because she refused to continue a relationship with him. His position of power over her combined with sex-role stereotyping of her as a woman in a traditional female occupation both help explain the resulting harassment. He harassed her because he was in a position of power that (he might have believed) would insulate him from her accusations (and entitle him to her attentions). In addition, he might have targeted her as a potential paramour because of her traditional female job—one that is often associated with a sexual relationship with the boss. Under either explanation, she is targeted because she was a *woman* who failed to accede to the demands of a man in power. The respective sexes of the actors play a part and render the harassment "because of sex."

The courts' continued difficulties with these cases seems particularly ironic. After all, the first Supreme Court case recognizing the cause of action—*Meritor*—involved a fact pattern that potentially could be considered "consensual." The Court in that case concluded that consent was not the key question in sexual harassment cases, but consent in failed relationship cases renders the harassment about something other than sex, in the view of some courts. Had the plaintiff in *Green* refused her boss's initial advances and had he continued to hound her for a relationship, the court would have had little problem characterizing the harassment as "because of sex." Her initial consent and later refusal, argued the employer, made it about something other than sex. This was nonsensical. She was still refusing to have a relationship with him; it was still "because of sex."

Coworker situations have a slightly different dynamic. Even though there is no status difference between the harasser and his or her target, power may play a role in these cases. In such situations, it may be societal power that plays a role—rather than workplace hierarchy—leading to the harassment. Taking *Galloway v. General Motors Service Parts Operations* as an example, the plaintiff in that case was harassed by her former boyfriend. He called her "sick bitch" repeatedly and also directed other derogatory comments at her, including an obscene gesture, while saying, "[S]uck this, bitch."[182] The court concluded that the harassment and the terms used were not based on gender. The harasser targeted the plaintiff because of their former relationship and did so in gender-specific terms. It is doubtful that the harasser would have targeted the plaintiff in such a manner had she not been a woman. In a sense, the harasser is making the plaintiff pay for being a woman who would not continue to date him. She had undermined his power—a result of societal patriarchy—and he was harassing her because of it.

2. A Practical Solution

Theoretically, the three categories of cases courts have difficulty with can be conceptualized as because of sex. I am concerned that this theoretical approach, however, is too obscure for courts. The facility with which human beings default to stereotypes when confronted with ambiguous information gives me further pause in setting up a standard for court use. What I propose the courts look at to determine whether the harassment is because of sex are the circumstances. This approach is consistent with Supreme Court precedent. The Court in *Oncale* directed lower courts to be sensitive to the factual circumstances and context in each case. I am taking the Court's guidance one step further. I am suggesting, based on social science, that the courts pay attention to specific factual factors that are likely to lead to discriminatory harassment. This multifactored approach, it is my hope, will give courts a concrete way to approach this issue that is consistent with what is known about the nature of sexual harassment.

This approach considers what psychologists have found about gender stereotypes and the ways that stereotypes can be undermined. Given the links between sexual harassment and stereotyping discussed earlier in this chapter, it makes sense to attempt to undermine stereotypes in setting up the legal standard. As Deaux and Kite explain:

> There are a number of ways in which one can weaken the grip of stereotypes. Simpler judgments are less likely to depend on stereotypes than are more complex judgments . . . and so one might want to split complex decisions (e.g., should a person be promoted) into smaller pieces where performance could be assessed more clearly. Ambiguous criteria also foster the use of stereotypes. If people are motivated to be accurate

when they make judgments about another person, then they are less likely to rely on stereotypes. . . . Similarly, if people are held accountable for their decisions, they are less likely to use broad generalizations.[183]

Deaux and Kite emphasize three areas in their stereotype research that have implications for reformulating sexual harassment law: (1) splitting up complex decisions into components; (2) using less ambiguous or unambiguous criteria; and (3) holding people accountable. There is no way for the legal system to hold jurors accountable, but the second and third means of undermining stereotypes—splitting up complex decisions into components and using less ambiguous criteria—could be used in this context to help in the decision making process. As for holding the other type of fact finders (judges) accountable, that has been part of the mission of this entire book in parsing their decisions and is the explicit duty of the appellate courts.

There are several factors that correlate consistently with the occurrence of sexual harassment in the workplace. Fact finders should examine whether these factors are present in a given case to help determine whether the harassment is because of sex. Included within these factors are (1) whether the workplace is gender homogeneous; (2) whether the target is isolated from others of the same gender; (3) whether the occupation is traditionally gendered female or male; (4) whether the environment is sexualized, for example, whether there are frequent sexual jokes, pinups, and so on; and (5) what is management's (including the immediate supervisor's) attitude toward harassment. No one factor need be present in every case in order for the fact finder to conclude that the harassment was "because of sex." Instead, the fact finder would look at the totality of all these factors to make the determination. By focusing on these factors, the fact finder is forced to assess the overall workplace environment. The factors help the fact finder concentrate on the circumstances that might lend themselves to harassment. They can be included in jury instructions, and their ramifications set out in those instructions. This allows for flexibility as well as an expansion of the types of facts that a court should consider based on increased knowledge about the functioning of sexual harassment in the workplace.

So, why have I chosen these factors and how will each be assessed? The first factor, whether the workplace is gender homogeneous, goes hand in hand with the second factor, whether the target is isolated from others of the same gender. Studies have consistently shown that a woman (and cases suggest, sometimes a man) who is placed in a predominantly male work environment is more likely to be sexually harassed. Such women challenge gender workplace norms in a way that makes them likely targets for harassment. Thus, if a woman experiences a series of targeted derogatory incidents, there is a significant likelihood that she has become such a target because of her sex. I am not the first legal scholar who has attempted to link gender integration of a workplace to the legal standard for sexual harassment. Law professor Vicki Schultz recently did so in creating a solution for the perceived problem of employers who overzealously enforce sexual harassment laws.[184] Interestingly, the gender segregation of the workplace is also helpful in understanding why men are harassed in predominantly male environments. These types of environments give rise to same-sexual harassment directed at men who violate gender norms, such as gay men. As Louise Fitzgerald and her colleagues have pointed out, assessment of the job-gender context is helpful in understanding whether the harassment was because of sex.

In addition, whether the occupation is traditionally considered gendered female or male plays a part in whether harassment is because of sex. Again, Fitzgerald and her colleagues suggested that the gendered nature of the job can lead to harassment because of sex. Thus, in occupations that are traditionally gendered male, women are more likely to be harassed for deviating from the gender norms of that occupation. Likewise, men who are in occupations that are traditionally gendered female may be more likely to be harassed as well for deviating from gender norms. In occupations that are gendered female, harassment can become the norm as well. Studies of nurses and secretaries have shown that in some predominantly female occupations, sexual harassment becomes a norm of the job. Thus, the gendered nature of the job results in its occupants becoming targets of harassment.

The fourth factor—whether the environment is sexualized, for example, whether there are frequent sexual jokes, pinups, and so on—correlates with increased incidents of sexual harassment in the workplace. Put simply, women who work in these types of environments are more likely to be sexually harassed. This is because sexual behavior, which often encompasses objectification of women, is condoned and sometimes even encouraged in these environments. In addition, it appears that for men who are likely to sexually harass, this type of atmosphere may act as a green light for them and lead them to harass when a work environment where such behavior is not tolerated might lead them to do otherwise.

The final factor is management's (including the immediate supervisor's) attitude toward harassment. Closely related to the fourth factor, this factor is included because of the many studies that have found a correlation between supervisors' attitudes about sexual harassment and the incidence of sexual harassment in the workplace. This information also is relevant to the *Ellerth/Faragher* affirmative defense discussed in chapter 5 because it forms part of the employer's efforts to prevent and correct harassment that has occurred. Evidence, including information about the supervisor's treatment of other allegations of harassment and supervisory attitudes toward harassment should be admissible and helpful in assessing whether the workplace is one in which sexual harassment is likely to occur.

Aside from more accurate fact finding, these factors also have a side benefit that should aid in eliminating sexual harassment in the workplace. Because fact finders (and, at initial stages, such as summary judgment, judges) will be looking at these factors to assess whether the harassment is because of sex, use of these factors also will force employers to look at harassment in a larger context than simply as a problem between one harasser and his or her target. Instead, employers will have to look at how their workplaces are structured and how the structure might foster harassment. This should lead to workplaces in which women and men who might become targets of harassment are less likely to be harassed. Employers may still attempt to bulletproof their workplaces in keeping with these factors in order to avoid liability,[185] but it will be much more difficult for them to address all these factors without making a sincere effort to evaluate and diversify their workplaces.

Psychologists have suggested such organizational remedies to limit the incidence of stereotyping, and therefore the incidence of harassment. In particular, Fiske and Glick suggest changing job descriptions and job titles in order to discourage segregation by gender.[186] In addition, how people in a particular job are treated can also "encourage or discourage stereotyping and harassment."[187] Advertising regarding sexual harassment policies and personnel recruitment of a significant number of nontraditional employees into traditionally segregated occupations can likewise have an effect.[188] Employers must also support these nontraditional employees, letting their coworkers know about their qualifications so that coworkers do not engage in affirmative action stereotyping.[189] As Fiske and Glick sum up: "Part of the impact of organizations adopting more interdependent and accountable structures is the message it sends about appropriate norms and standards. If those in authority communicate that stereotyping and harassment will not be tolerated and that this is a standard central to the organization's mission, then such policies have optimal impact. Those in power can create real change."[190] Thus, adoption of these factors, along with creating a better approach for fact finders grappling with these issues in lawsuits, should lead to better working environments for workers generally.

5

Reality Bites the *Ellerth/Faragher* Standard for Imputing Liability to Employers for Supervisor Sexual Harassment

Perhaps the legal standard that is most out of synch with the reality of sexual harassment in the workplace is the standard for imputing liability to the employer. It is not enough for a target to prove the harassment met the "severe or pervasive" standard. She also must establish that the employer is liable for this workplace conduct. The Court's decisions in *Faragher v. City of Boca Raton* and *Burlington Industries, Inc. v. Ellerth*, while theoretically creating an affirmative defense for employers in cases of supervisory harassment, result in a significant burden on the harassed employee to come forward and report the harassment as early as possible. This might make sense in terms of giving the employer the opportunity to nip the harassment in the bud, but it does not reflect the manner in which many targets respond to harassment. Instead, the courts appear to be engaging in "assumptions" about the way women "should" or "ought" to behave. In addition, these cases encourage and credit employer efforts to formulate sexual harassment policies and address harassment in the workplace through training and remedial measures. Yet, there is little evidence that such employer efforts are effective. Once again, courts assume an employer's attempts will be effective in remedying or preventing harassment when there is little empirical support for this position. The result is that the legal standards and the factual assumptions that underlie those standards, rather than tending to eliminate harassment in the workplace, amount to mere window dressing.

In this chapter, I begin by discussing the current legal standards for imputing liability to employers for the harassing acts of supervisors, focusing particularly on the newly created defense established in the *Ellerth* and *Faragher* decisions. I then discuss social science studies and medical science findings about various aspects of sexual harassment that are relevant to this standard. Included in this discussion are (1) what employer strategies lead to more or less harassment in the workplace; (2) whether employer training helps eliminate harassment in the workplace; and (3) how targets respond to harassment. Finally, in light of this social science data, I suggest modification of the standards to create healthier workplace environments where all workers will be respected and sexual harassment will be discouraged more effectively.

A. Supreme Court Precedents

Since the Supreme Court's decision in *Meritor*, the lower courts have struggled to determine under what circumstances to impute liability to the employer for harassing acts of supervisors. They have not been similarly confused regarding harassment by coworkers, about which consensus has formed that if the employer knew or should have known of the harassment and failed to take effective remedial measures, the employer will be liable.[1] There is also consensus on quid pro quo cases: when a "tangible employment action is taken" against an employee by a supervisor for failing to engage in a relationship or sexual activities with a supervisor, the employer is liable.[2] There is some debate in the lower courts about what constitutes a "tangible employment action" for purposes of this standard.

When it came to hostile environments created by supervisors, the *Meritor* Court established no precise rule. Caught between the trial court's standard of actual notice and the Court of Appeals' standard of strict liability, the Supreme Court "agree[d] with the EEOC that Congress wanted courts to look to agency principles for guidance in this area."[3] The Court referred to agency rules because the language of Title VII defined "employer" to include an "agent" of the employer. It also acknowledged that common law agency principles might not be "transferable in all their particulars to Title VII."[4] With so vague a standard, it is not surprising that it led to confusion among the lower courts and scholarly debate as to the appropriate standard for imposing liability on employers for supervisor harassment.[5]

Since *Meritor*, the Court has clarified this standard in *Faragher v. City of Boca Raton* and *Burlington Industries, Inc. v. Ellerth*. In *Faragher*, the Court addressed the circumstances under which an employer may be held liable for a supervisor's acts of harassment that create a hostile work environment. In order to frame a standard, the Court looked at various theories of imputing liability to employers for the actions of their supervisors. It took into consideration that supervisors can easily misuse their authority and that the threat of an adverse employment action is always there for an employee who does not act in the manner a supervisor wishes. On the other hand, the Court acknowledged its statement in *Meritor* that employers would not automatically be liable for the acts of their supervisors.[6]

With this in mind, as well as the Court's current emphasis on correcting problems before they reach litigation, the Court provided that employers would be vicariously liable for supervisor-created hostile environments, subject to an affirmative defense:

> When no tangible employment action is taken, a defending employer may raise an affirmative defense to liability or damages, subject to proof by a preponderance of the evidence. . . . The defense comprises two necessary elements: (a) that the employer exercised reasonable care to prevent and correct promptly any sexually harassing behavior, and (b) that the plaintiff employee unreasonably failed to take advantage of any preventive or corrective opportunities provided by the employer or to avoid harm otherwise.[7]

The Court did not design the defense to act as a complete bar to liability in every instance. Instead, it explicitly stated that the defense may limit "liability or damages." It also made clear that the defense does not exist if the supervisor's harassment involves a "tangible employment action" against the harassed employee, such as a demotion, pay cut, and the like.[8] In such cases, the employer is liable.

In *Faragher*, the Court stated that it arrived at this "compromise" affirmative defense after considering common law distinctions in agency law between supervisory acts that benefit the employer and those it characterized as a personal "frolic."[9] While acknowledging that sexual harassment was prevalent enough in the workplace for employers to "reasonably anticipate" such conduct occurring, the Court stopped short of holding employers liable for all acts of harassment by supervisors, instead preferring to provide the affirmative defense.[10]

In *Ellerth*, the Supreme Court addressed whether an employee must prove a tangible job detriment in order to maintain a quid pro quo harassment claim. The Court recharacterized the issue as whether the company was vicariously liable for the acts of its supervisor. The Court reasoned that the terms "quid pro quo" and "hostile environment" are useful in separating harassing situations in which a threat is carried out and one in which the threat is not carried out, but beyond that, they have little significance. Thus, although Ellerth's claim involved unfulfilled threats, this was not fatal to her harassment claim; it simply meant that she had a hostile environment claim instead of a quid pro quo claim. In rejecting threats as a basis for liability for quid pro quo harassment, the Court departed from precedent in some jurisdictions holding threats sufficient.[11] In addition, it opened up debate about what would constitute a "tangible employment action" that eliminates the *Ellerth/Faragher* affirmative defense, an issue the Supreme Court attempted to resolve in 2004.[12]

The *Ellerth* Court adopted the identical affirmative defense as it had adopted in *Faragher*.[13] It also described what sorts of evidence might suffice to prove the affirmative defense:

> While proof that an employer had promulgated an anti-harassment policy with complaint procedure is not necessary in every instances as a matter of law, the need for a stated policy suitable to the employment circumstances may appropriately be addressed in any case when litigating the first element of the defense. And while proof that an employee failed to fulfill the corresponding obligation of reasonable care to avoid harm is not limited to showing any unreasonable failure to use any complaint procedure provided by the employer, a demonstration of such failure will normally suffice to satisfy the employer's burden under the second element of the defense.[14]

The Court's description supports the use of antiharassment policies by employers. The Court suggests that the one-two combination of an employer-promulgated antiharassment policy and the employee's "unreasonable failure to use" such a policy can provide necessary proof of both elements of this defense. Although the burden of proof for this affirmative defense is obviously on the employer, depending how the lower courts apply this defense, *Ellerth* and *Faragher* may not establish a very difficult burden for employers.

B. Lower Courts' Interpretations

While the lower courts have been assesssing the applicability and contours of the *Ellerth/Faragher* affirmative defense for only six years, several themes have already begun to emerge. First, consistent with *Ellerth*, threats that are not carried out do not constitute quid pro quo harassment. Instead, the courts have struggled to determine what constitutes a tangible employment action for purposes of eliminating the defense. Second, although courts are careful to note that an employer's antiharassment policy does not, in and of itself, meet the requirements of the defense, as a practical matter, that is the implication of many rulings. Third, courts appear skeptical of plaintiffs' reasons for not reporting harassment at the earliest moment, which helps employers maintain the second element of the defense—that the plaintiff unreasonably failed "to take advantage of preventive or corrective opportunities provided by the employer or to avoid harm otherwise."[15] Finally, cases applying the defense generally have used it as a complete defense and not simply as a means of limiting damages. The defense also is used to take the case away from the jury, either through granting summary judgment or judgment as a matter of law.

Courts discussing the *Ellerth/Faragher* defense acknowledge that simple implementation of an anti–sexual harassment policy may not insulate an employer from liability. However, implementation of such a policy seems to have the net result of satisfying the first prong of the defense in many cases. As the Fourth Circuit explained in *Watkins v. Professional Security Bureau, Ltd.*, the sexual harassment policy's "'existence . . . militates strongly in favor of a conclusion that the employer exercised reasonable care to prevent and promptly correct sexual harassment.'"[16] Employers, likewise, have used training programs to bolster their position that they took reasonable steps to prevent harassment.[17] Even if the employer is unsuccessful in stopping harassment following a complaint pursuant to such a policy, the employer may satisfy the first prong of the defense. As the court in *Caridad v. Metro-North Commuter Railroad* explained, "An employer need not prove success in preventing harassing behavior in order to demonstrate that it exercised reasonable care in preventing and correcting sexually harassing conduct."[18] Thus, an employer's response to harassment may have been reasonable even though the conduct continued.

Further, the existence of such a policy is useful in meeting the second element of the defense. As the *Watkins* court explained, "When an employer has in place a viable anti-harassment policy, a demonstration that an employee unreasonably failed to utilize the complaint procedure provided by the employer 'will normally suffice to satisfy the employer's burden under the second element of the defense.'"[19] Often, the result is that if a plaintiff delays in reporting harassment under a policy, the courts hold that the second element has been satisfied. For example, the plaintiff's delay in reporting her rape by a supervisor in *Watkins* was about four months.[20] In *Caridad v. Metro-North Commuter Railroad*, the employee did not report the harassment for three months.[21] The plaintiff in *Savino v. C.P. Hall Co.* likewise delayed reporting for about four months.[22] In these cases, this delay furthered defendants' showings on the second element of the defense.

The plaintiffs in these cases tried to explain their reasons for not reporting the harassment earlier, but the courts were unreceptive to their explanations, deeming them unreasonable. As the court in *Caridad* explained, "We do not doubt that there are many reasons why a victimized employee may be reluctant to report acts of workplace harassment, but for that reluctance to preclude the employer's affirmative defense, it must be based on apprehension of what the employer might do, not merely on concern about the reaction of co-workers."[23] The court in *Caridad* ignored that the plaintiff was the only woman electrician among the twelve electricians in her work unit. She initially did not report the harassment she experienced from her supervisor and coworkers because "she did not think an investigation would improve matters."[24] She also did not trust the company's equal employment office. Caridad alleged that her supervisor harassed her, which included sexual touchings, over a seven-month period. Her coworkers treated her in a hostile manner as well, telling her that "nobody cares what happens to you" and that she had "walked into a lion's den."[25] Eventually, she broke down during a disciplinary hearing about her absenteeism and told the employer, including the affirmative action director, about the harassment. Even though the employer offered to transfer her to another shift, Caridad refused the offer because she believed it would not help; all other work areas, like her current work area, were predominately male.

Similarly, the plaintiff in *Watkins* did not report her rape by a supervisor until four months after it happened. When a succeeding incident that was less severe occurred, she did inform another supervisor.[26] Once again, the court of appeals held that no reasonable jury could find for Watkins and upheld the lower court's granting of judgment as a matter of law. As the Seventh Circuit Court of Appeals in *Shaw v. Autozone, Inc.* explained, "[A]n employee's subjective fears of confrontation, unpleasantness or retaliation do not alleviate the employee's duty under *Ellerth* to alert the employer to the allegedly hostile environment."[27]

The *Watkins* court pushed this one step further. Faced with a situation in which the plaintiff testified that she was unaware of the employer's antiharassment policy, the court found that she could be found "constructively aware" based on the employer's having placed the policy in the employee handbook (which the plaintiff stated she never received), having posted the policy in an area frequented by employees, and having placed the employee handbook at work sites. "Under these circumstances, a reasonable jury could only conclude that Watkins was at least constructively aware of the policy."[28]

Failure to aggressively pursue a claim can also result in the court's finding that the plaintiff "failed to avoid harm otherwise," which will also satisfy the second prong of the defense. In *Brown v. Perry*, the plaintiff was physically attacked by a supervisor in his hotel room while attending a conference. She told her bosses about this attack but decided that she did not want to pursue the matter formally. Six months later, she was again attacked in a hotel room by the same supervisor. The court stated that "[t]he record in this case is replete with uncontroverted evidence that Brown [the plaintiff] utterly failed to 'avoid harm otherwise.' Less than six months after rebuffing advances from Boyd in his hotel room late at night, Brown unnecessarily put herself in a situation that permitted repetition of precisely the same kind of advances."[29]

The net effect of these cases is that lower courts often are placing a significant burden on the plaintiff to report harassment, even though the burden of proof for the affirmative defense is on the defendant. As the *Shaw* court put it: "[T]he law against sexual harassment is not 'self-enforcing' and an employer cannot be expected to correct harassment unless the employee makes a concerted effort to inform the employer that a problem exists. . . ." In short, Shaw [the plaintiff] acted in precisely the manner that a victim of sexual harassment should *not* act in order to win recovery under the new law.[30]

The courts in *Caridad* and *Brown* did not directly address the "failure to avoid harm otherwise" aspect of the second prong, but both likewise concluded that both plaintiffs' reluctance to have the employer pursue the claim after they reported it aided the employer in establishing the second element of the defense. In *Brown* the court held the employer's response adequate (not doing anything pursuant to the plaintiff's wishes) even though the employer's own policy required that all instances of sexual harassment be reported to a resources manager. Brown reported the harassment to her supervisors, but they did not pass this information on to a resources manager pursuant to company policy. Instead, the court placed the entire burden on the plaintiff:

> We believe that in these circumstances offering immediate unconditional support to the victim and suggesting that she pursue her EEO remedies constitutes an entirely reasonable effort to prevent further incidents. That this effort proved unsuccessful is unfortunate, but it does not mean that the effort was unreasonable. Sometimes, as in this case, an employer's reasonable attempt to prevent harm will be frustrated by events that are unforeseeable and beyond the employer's control. The law requires an employer to be reasonable, not clairvoyant or omnipotent.[31]

The effect, however, is that the court required the plaintiff to be clairvoyant and predict subsequent harassment by a superior.

The *Watkins* court also suggested that the defendant need not satisfy the second prong of the defense in order to be successful using the defense. As the court explained:

> Even if Watkins' disclosure of the harassment of Dowling were adequate to establish that she took advantage of available preventive or corrective opportunities, our result would be the same. Although the Supreme Court did not speak to this issue in *Burlington Industries*, we cannot conceive that an employer that satisfied the first element of the affirmative defense and that promptly and adequately responds to a reported incident of sexual harassment . . . would be held liable for the harassment on the basis of an inability to satisfy the literal terms of the second element of the affirmative defense. . . . Such a result would be wholly contrary to a laudable purpose behind limitations on employer liability identified by the Supreme Court in *Burlington Industries*: to promote conciliation.[32]

This interpretation is at odds with the Equal Employment Opportunity Commission's guidance on this issue.[33]

Some courts have been a bit more lenient in their interpretation of the second element. For example, in *Watts v. Kroger Company*, the Fifth Circuit Court of Appeals reversed in part the granting of summary judgment because a jury could find that waiting a couple months to report harassment was not unreasonable. Further, the plaintiff's use of a union grievance mechanism rather than the employer's internal procedure could satisfy the plaintiff's obligation to take advantage of corrective opportunities or to avoid harm otherwise.[34]

The end result in many cases is that *Ellerth/Faragher* was used to formulate a complete defense to liability. The courts did not even entertain the possibility that the defense might simply limit damages. In *Savino*, the trial court's jury instruction contemplated that the jury could choose to reduce the damages based on the affirmative defense, and the court of appeals supported this position. However, the jury itself decided that it formed a complete defense to employer liability in that case.[35] In light of these decisions, in the next section, I examine how well these interpretations reflect the reality of employer and target responses to sexual harassment in the workplace.

C. Social Science Data

The *Ellerth/Faragher* affirmative defense places responsibility on both the employer and the harassed employee. The employer has a duty to prevent and correct harassment once it becomes aware of it, and the employee, under many circumstances, has a duty to tell the employer about harassing incidents, thereby taking action to protect herself. The findings of social scientists on both employer control over the work environment and the reporting behavior of harassed employees have implications for the duty of employer and employee. In this section, I review various studies in an effort to assess whether this affirmative defense is likely to further Title VII's primary purpose: elimination of discrimination in employment.

1. The Effect of Threats

In chapter 1, social science data on the perception of sexual harassment involving threats was discussed. Looking at that data, there is near-universal agreement among workers that sexual bribery as well as sexual coercion constitute sexual harassment. Studies of both working and student populations overwhelmingly show that people agree that sexual propositions tied to a job threat or a job enhancement constitute sexual harassment.[36] Although such propositions are consistent with the quid pro quo category of harassment, the Court has separated out harassment that results in an tangible employment action from harassment that is, as the Court characterizes it, a "mere threat." Thus, for example, if a supervisor threatens to cut a target's salary for refusing to have a relationship with him, but the supervisor never carries out that threat, the employer could still use the *Ellerth/Faragher* defense. However, if the target's pay was actually reduced because of her refusal, the defense would no longer be available to the employer. Given the perception data on threats, this distinction between threats that are carried out versus those that are not can be questioned.

2. The Employer's Influence over the Work Environment

As developed more fully in chapter 4, certain workplace characteristics appear to lend themselves to more sexual harassment than others. For example, social science reveals that workplaces where there are few women, where demeaning images of women are present, and where supervisors do not take sexual harassment seriously tend to have more sexual harassment. The implications for the employer's prevention efforts—key to the first element of the *Ellerth/Faragher* defense—are obvious. To the extent that employers can influence these aspects of their workplaces, their efforts could go a long way toward lessening sexual harassment. In addition, studies suggest that these norms may even influence men who are likely to sexually harass. Thus, they may even curb harassment by those who would do so if the behavior had little consequence for them. Employers can influence local norms by setting and enforcing anti–sexual harassment policies as well. All these factors are helpful in evaluating whether an employer has adequately attempted to prevent sexual harassment in the workplace.

Some preventive measures require particular mention here because of their influence on court outcomes. Anti–sexual harassment policies and training programs have an impact on the outcomes of cases. It seems intuitive that sexual harassment training programs should have an effect on local norms, but the effects of such training have yet to be extensively studied. Indeed, "[l]ittle empirical research has assessed the effects of training on potential harassers' knowledge, behaviors, or attitudes regarding sexual harassment."[37] This has led law professor Susan Bisom-Rapp to question the validity of the Court's reliance on training as the key to preventing sexual harassment.[38]

For example, in a study of the effects of a training video on sexual harassment, Perry and her colleagues found that a twenty-minute training video did not affect viewers' knowledge of sexual harassment or of a harasser's propensity to touch a woman during a subsequent golf lesson. Although the study may be less generalizable because of the rather small sample size, Perry et al. did find that sexual harassment awareness training "appeared to be more effective" for high LSH men than for low LSH men. To illustrate, high LSH men who viewed the video engaged in less inappropriate touching than those who had not viewed the video. Finally, the researchers also found that viewing the video "was not effective in changing long-term attitudes and belief systems associated with the propensity to harass."[39] This might not be all that surprising, but it does suggest that courts (and employers) should be hesitant to accept the use of training videos as an effective preventive strategy.[40] One study of the effect of written training materials showed that they affected what men considered to be sexual harassment in a positive manner.[41] Like the earlier study described, this study was also hampered by a somewhat small sample size.[42]

In addition to the questionable positive value of such programs, scholars have noted that sexual harassment training and diversity training can lead to backlash against the groups the employer is trying to help. Such training can bolster or create new stereotypes about protected groups that run counter to the point of such training. There are several theoretical reasons for this result, including attitude polarization. In the presence of attitude polarization, a subject's beliefs become reinforced and entrenched, rather than lessened, through training.[43] Whatever the reasons for the negative consequences, it is clear that training has the potential to backfire and should be viewed skeptically by the courts, especially in workplaces where harassment is widespread in spite of such training.

Instead, the courts should examine whether a given program actually works to eliminate discrimination in the particular workplace.[44] For example, employers whose workplaces are dominated by or contain sections that are traditional male workplaces versus those with traditional female work sections may have to adjust their training because of differences in the phenomenon of harassment in these two contexts.[45] Law professor Joanna Grossman, reviewing studies of sexual harassment training, sees more potential for training to play a role in changing employee attitudes about sexual harassment. Some studies indicate that sexual harassment training may have an impact on assessments of behavior people perceive as harassing.[46] However, Grossman concedes that "[s]ocial science tells us that current preventative efforts employers take may help, but are not sufficient to effect a meaningful reduction in the level of harassment."[47] She bases this in part on studies such as the USMSPB's, which have shown little reduction in overall reported rates of harassment in spite of training programs.

Bisom-Rapp argues that the Court's acceptance of training as a fundamental part of defending a sexual harassment claim is a result of what sociologist Lauren Edelman and her colleagues call "legal endogeneity." Under this theory, suggestions for modification of legal standards by groups subject to those standards end up finding their way into the actual legal standard that the courts adopt.[48] In the case of employment discrimination law, the courts have accepted training programs as an effective measure to prevent and correct harassment when it is unclear whether these programs are effective. It should come as no surprise that these standards then work to the advantage of the employers who suggested them. The fox is not only watching the hen house but also designing its fences (with appropriate gaps), while the farmer blissfully watches, occasionally nodding with approval. The result is that employers wiggle out of claims while doing very little to realistically end or limit workplace sexual harassment.

Although training may be of questionable value, studies show that employers who have policies aimed at addressing harassment are more likely to receive complaints about harassment than are employers without such policies in place, and therefore are more likely to have an opportunity to correct harassing behavior.[49] The type of policy appears to have an impact as well. In his study of nearly two thousand Canadian women workers, Gruber found that "providing workers with information about sexual harassment does have a modest effect on reducing its occurrence, although proactive methods [such as official complaint procedures or training programs] are much more effective."[50] In particular, the lack of proactive polices is a relatively strong predictor of environmental forms of harassment, such as sexual materials and "sexual categorical remarks."[51] In this respect, proactive employer methods appear to change or influence "local norms."[52]

These studies lead to the conclusion that harassment can be controlled by an employer's careful attention to the workplace environment and the creation of appropriate local norms. Employers can benefit from instituting an effective complaint procedure. Such a procedure can not only signal to employees that the employer takes sexual harassment complaints seriously but also can lead to earlier resolutions of such complaints. Because sexual harassment often leads to absenteeism, turnover, and lowered productivity,[53] an effective complaint procedure has the potential to create a win-win situation for both the employer and employee. Such a procedure can eliminate both the harassment and the workplace problems it spawns. It should take into account the status of the harasser, i.e., supervisor or coworker, in its design.[54] Avoiding or eliminating sexually explicit or sexually demeaning materials, hiring a more diverse workforce, and taking allegations of harassment seriously all appear to lead to less harassment in the workplace.

This research, however, has one notable glitch. There is little research on what procedures are effective for handling sexual harassment complaints once they are received, as well as what types of employer responses to harassing behaviors are effective in stopping harassment.[55] Thus, although the courts are eager to find the employer's remedy sufficient for purposes of the *Ellerth/Faragher* defense, there is scant social science literature to support what actually works. Indeed, Grossman has canvassed the literature and found a variety of problems with internal grievance mechanisms.[56] In the absence of a response that actually stops the harassment, the courts should be circumspect in assessing the employer's response as "reasonable."

3. The Effect on Targets Who Report Incidents of Sexual Harassment

Two types of evidence should be helpful in understanding women's responses to incidents of harassment. One comes from medical science. As I explain below, posttraumatic stress disorder (PTSD) explains why some harassment victims do not report harassment or delay in reporting harassment. Evidence of PTSD is especially helpful in cases of extreme harassment—incidents involving rape or physical abuse—in which it is more likely than not that the target will experience PTSD. Another helpful form of evidence comes from traditional social science—what I will refer to as "social context" evidence. This kind of evidence is useful to explain why targets of harassment might not complain in situations where the harassment is less severe than the types of situations that would trigger PTSD. The combination of the findings from medical science as well as social science provide an explanation of victim responses to harassment.

A. MEDICAL EVIDENCE

PTSD provides an evidentiary explanation for a victim's reluctance to report harassing behavior. Medical science tells us that women or men who have been physically or sexually assaulted in the course of being sexually harassed may suffer from PTSD.[57] The common perception of sexual harassment among the public is that it involves fairly "minor" conduct, such as commenting on someone's dress or asking someone out on a date, but some cases do contain allegations of physical and/or sexual assault. In addition, PTSD can be triggered by less severe incidents for persons who have suffered from PTSD in the past (for example, have been sexually or physically assaulted or sexually or physically abused as a child).[58] Medical studies show that 60% of rape victims experience PTSD.[59] Thus, it is more likely than not that a victim of sexual harassment who is raped during the harassment will experience PTSD. Evidence of PTSD should be admissible to explain the plaintiff's behavior. Although many cases mention that the target has been diagnosed as suffering from PTSD,[60] few cases discuss how PTSD might affect actions of harassment victims.

PTSD is a medical diagnosis contained in the American Psychiatric Association's *Diagnostic and Statistical Manual of Mental Disorders* (DSM-IV).[61] As such, the diagnosis is generally accepted by the medical community and should be accepted as a matter of scientific evidence by the courts in the appropriate case. Looking at the requirements for the diagnosis and symptoms associated with PTSD makes obvious how it might help explain the actions of harassment victims.

First, PTSD is experienced by individuals in situations "following exposure to an extreme traumatic stressor involving direct personal experience of an event that involves actual or threatened death or serious injury, or other threat to one's physical integrity."[62] Specifically included in the types of threats or injuries that can lead to PTSD are sexual assault and physical attack, both of which are experienced by sexual harassment victims. The diagnosis becomes significant because of the manner in which people who suffer from the disorder respond to stimuli associated with the traumatizing event. As the DSM-IV explains: "The person commonly makes deliberate efforts to avoid thoughts, feelings, or conversations about the traumatic event . . . and to avoid activities, situations, or people who arouse recollections of it."[63] Social science shows that targets of sexual harassment frequently go into "avoidance" mode, which is consistent with the symptoms of persons experiencing PTSD. The upshot is that a target may avoid reference to the stressor for quite some time and therefore be unable to report severe harassment as early as the courts are demanding.

The *Watkins* case described earlier in this chapter provides an example of how PTSD evidence could be used to explain the target's behavior. In *Watkins*, the plaintiff delayed reporting a rape for four months. In addition, she did not want to pursue instances of "lesser" forms of harassment involving the same person in the interim. Though no medical diagnosis appears in the court's decision, it is more likely than not that Watkins was suffering from PTSD following the rape. If that was so, her reasons for delaying reporting the rape as well as for avoiding further trauma with respect to the other incidents by being reluctant to have them pursued are entirely reasonable, given that medical diagnosis. She was behaving like persons suffering from PTSD behave when confronted with the stressing incident. In this context, her behavior was reasonable and a result of the misconduct of the harassing supervisor. Yet, the court in that case found no liability as a matter of law.[64]

Even though using such evidence becomes more complicated in cases involving preexisting PTSD,[65] attorneys representing plaintiffs should consider using PTSD evidence to support explanations of their clients' behaviors. Examining how PTSD affects targets of harassment shows that their behavior is not "unreasonable" but, instead, consistent with a person who is suffering from the disorder.

B. SOCIAL CONTEXT EVIDENCE

Psychologists have studied the responses of targets to sexual harassment. In chapter 2, studies are discussed that reveal the most common target responses to harassment: to ignore it or to avoid it. The implications of this data were considered for their impact on the unwelcomeness standard; this information also has ramifications for the new defense set out in *Ellerth* and *Faragher* as well. These studies alone suggest that the courts' requirement that plaintiffs report harassment early does not reflect what they most often do—avoid the harassment until it gets intolerable. In addition, other studies reveal that victims often fail to recognize their situations as sexually harassing. Hence, they might not report initially because they do not label their experiences as sexual harassment at all or until the harassment reaches a certain level of severity or frequency. Finally, there are many potential negative outcomes from reporting harassment, which might lead targets to the rational decision to ignore it or not report it. In effect, targets are caught in a classic catch-22. If they do not report the harassment, they risk losing a potential claim. If they do report it, they risk being subject to a variety of adverse ramifications—ramifications that affect not only their jobs and careers but also their psychological well-being. It appears that the courts have in mind some idealized harassment victim who is far more empowered than the average worker.

i. Labeling Experiences as Sexual Harassment To begin with, for some women, there appears to be a disconnect between what, in theory, they believe harassment to be and how they apply that concept to their own situations. In essence, it is one thing for a woman to assess a particular behavior as sexually harassing and another for her to perceive it to be so when she confronts it in her own work environment. Apparently, the process of a victim's acknowledging sexual harassment is complicated.[66] One study showed that "large numbers of women who have experienced relatively blatant instances of such behavior fail to recognize and label their experiences as [sexual harassment]."[67] In a study of how women recall and reconstruct potentially harassing experiences, Kidder and her colleagues found that it was only upon reflection that the women recalled the experiences as harassing. They recalled feeling uncomfortable in the situations they were describing, and often felt gullible, naive, or ashamed for not seeing that the harassing incident was coming. The authors of the study theorize that "[h]aving the words, a name, a category (even if the category is flawed as any box or set of boxes must be) enables women to recognize and recall what happens to them with less shame, guilt, or embarrassment. A social context in which the telling does not shame or blame the teller makes telling more likely."[68] Like other social science research, this suggests again that the employer's attitude toward harassment will have an effect on whether women report it. If the employer creates an environment in which complaints are encouraged and resolved, women will more likely report harassment.

Fitzgerald and her colleagues cite a study showing "that organizational factors were the best predictors of response when severity of harassment was controlled."[69] In general, "frequency of reporting [harassment] can be expected to rise in the wake of increasing sensitivity to this issue and there is some evidence that it has begun to do so."[70] Obviously, sexual harassment policies should be helpful in encouraging targets to report. However, the policy must be one that targets will actually put into practice. Stephanie Riger has suggested that many policies fall short of meeting the needs of female targets because of the policies' inherent gender bias.[71] Employers must be careful to make employees aware of the policy, and the policy must be drafted with sensitivity to harassment targets.

Determining why women do not perceive their situations as harassing is difficult and complex. Stockdale and her colleagues attempted to assess the correlation between various factors and a target's acknowledging an experience as harassment. In their study of university students, faculty, and staff, they found that a victim was more likely to acknowledge "unwanted sexual attention, such as sexual looks, gestures, or touching [as harassment], if (a) the offenses were frequent and pervasive, (b) negative affect resulted, (c) the respondent was harassed by a higher status perpetrator, and (d) the respondent was a woman."[72] As these researchers found from their survey, "[t]he higher the occupational status of the perpetrator in relation to the respondent, the more likely was the respondent to acknowledge being sexually harassed."[73] Also, studies have shown that younger women are less likely to label their experiences as "sexual harassment."[74]

Barbara Gutek and Bruce Morasch argue that because harassment on the job may be the norm, women fail to see behaviors as harassing; this results in women underreporting sexual harassment in female-dominated jobs.[75] In addition, studies show that employers can essentially create sexualized working environments by, for example, requiring female waitpersons to wear skimpy uniforms. Workers in these environments also may not consider their experiences as sexually harassing.[76]

Giuffre and Williams posit another explanation for the failure of targets to label their experiences as sexual harassment. They argue that sexual interaction between coworkers of the same race and sexual orientation is viewed as less problematic because of heterosexual norms that are pervasive in the workplace.[77] However, once sexual interaction crosses race, sexual orientation, or power levels, targets are more likely to label their experiences as sexual harassment.[78] This explanation suggests possible problematic interactions between race and sexual orientation in perceptions of sexual harassment that warrant further study.

ii. Why a Target Might Choose Not to Report Harassment In their study of women's responses to harassment, Fitzgerald and her colleagues noted that the public perception of the manner in which targets of harassment should respond to such incidents and the manner in which they actually respond are quite different.[79] Indeed, early studies of responses to harassment showed that people would respond more assertively in theory; research on actual sexual harassment targets reveals that they respond much less assertively when faced with an actual harassing situation.[80] There are a variety of possible reasons that women choose not to report harassment, as Fitzgerald et al. explain:

> The question most commonly asked concerning victim response is, "Why didn't she just report him?" Faced with this question, women give a variety of answers. They believe that nothing can or will be done, and many are reluctant to cause problems for the harasser. The most common reason, however, is fear—fear of retaliation, of not being believed, or hurting one's career, or of being shamed and humiliated.[81]

As one researcher put it, women complain through official channels as a "last ditch effort," when other responses, such as ignoring the harassment, have failed.[82]

The USMSPB study paints a slightly different picture of why targets fail to report harassment. Half of those responding that they experienced harassing behavior thought the harassment was not serious enough to warrant reporting it. This could be the result of being accustomed to such behavior or of avoiding such behavior. Or, it could simply be that the incident was too insignificant for the employee to believe a complaint was necessary. Indeed, many of these incidents, if not repeated, would not meet the legal definition—they are not sufficiently severe or pervasive, as explained in detail in chapter 1. Table 1, below, shows the various reasons targets of harassment gave for failing to report the harassment. As is obvious in the percentages therein, some gave more than one reason. This information is particularly interesting because the federal government has made significant efforts to inform its employees regarding its sexual harassment policy and complaint procedure. Indeed, this survey suggests that the vast majority of its employees were aware of the government's anti–sexual harassment policies.[83]

TABLE 1: *Why Targets Are Reluctant to Take Formal Action*[84]

Reason Targets Are Reluctant to Report	Percentage Agreeing with Statement
Did not think it was serious enough	.50
Other actions resolved the situation satisfactorily	.40
Thought it would make my work situation unpleasant	.29
Did not think anything would be done	.20
Thought the situation would not be kept confidential	.19
Did not want to hurt the person who had bothered me	.17
Thought it would adversely affect my career	.17
Was too embarrassed	.11
Thought I would be blamed	.9
Did not think I would be believed	.8
Supervisor was not supportive	.6
Did not know what actions to take or how to take them	.5
Would take too much time or effort	.5
Other	.4

Jensen and Gutek studied whether targets of harassment might experience self-blame, which could lead to less reporting of harassing incidents. Of their 135 targets, the majority did not appear to experience self-blame. However, about 21%–29% did experience it. Those who did acknowledge some self-blame for the harassing incidents were less likely to report it. Also, women who have traditional beliefs about the role of women were more likely to assign greater responsibility to the victim.[85]

The USMSPB study suggests that a significant number of harassment targets do not report it because of fear that it would make their work situations unpleasant (29%); did not think anything would be done about it (20%); thought it would adversely affect their careers (17%); thought they would be blamed (9%); or thought they would not be believed (8%).[86] A recent study of the 1988 USMSPB data has cast doubt on the responses of women who believed that more assertive responses actually made things better. Contrary to perceptions of the targets who participated in that study, Hesson-McInnis and Fitzgerald found:

Contrary to conventional wisdom, assertive and formal responses were actually associated with more negative outcomes of every sort. Women who reported harassment to their supervisors or who filed complaints were more likely to quit, be fired, or be transferred; to need or utilize medical or psychological assistance; to feel worse about their jobs; and so forth.[87]

While noting that this study was conducted prior to increased public awareness about sexual harassment, they conclude that their "findings should give pause to those who advise 'Just tell your supervisor' as a matter of course."[88]

Hesson-McInnis and Fitzgerald also found differing relationships between various consequences and reporting harassment. In particular, psychological and physical symptoms appear related to the harassment itself—specifically, the intensity of the harassment. However, the data suggests that "negative job outcomes may derive more from retaliation and negative organizational response (e.g., victim blaming) than from the sexually harassing behavior itself."[89] Although more research is needed on the effects of harassment on its targets, these potential relationships between work-related outcomes and reporting are extremely important in determining the reasonableness of a target's choice not to report.

In a study of the impact of potential outcomes on whether someone reports harassment, "Ormerod found that fear of negative outcomes was the most powerful predictor of responses to sexual harassment."[90] Ormerod also found that "[o]nly in situations involving explicit sexual coercion did the expectation of stopping the behavior outweigh the fear of retaliation."[91] Information is available about some effects of sexual harassment on both targets and organizations. The impact on targets is somewhat difficult to study because it is multidimensional, including impacts on physical health, mental health and "work variables including attendance, morale, performance, and impact on career track."[92]

Other studies of work effects have shown a variety of downsides to reporting harassment. Murrell and her colleagues have recounted many early studies showing the bad outcomes resulting from reporting harassment. They explain, "One of the frequent responses to harassment is to quit one's job. . . . Women who do complain are often fired (Coles, 1986) or are not able to work in their field because of bad references. . . . This fear of job loss can cause women to be afraid to report the harassment."[93] The studies cited by Murrell et al., as well as by Gutek and Koss[94] support these many downsides. Coles's study of employees who filed formal sexual harassment complaints in California found that half were fired.[95] In addition, 25% resigned due to the harassment or the complaint process.[96]

The USMSPB also looked at some of the job effects experienced by targets of harassment. It found that 8% of sexual harassment targets reported using sick leave; 8% reported using annual leave; 1% took leave without pay; 3% sought medical or emotional help; 7% "would have found medical or emotional help beneficial"; 2% were reassigned or fired; 2% were transferred to a new job; and 21% reported a decline in productivity.[97] Very few—only 0.1%—quit without a new job. Unlike the subjects of the California study, far fewer lost their jobs in the federal system. However, these responses encompassed many employees who took no formal action to address the harassment. Therefore, the difference between the two studies might well be that the effects of filing a formal complaint in court are far more detrimental to the target's career than using the varying coping strategies that federal employees reported using. Also, the Coles study is rather dated; it was conducted prior to the heightened awareness of sexual harassment that was generated by the Clarence Thomas/Anita Hill hearings. However, it does suggest that it might be a rational response not to formally report the harassment and instead ignore it, given the potential for bad job outcomes.

A recent study by Mindy Bergman and her colleagues supports the relationship between work environment and harassment reporting. In a study using subjects in the United States military, these researchers attempted to integrate reporting into Fitzgerald et al.'s integrated model of responses to reporting harassment. They relied, in part, on studies of whistle-blowing. That "literature suggests that organizational climate should influence organizational responses to reporting."[98] They posited three forms of organizational responses to harassment reports: (1) the organization may support the complainant (referred to as "organizational remedies"); (2) the organization may ignore the complaint (referred to as "minimization"); and (3) the organization may retaliate against the reporting employee (referred to as "retaliation").[99]

The results of their study have implications for the *Ellerth/Faragher* affirmative defense. First, they found that reporting harassment often triggered retaliation against the reporting employee. In addition, reporting resulted in lower job satisfaction and increased psychological distress, which led them to conclude that "at least in certain work environments, the most 'reasonable' course of action for the victim is to avoid reporting."[100] They opined that the key to increasing reporting, while lowering the potential for bad effects for reporting employees, was organizational climate. Although they noted that "organizational climate did not directly affect reporting, it did influence reporting and its outcomes through sexual harassment history, frequency of sexual harassment, organizational minimization of reporting, retaliation, and procedural satisfaction."[101] Thus, they theorized how courts might consider reporting in the *Ellerth/Faragher* context:

> The findings that we report suggest that legal scrutiny might better focus on the organization's responsibility to create a climate in which victims have no reason to fear reporting mechanisms or their aftermath. That is, courts should require that the organization demonstrate a climate intolerant of sexual harassment through a documented history of taking complaints seriously, protecting complainants from retaliation, and holding perpetrators responsible for their actions. Only in such an organizational context would it be reasonable for victims to avail themselves of grievance mechanisms. The burden should be on the organization, not the victim to prove reasonableness.[102]

The research described above concerning responses to sexual harassment suggests that there are many good reasons that targets of harassment might not report it. It also begs for modification of the current framework used by the courts, which places so much emphasis on the targets' reporting behavior.

D. Reformulating the Legal Approach for Imputing Liability

The social science research above reveals several gaps between how courts evaluate the defense coming out of the *Ellerth* and *Faragher* cases and the manner in which harassment targets respond, as well as the employer's influence over the work environment. Although at first glance the defense may seem to place a significant burden on the employer, in actuality it mistakenly places a significant burden on the harassed employee to explain his or her inaction—or failure to report—in the face of harassment. In addition, it does not sufficiently take into account the significant role the employer plays in creating, condoning, or refuting an environment that could result in more or less harassment. Because of these anomalies, along with the Supreme Court's overemphasis on encouraging employer compliance, it is time to take a close look at the defense and suggest changes that would make sexual harassment law more effective. Encouraging compliance is one of the collateral purposes of Title VII, but it is not the only or primary purpose of the statute.

1. Tangible Employment Actions

I will not go into detail about claims for quid pro quo harassment (although I acknowledge the need for some policy work on the subject), yet I do want to point out one aspect of this claim that appears problematic based on social science. Sexual harassment that includes sexual or physical coercion, including threats of negative job outcomes as a result of the target's refusal to engage in sexual acts with the harasser, are considered very serious forms of sexual harassment by almost all workers. Even so, distinguishing between cases in which threats are carried out and those in which they are not, the Court in *Ellerth* concluded that an employer could still raise the defense so long as the threat was not carried out. This appears to put form over substance. Carrying out a threat often has an economic impact (for example, a decrease in pay or termination) on the target; once the target believes her job is conditioned on submitting to sexual interactions with a supervisor, her terms of employment have been altered in a tangible way. Not agreeing to the demands—calling the supervisor's bluff, perhaps—with no resulting financial penalty may mean that the target has been damaged less, but she still has had her terms of employment altered in a discriminatory manner. She waits in daily fear for the proverbial shoe to drop—for the supervisor to actually act on his threat. The supervisor should be enjoined from carrying out the threat. The plaintiff should be compensated for stress related to working under this threat. The employer placed the supervisor in a position to make such a threat; the harasser was certainly aided by his or her status in being able to make this threat. Thus, the employer should be liable without the benefit of any defense.

There is some precedent for holding that employers should not have the *Ellerth/Faragher* affirmative defense available to them when the threat is not carried out. However, the cases that have so held all involved situations in which the target agreed to the supervisor's demands. The Ninth

Circuit recently held that if an employee complied with a supervisor's coercion to engage in a relationship with him under a threat of a negative job outcome, this constituted a tangible job action, making the *Ellerth/Faragher* defense unavailable to the employer. Reasoning that the unwanted sexual acts become a condition of a plaintiff's employment, the court stated that this constituted a substantial change in the terms of the plaintiff's employment. The supervisor's decision not to fire her under these circumstances was the tangible job action.[103] The Second Circuit held similarly, reasoning that the employee's submission to her supervisor's sexual demands constituted a tangible employment action.[104] Thus, there is already beginning to be some give in the tangible employment action standard. It takes only a relatively small step to extend this analysis to situations in which the plaintiff does not accede to sexual demands under threats by her supervisor.

2. Evaluating Whether the "Employer Exercised Reasonable Care to Prevent and Correct Promptly Any Sexually Harassing Behavior"

The first prong of the *Ellerth/Faragher* defense has two components. The employer must exercise reasonable care (1) to prevent harassment from occurring, and (2) to correct harassment after becoming aware of it. If the employer's factual showing fails under either component, the employer has not proven the defense. There are two facets of social science that come into play in reevaluating the use of the first prong of the *Ellerth/Faragher* defense. One is the employer's impact in setting a local norm that will discourage harassment. The second is the use of training programs and anti-harassment policies to either prevent or correct harassment.

A. REASONABLE CARE IN PREVENTING HARASSMENT

The *Ellerth/Faragher* defense places an obligation on employers to prevent supervisory harassment. The Supreme Court suggested that a sexual harassment policy would provide a sufficient showing on this prong, but social science reveals that more is required. First, given the potential positive or negative effect that the employer has on the work environment, evidence related to the employer's general efforts (or lack thereof) to raise awareness about and to curb harassing behavior should be admissible on this aspect of the defense. Fact finders should evaluate the totality of the circumstances related to the working environment. They already look at the totality of the circumstances in deciding whether an environment meets the severe or pervasive standard. This would merely be an extension of that principle to aid in assessing the environment the employer is creating for its employees. Along with showing it has an effective policy in place, the employer should be required to submit evidence on the local norm in the workplace.

Things like pinups, the manner in which the employer handled other harassing incidents,[105] and attitudes of supervisors should be relevant to this analysis regardless of their direct relevance to the particular incident of harassment involved. Social science suggests that if an employer allows other harassing incidents to occur in the same employment area, this could help create a local norm in which harassment is viewed as being "normal," "okay," or "no big deal." Although an antiharassment policy will be relevant to this inquiry, it should not be enough standing alone. Instead, the employer must show that it distributed the policy, took it seriously, and conscientiously handled complaints falling within the policy. One recent suggestion by law professor Martha West is that employers tell employees how actual harassment complaints are handled.[106] This informs employees that the employer takes sexual harassment seriously. The courts usually protect employee records from disclosure in the course of a court proceeding, but tools like redaction and in camera review could protect other employees while allowing in evidence that reflects the employer's efforts at combating sexual harassment. Local norms evidence necessarily goes well beyond the alleged harassing incidents directed at the particular plaintiff in the case. However, given the social science data on this point, such additional evidence—including the handling of other incidents of harassment directed at other employees, the prevalence of sexually demeaning material, and so on—is relevant to the determination of whether the employer "exercised reasonable care to prevent" sexual harassment.[107] This will allow the courts to assess the workplace without invading the right of privacy that other employees might have in their personnel records.

One possible argument against this searching look into the workplace environs is the chilling effect it may have on employee speech. Much has been written on the First Amendment implications of sexual harassment law by legal scholars, yet courts rarely have found such arguments compelling.[108] Engaging too deeply in this debate is beyond the scope of this chapter, given how infrequently the courts have actually held such arguments meritorious. Thus, at a practical level, the First Amendment "issue," though intellectually interesting, is of very little practical import. My treatment of it is therefore brief.

There are a number of ways in which to address the potential First Amendment implications of this approach. First, a finding of harassment generally includes at least some acts that are not protected by the First Amendment. As I explain in chapter 1, the courts have set the standard for severity and pervasiveness so high that it is unlikely that anything approaching "pure speech" would be found actionable. Indeed, many of my suggestions for broadening the concept of sexual harassment in chapter 1 involve conduct. Even First Amendment proponents have conceded that many forms of harassment have no First Amendment implications. For example, quid pro quo harassment generally is considered unprotected speech, with no First Amendment protection. Another example is fighting words.[109] Kingsley Browne, one of the first legal scholars to make a First Amendment attack on sexual harassment law, described several other exceptions to the amendment, including labor speech; speech directed at captive audiences; time, place, and manner regulations; defamation; obscenity; indecency; and privacy.[110] These exceptions may apply to many hostile environment fact patterns. In *Robinson v. Jacksonville Shipyards Inc.*, the court rejected a First Amendment argument on a variety of grounds, including that the harassment consituted conduct, that it was only a time, place, and manner restriction, and that the plaintiffs were a captive audience.[111] Others have argued that when harassment is directed at a particular employee (which it often is), it is entitled to no First Amendment protection.[112] In this context, it can constitute an assault. Others have suggested establishing a new subcategory of speech that is unprotected or is entitled to a lesser amount of First Amendment protection.[113] Given the many First Amendment exceptions potentially applicable as well as the severe or pervasive requirement, my proposal that courts examine the workplace environment in assessing whether the employer has made reasonable efforts to prevent harassment should not pose a significant First Amendment problem.

Instead, evidence of local norms simply places the harassing incidents in a context that might better explain their meaning and genesis. The employer is not being held liable for the local norm itself. Instead, the local norm is useful in determining whether the employer took seriously or condoned behavior that could escalate into sexual harassment. The plaintiff will still need to show that the harassment was sufficiently severe or pervasive to alter her working conditions. Thus, it is no longer discrimination in thought but has become discrimination in action—having a direct effect on the plaintiff's ability to work. There is much speech that would be "protected" but yet is admissible in the context of proving elements of criminal or even civil wrongdoing. For example, a political bribery case will no doubt involve speech—including discussions regarding the terms of the bribe. Yet, those discussions are clearly admissible in the context of proving that the bribery occurred. Likewise, it seems reasonable to admit evidence of workplace norms to assess the employer's prevention efforts.

Training programs have implications for this component of the defense as well. Employers may use training programs to show that they took reasonable care to prevent harassment. If an employer commits the time and effort that go into training employees about sexual harassment, this indicates that the employer is trying to create a local norm in which harassment is not tolerated. However, given the few studies on what training is effective, the courts need to look closely at how seriously the employer takes such training and how effective that training is likely to be. Indeed, if the employer has not studied the effects of its training program or has done little else to curb harassment, a video training program, for example, is unlikely to have much effect. Many employees have sat through employee training programs while completing crossword puzzles or otherwise ignoring the presentation. That's why interactive programs, which require employee participation, are more effective in training. The upshot is that the courts should not simply accept that the employer did training. It must examine the nature of that training to see how it affects an employee who is likely to sexually harass. A halfhearted attempt at training should not be enough to show that the employer made a reasonable effort to prevent harassment.

B. REASONABLE CARE IN PROMPTLY CORRECTING ANY SEXUALLY HARASSING BEHAVIOR

The second component of this part of the defense involves the reasonableness and promptness of the employer's corrective response to allegations of harassment. Courts have given employers wide latitude in this regard. Thus, there are instances in which the harassing behavior continued in spite of the employer's alleged "corrective action," and the courts have still found the employer's response sufficient because it was deemed "reasonable." At a minimum, if the employer's actions do not stop the harassment, they should not be deemed "reasonable."[114] At the least, the plaintiff should be compensated for her continued harassment.

Like the other component of this part of the defense, training programs have implications here as well. Specifically, they are sometimes used by employers as a means of correcting harassers' behaviors. Once again, the use of such programs to achieve this purpose should be viewed cautiously. First, the courts should be skeptical in their acceptance of training programs as a way to correct harassing behavior. There is no significant body of evidence about what sorts of training programs do and do not work to counter sexual harassment. An effective training program might be very helpful, but it should be the responsibility of the employer to show that the program it is using has the effect of stopping harassment. Indeed, if a supervisor continues to harass after going through a training program, it is obvious that the program was unsuccessful. Subsequently harassed employees should not bear the burden of the employer's failure. Once such a program fails, the employer should be liable for any harassment that results.

3. PRONG TWO: THE PLAINTIFF'S OBLIGATION TO REPORT OR AVOID HARM OTHERWISE

There are two problems with the second prong of the *Ellerth/Faragher* test. First, the portion that indicates that the employee "fail[ed] to avoid harm otherwise" is so vague as to be unworkable. This prong should be entirely eliminated. It is open for any meaning the courts wish to give it. Indeed, already the lower courts have begun to use it with very perverse results.[115]

The second problem with this prong is its failure to take into account the most common reactions of employees faced with harassment. Courts apparently are not in the best position to understand the target's perspective, especially at the summary judgment stage, where many cases are decided. Cases should not be thrown out because a target failed to report initially or delayed reporting until the incidents were repeated or became more severe. Indeed, it is counterintuitive, especially given that the harassment might not have reached an actionable level yet. Thus, the target of harassment is caught in a difficult catch-22. If she does not report minor incidents of harassment, she risks providing support for the employer's showing on the second prong of the *Ellerth/Faragher* defense. Yet, the incidents of harassment may well not have reached an actionable level yet or a level that the target believes she can no longer handle. On the other hand, the courts also want to give the employer the earliest opportunity to correct harassment—preferably before it reaches an actionable level. Some sort of balance must be struck between forcing employees to report minor incidents and letting employers defend based on an employee's failure to report them. One could envision a workplace coming to a standstill if every minor incident of potentially harassing behavior were reported. Indeed, it might well benefit the employer that much harassment is ignored or handled informally by the employees involved.

Courts must understand that targets often do not report harassment for, as social science corroborates, some very good reasons. Although it is understandable for the courts to encourage an employer to nip harassment in the bud, targets of harassment choose to ignore lesser forms of harassment until they become unmanageable. It seems equally reasonable for employees to wait to see what happens before risking their jobs in order to report harassment. The courts need to be more sympathetic to the not unreasonable approach that is most common to employees, especially given the many bad potential outcomes for targets who report harassment. Thus, the courts should accept delays of several months in reporting harassment. In addition, if a target is suffering from PTSD, delays should be commonplace and understood by the courts as the normal response of avoiding the stressor.

A. A REASONABLE SOLUTION: CREATIVITY WITH DAMAGES

A reasonable solution that resolves this dilemma and furthers the underlying purposes of Title VII is to encourage the employer's prevention and correction efforts using punitive damages. After the Civil Rights Act of 1991, punitive damages are available to plaintiffs in sexual harassment cases if the employer engages in a discriminatory practice with "malice or with reckless indifference to the federally protected rights of an aggrieved individual."[116] In addition, compensatory damages are available in all cases of intentional discrimination. Depending on what the employer has done with respect to preventing and correcting harassment, the employer may or may not be liable for punitive damages. In any event, the employee should be compensated for the damages she sustained as a result of harassment by her supervisor. This solution is consistent with both the language of *Faragher* and *Ellerth* as well as the purposes behind the Civil Rights Act of 1991.

Acts relevant to liability for harassment occur in several stages for purposes of this defense. First, the employer must set up an effective program to prevent harassment. Second, it must have a procedure for dealing with complaints of harassment that effectively ends the harassment once reported or the employer becomes aware of it. Depending on what the employer has done to prevent and correct harassment, it may or may not be liable for punitive damages. In this manner, the *Ellerth/Faragher* defense would not eliminate liability entirely; it would simply limit liability for punitive damages. The employer would still be liable for compensatory damages. An employee should not be required to incur the costs of psychiatrists, psychologists, or other medical professionals because of harassing acts of a supervisor who was placed in the position to harass by the employer. This strikes a balance between the compensatory nature of Title VII and the policy of encouraging employers to address and correct sexual harassment.

Perhaps it is easiest to explain how this would work by example. If the employer can prove that it has a clear and effective policy for redressing sexual harassment, it should not be liable for any punitive damages for acts of harassment that occur prior to the employer's becoming aware of the harassing behavior. However, if the employer has made no effort to prevent harassment and, perhaps, has even encouraged it (based on the evidence of the local norm), the plaintiff should be eligible for punitive damages against the employer. This amounts to reckless indifference to the employee's rights.

Likewise, if an employer unreasonably fails to correct harassing behavior after an employee's complaint, it has effectively engaged in a discriminatory practice with "malice or with reckless indifference to the federally protected rights of an aggrieved individual" and should be liable for punitive damages for its failure to correct harassing behavior. However, if the employer corrects the harassment, it will not be liable for punitive damages but, instead, will be liable only for compensatory damages for the harassment that has actually occurred. Of course, if the employer did not have a prevention program in place, it could be held liable for punitive damages for harassment that occurred prior to the employer's becoming aware of the harassment.

Although it is not entirely clear from the policy explanations in *Faragher* and *Ellerth*, such an approach is consistent with the purposes of Title VII and the Civil Rights Act of 1991. The employer placed the supervisor in a position of authority, with the opportunity to harass subordinates. Although the employer should be encouraged to curb harassment by receiving some credit for eliminating the harassment, it is consistent with the purposes of Title VII that the employer compensate plaintiffs for harassment by supervisors that has already occurred.

Instead of focusing on the deterrence and compensatory aspects of Title VII, the Supreme Court and the lower courts recently have shifted their focus to a latent purpose of Title VII: encouraging prevention.[117] The primary objective of Title VII is to eradicate discrimination in the workplace.[118] In emphasizing prevention, the courts have given little weight to the usefulness of damages in deterring discriminatory conduct. For example, in *Ellerth*, the Supreme Court stated that

> Title VII is designed to encourage the creation of antiharassment policies and effective grievance mechanisms. Were employer liability to depend in part on an employer's effort to create such procedures, it would effect Congress' intention to promote conciliation rather than litigation in the Title VII context. . . . To the extent limiting employer liability could encourage employees to report harassing conduct before it becomes severe or pervasive, it would also serve Title VII's deterrent purpose.[119]

Likewise, in *Faragher*, while acknowledging that Title VII seeks "to make persons whole for injuries suffered on account of unlawful employment discrimination," the Court stated its "'primary objective,' like any statute meant to influence primary conduct, is not to provide redress but to avoid harm."[120]

By overemphasizing prevention, the Court ignores both deterrence through damages and compensation (to make plaintiffs whole) as other important goals of Title VII. If interpreted as a complete defense, the Court's holdings in *Faragher* and *Ellerth* will prevent plaintiffs from being compensated for losses they incurred due to harassment. For example, the employer would not be liable for any resulting medical expenses (including psychiatric or medical visits) that the harassed employee incurred. In addition, cutting off damages does not encourage employers to raise awareness about harassment and engage in more effective prevention efforts. The result is a lesser deterrent effect than might be gained if the employer knew it would be liable at least for compensatory damages. Compensation is a significant policy underlying Title VII that the Court has devalued. As the Court explained in *McKennon v. Nashville Banner Publishing Co.*, a private litigant furthers both the "deterrence and compensation objectives" of the antidiscrimination laws.[121] Providing complete defenses to employers under these circumstances also discourages litigants and attorneys from bringing these cases, further undermining the deterrence and compensation purposes of Title VII. Victims of employment discrimination have difficulty accessing the legal system.[122] One significant problem is that these cases, at least prior to the Civil Rights Act of 1991, did not provide enough damages to justify a contingent fee arrangement with attorneys who might represent plaintiffs. The result, as Congress recognized in enacting the Civil Rights Act of 1991, was that targets of harassment were unable to seek effective redress in the court system.

The Court in *Faragher* makes much of the Civil Rights Act of 1991's avoidance of the agency issues discussed in *Meritor*,[123] but the legislative history of the act does tell quite a bit about the purposes of Title VII and the 1991 act as well. In the act, Congress sought to further the "make whole" aspect of Title VII by providing for compensatory and punitive damages for intentional discrimination. In the legislative history, Congress was emphatic that its purpose in enacting Section 1981a was both to compensate targets in a more meaningful manner (particularly in harassment cases) and to further the deterrent effect of Title VII by creating higher damages that will force employers to take discrimination seriously. As was explained in the House Report on the law,

> Monetarty [*sic*] damages also are necessary to make discrimination victims whole for the terrible injury to their careers, to their mental and emotional health, and to their self-respect and dignity. Such relief is also necessary to encourage citizens to act as private attorneys general to enforce the statute. Monetary damages simply raise the cost of an employer's engaging in intentional discrimination, thereby providing employers with additional incentives to *prevent* intentional discrimination in the workplace before it happens.[124]

The House Report repeatedly alluded to sexual harassment plaintiffs as examples of discrimination victims who are not being fully compensated. Further, the House explicitly linked the use of damages to not only compensating targets but also deterring and preventing intentional discrimination. Indeed, even members of industries that would be affected by the act admitted that "under Title VII's current [pre-Civil Rights Act of 1991] remedial scheme, 'there is little incentive to set up the kinds of internal controls that companies need to set up.'"[125]

During consideration of the Civil Rights Act of 1991, Congress clearly contemplated the effect of damages on conciliation efforts and concluded there was no evidence supporting a negative effect.[126] In this context, Congress discussed the goal of encouraging voluntary settlement. It did not appear to directly contemplate or even be concerned with the negative effect damages might have on employer voluntary compliance with Title VII. This is not surprising because damages can only serve to encourage voluntary compliance. Thus, aligning an employer's efforts to prevent and correct sexually harassing behavior to the ability of the plaintiff to collect punitive damages is a fair compromise that furthers the purposes of Title VII and the Civil Rights Act of 1991.

The only possible stumbling block to the use of punitive damages in this manner is the Court's recent decision in *Kolstad v. American Dental Association*. However, a careful review of that case in light of the language of the Court in *Faragher* and *Ellerth* reveals that the use of punitive damages is consistent with both the language of Section 1981a and the *Kolstad* decision. The *Kolstad* Court aligned liability for punitive damages with "the employer's knowledge that it may be acting in violation of federal law."[127] Given the Court's acknowledgment in *Faragher* that "[i]t is by now well recognized that hostile environment sexual harassment by supervisors . . . is a persistent problem in the workplace,"[128] and the clear illegality of this conduct since the Court's decision in *Meritor* in 1986, courts can reasonably assume employers are aware that sexual harassment by supervisors is prohibited by Title VII. It is not a novel theory.

A more difficult problem is presented by the *Kolstad* Court's renewed emphasis on employer prevention efforts. The Court held:

> Recognizing Title VII as an effort to promote prevention as well as remediation, and observing the very principles underlying the Restatements' strict limits on vicarious liability for punitive damages, we agree that, in the punitive damages context, an employer may not be vicariously liable for the discriminatory employment decisions of managerial agents where these decisions are contrary to the employers' "good-faith efforts to comply with Title VII."[129]

Preceding this holding, the Court discussed the importance of encouraging employer antidiscrimination programs, including grievance mechanisms and employee education programs. Although this holding could be read to eliminate the possibility of punitive damages for an employer who sets up a complaint process and training program, there is room for interpretation in the Court's holding.

The key to the standard set out by the Court is in assessing whether an employer has indeed made good-faith efforts to comply with Title VII. The courts should not consider perfunctory efforts—such as simply setting up a policy—as sufficient to meet this good faith requirement. Likewise, if an employer implements a training program without any reason to believe that it works, the courts should be skeptical that such efforts were made in good faith. The employer may have been making a good faith effort to avoid liability, but the real issue is whether the employer was making a good faith attempt to prevent sexual harassment. The courts should understand that there is a distinction between these two objectives.

To the extent that the *Kolstad* Court meant any training or preventive efforts would suffice without considering the efficacy of such programs, the decision will not, in the end, further the policies underlying Title VII. Instead, the decision will lead to employers establishing superficial training and antiharassment policies with little concern that they work. Given that there is little evidence about what training, preventive, and corrective measures do work, putting the burden on the employers will spur the kind of inquiry into these programs that will actually result in effective methods for eliminating sexual harassment in the workplace. Certainly, letting an employer avoid liability will not spur such efforts.

The courts do not seem to understand the impact that employers have in condoning, encouraging, or preventing harassment by their simply paying attention to the workplace environment. Further, the courts' emphasis on making targets report does not comport with the reality of working Americans' lives—lives that include a fundamental need for employment that will lead them to ignore, reinterpret, and tolerate workplace harassment. A careful look at the standard set out by the Court in the *Ellerth* and *Faragher* cases in light of social science leads to a different approach, one—it is hoped—that will more adequately meet the goals of Title VII (to compensate and make targets whole) while encouraging employers to truly prevent workplace harassment.

I have suggested in this chapter two solutions that are consistent with the factors developed in chapter 4 to determine whether harassment is because of sex. One is for the courts to pay careful attention to the workplace environment in assessing the "totality of the circumstances" that made the harassment of the target possible. The other is for the courts to use punitive damages in a creative manner to punish employers who do not take harassment seriously while rewarding those (by not awarding punitive damages) who seek to actively address harassment. This solution provides a key to furthering all Title VII's purposes and at the same time addresses harassment in the workplace in a fashion that acknowledges the complexity of as well as the employer's influence on the phenomenon.

6

Making Targets Whole and Deterring Defendants

Title VII is designed to accomplish two primary goals. First, to promote equality in the workplace by encouraging employers to treat employees the same regardless of protected characteristics. Since enactment of the Civil Rights Act of 1991, it does this in part by using potential damage awards to deter employers from engaging in discrimination. The second goal is one typical of tort-based schemes: to compensate victims and make them whole. However, damage awards under Title VII are limited by caps—limits on the amount of damages a plaintiff can receive based on the size of the employer. Thus, to the extent that the caps do not reflect the nature of the harm experienced by sexual harassment targets or are insufficient to deter employers from discriminating, Title VII may be less effective than it was intended to be in achieving its goals.

Damage caps are particularly problematic, given what social science reveals about the harm caused by sexual harassment. Harms are not limited to workplace consequences (such as job loss or decreased job satisfaction) but also include personal and psychological effects. In this chapter, I review both statutory and case law on damage awards for sexual harassment. I then review social science data on the effects of sexual harassment on its targets. Studies looking at how juries make damages determinations are also discussed because proponents of damage caps are worried about exorbitantly large jury awards. As in prior chapters, I suggest reform to the legal standard based on social science.

A. *The Law of Damages for Sexual Harassment*

1. Congress and the Supreme Court

Initially, Title VII limited plaintiffs to equitable relief as the only form of compensation for an employer's violation of the statute's antidiscrimination provisions. This meant that traditional compensatory damages were unavailable to plaintiffs. The courts did characterize certain forms of monetary relief as "equitable." Included in this relief were back-pay awards (available to plaintiffs who were fired, not hired, or not promoted due to discrimination) and front-pay awards (available to plaintiffs when reinstatement was inappropriate).[1] As is obvious based on the nature of this monetary relief, many sexual harassment victims were left with little relief except in cases of quid pro quo harassment or where the harassment had an economic impact. If a plaintiff was harassed and continued to work, the most she could hope for was an injunction against any future harassment. Yet, the plaintiff might be undergoing psychiatric care or counseling due to emotional distress as well as experiencing physical illness brought on by the harassment.

Eventually, Congress realized victims of harassment and other forms of employment discrimination were not being made whole. As discussed in chapter 5, employers did not believe Title VII was a significant threat to them because of the low (and sometimes nonexistent) monetary damages awarded against them. Congress designed the Civil Rights Act of 1991 to remedy this situation by permitting juries to award compensatory and punitive damages under certain circumstances. The key component of the act, Section 1981a, provides that in cases of intentional discrimination, which is how sexual harassment is typically characterized,[2] a plaintiff can recover compensatory and even punitive damages. For punitive damages, the plaintiff must show that the employer "engaged in a discriminatory practice or discriminatory practices with malice or with reckless indifference to the federally protected rights of an aggrieved individual."[3] Punitive damages are designed to deter and punish defendants.[4] In addition, the statute provides a broad range of examples of compensatory damages, including "future pecuniary losses, emotional pain, suffering, inconvenience, mental anguish, loss of enjoyment of life, and other nonpecuniary losses."[5] These damages are designed to compensate plaintiffs for actual losses resulting from the defendant's conduct.[6]

There is one significant caveat, however. The amount of compensatory and punitive damages is limited by caps based on the size of the employer. Ranging from a cap of $50,000 for employers with 15 to 100 employees to $300,000 for employers of more than 500 employees, Congress statutorily limited the amount of damages a plaintiff could collect.[7] The caps include compensatory and punitive damages combined.[8] Courts have not interpreted these caps broadly. Although each individual who has experienced discrimination can be awarded up to the maximum under the cap, some courts have limited plaintiffs to the cap even though the plaintiff had multiple claims under Title VII or Title VII combined with another antidiscrimination statute.[9] Thus, employees who experience serious and multiple forms of harassment may be undercompensated.

Damages caps were the result of a political compromise between President George H. W. Bush and members of Congress who wished to provide victims of discrimination with a remedy that went beyond equitable relief as well as make the same damages available to victims of sex, religious, and other forms of employment discrimination that were already available to race discrimination victims under Section 1981.[10] The concerns that led to the damages caps are reflected in their graduated nature. Congress was concerned that small business owners would be put out of business by high damages in discrimination suits.[11] On the other side of the issue were those who argued that compensatory damages were necessary to make discrimination victims whole and punitive damages were necessary to curb actions by those engaged in intentional discrimination.[12] This, along with the concern that race discrimination victims already had these damages available to them under other civil rights legislation that had no caps, fueled the argument against caps.

As described in chapter 5, the Supreme Court's decision in *Kolstad v. American Dental Association*[13] adds another layer to the punitive damages inquiry. The Court held that the plaintiff need not show that the employer acted in an egregious manner in order to be eligible for punitive damages.[14] Instead, Section 1981a requires only that the "employer must act with 'malice or with reckless indifference to [the plaintiff's] federally protected rights.'"[15] The Court further explained that the "terms 'malice' or 'reckless indifference' pertain to the employer's knowledge that it may be acting in violation of federal law, not its awareness that it is engaging in discrimination."[16]

In addition, recognizing that encouraging employers to comply with Title VII was one of the statute's "primary objectives,"[17] the Court held that "in the punitive damages context, an employer may not be vicariously liable for the discriminatory employment decisions of managerial agents where these decisions are contrary to the employer's 'good-faith efforts to comply with Title VII.'"[18] Lower courts evaluating punitive damages claims have noted that an antidiscrimination policy is relevant to the good faith defense, but is insufficient on its own to avoid liability for punitive damages.[19] Some courts have argued that individual cases did not involve vicarious liability but, instead, direct liability, to which the good faith defense did not apply.[20] It is unclear how this standard would apply in the context of sexual harassment, where the Court has clearly established in both *Faragher* and *Ellerth* that the employer is vicariously liable for the harassment of supervisors absent the employer's proving the affirmative defense set out in those cases.

Some courts view the inquiries under the *Faragher/Ellerth* affirmative defense and punitive damages differently. In *Hatley v. Hilton Hotels Corp.*, the court held that punitive damages instructions were unnecessary in a case in which the defendant failed to prove the *Ellerth/Faragher* defense. Although the appellate court found sufficient evidence to support the inadequacy of the employer's investigation into the plaintiff's complaint to support the jury's rejection of the defense, it still held that the trial court was correct in refusing to give a punitive damages instruction.[21] Instead, because the employer had an antiharassment policy that was well publicized and included training and a grievance process, as well as investigated the plaintiff's complaints (although the investigation was found inadequate), the court held that the employer had made out the good faith defense to punitive damages as a matter of law.[22]

The Supreme Court also has weighed in on the constitutionality of punitive damages in several recent cases. Specifically, it has addressed when punitive damages become so excessive that they violate the Fourteenth Amendment's due process clause, which is applicable to the states. Although the Court may set a different standard for the Fifth Amendment's due process clause, which is applicable to the federal courts, recent decisions on other issues have suggested that the Court will impose identical standards for state and federal governmental actors under the Fifth and Fourteenth Amendments.[23] A detailed analysis of these cases is beyond the scope of this chapter. Suffice it to say that the Supreme Court has recently hemmed in punitive damages awarded under state law.[24] How this will affect the Fifth Amendment remains to be seen.

2. Lower Courts and Caps

Lower court cases reveal that the caps sometimes reflect neither the harm jurors believe the employee experienced nor the amount necessary to punish and deter the employer for its part in a plaintiff's harassment. In many cases, jurors award more damages than the caps allow, only to have their verdicts reduced to the statutory cap by the trial court. In case after case, jury awards are reduced to comply with caps. The question becomes whether the caps are resulting in plaintiffs getting less than what is adequate for compensation. Congress can certainly set caps low, but that does not mean that setting them low makes them fair or sufficient to compensate or to deter and punish.

A recent case from Utah provides an example. In *Parker v. Olympus Health Care, Inc.*, the plaintiff was raped by a coworker. The plaintiff presented evidence that her harasser had raped and sexually assaulted four other female employees before he raped her. At least two of these women testified that they reported the conduct to supervisory personnel. Needless to say, the jury was concerned that the employer had not taken sufficient action to prevent plaintiff's rape. They awarded $750,000 in compensatory and $1.75 million in punitive damages. The award was lowered to the cap of $300,000.[25] Similarly, in *Coleman v. State of Tennessee*, one of the plaintiffs was subjected to severe harassment, including the harasser (a supervisor) feeling her breasts and sexually assaulting her. The plaintiff testified, along with her therapist, as to the mental anguish and pain she experienced and its effect on her ability to sleep and interact with others. The jury's award of $700,000 for pain and suffering was reduced to the cap of $300,000.[26] Finally, in another case in which the plaintiff was, by the court's own assessment, subjected to "egregious, unremedied harassment," the court itself noted that the jury's award of $735,000 for emotional distress was "not grossly excessive."[27] Yet, the court reduced the award to the $300,000 cap, as required by statute.

In *Madison v. IBP, Inc.*, plaintiff suffered repeated racial and sexual harassment of an egregious nature. Plaintiff, a white woman married to an African American man, was subjected to pervasive harassing behavior both verbally and physically. This behavior frequently occurred before supervisors, who also participated in some of the activity. Plaintiff complained repeatedly about the harassment, and yet nothing was done to stop it. Given the outrageousness of the conduct in this case, it is unsurprising that the jury awarded $266,750 for emotional distress, $76,667 for backpay and benefits, and $2,069,000 in punitive damages. The award for compensatory and punitive damages was reduced on her Title VII claim to the $300,000 cap.[28] These do not appear to be cases of jurors out of control. Instead, it appears that in at least some cases the caps are not high enough to compensate plaintiffs and deter and punish employers in a manner that jurors believe is appropriate.

B. Social Science of Harm, Damages, and Jury Awards

There are two aspects of social science inquiry that are helpful in assessing whether damages are being properly awarded in sexual harassment cases. The first is information about the effects of sexual harassment. It has already been noted that sexual harassment has significant consequences for workplaces. Psychologists and other social scientists also have documented the effects of sexual harassment on its victims. It affects not only career opportunities and job satisfaction but also has personal implications that go beyond the workplace. The impact on victims is somewhat difficult to study because it is multidimensional, including effects on physical health, mental health, and "work variables including attendance, morale, performance, and impact on career track."[29] This is not the only social science data of interest on the damages issue, however. Given the salience of the tort reform movement, no discussion of damages is complete without an assessment of the implications of leaving damages to the sole discretion—some might argue whim—of a jury. Thus, the latest studies of jury decision making on damages will be discussed so that potential solutions can take those findings into consideration.

1. The Damage That Sexual Harassment Causes

Sexual harassment has a variety of personal and professional effects on working women. Some researchers have documented lower job satisfaction and other negative job outcomes for women experiencing harassment.[30] In addition, there is a growing body of research on the relationship between certain types of psychological harm and sexual harassment. Psychologists Barbara Gutek and Mary Koss have outlined the effects of harassment on its victims. They detail a range of outcomes—including work-related effects, psychological and physical (often referred to as somatic) effects, as well as organizational effects.[31] In 1999 Vicki Magley and her colleagues explained that "[t]here is a large body of research on the effects of sexual harassment on women. The effects . . . have been found in studies with sound methodology such as large samples and the use of independent outcome measures (i.e., measures assessed separately from and prior to the measurement of sexual harassment, thus reducing potentially biased responses)."[32] Such effects vary from person to person and circumstance to circumstance; this section provides a general overview of the nature and types of injuries sexual harassment victims experience.

Beginning with job effects, in chapter 5, I detailed studies showing that targets who report harassment risk losing their jobs. Whether they resigned or were fired, studies show that targets of sexual harassment lost their jobs somewhere between 4% and 50% of the time, depending on the study.[33] Just to use one example, the 1987 USMSPB study estimated that during the two-year period studied in that report, more than 36,000 federal employees quit, were transferred or reassigned, or were fired because of sexual harassment.[34] Likewise, studies have shown a relationship between experiencing or witnessing sexual harassment and increased intention to quit.[35] Thus, sexual harassment can have significant effects on the employment prospects of targets. Research shows that there are a variety of negative psychological as well as physical reactions to job loss. Reactions vary and can include grief due to lost relationships and connections at work as well as anxiety related to financial difficulties caused by unemployment.[36] Thus, the psychological and financial costs of job loss can be elements of damage resulting from sexual harassment.

In addition, sexual harassment can affect the day-to-day work of the target even when he or she does not suffer job loss. It may cause problems in interpersonal working relationships with coworkers and supervisors as they are forced to take sides on the harassment. It may lead to self-esteem problems as targets wonder whether they were successful in their jobs or merely found attractive by the person who hired them. Harassment that takes the form of ostracism by coworkers or supervisors can lead to decreased learning and networking opportunities, which can lead to decreased work opportunities.[37]

Sexual harassment appears to have an effect on job satisfaction as well. In a study of sexual harassment in the legal profession, Laband and Lentz analyzed survey data collected by the American Bar Association in 1990. They found that job satisfaction was significantly lower for women lawyers who had experienced or witnessed sexual harassment during the two years prior to the survey as compared to women who had not in the prior two years.[38] This was most significant for women who experienced or observed harassment by a supervisor. In this study, researchers also found that job satisfaction is positively correlated with increases in income but more than twice as strongly influenced by supervisor harassment than by increases in salary.[39] Paula Morrow and her colleagues, in a study of workers at a midwestern government agency, found incidents of supervisor harassment correlated to women's lower levels of satisfaction with work, supervision, and promotion as well as with higher levels of role ambiguity, role conflict, and stress. In addition, coworker harassment correlated with lower levels of organizational commitment and satisfaction with coworkers.[40] Interestingly, although they found similar correlates for men experiencing supervisor harassment, there were no statistically significant correlations for men experiencing coworker harassment.[41] These correlations occur even if the employees do not perceive themselves as being sexually harassed.

Magley and her colleagues found similar results in a study of the military. Military personnel who had experienced forms of sexual harassment as defined by the Department of Defense's version of the SEQ were less satisfied with work, colleagues, and supervisors. They also were less committed to the military and reported reduced work productivity. The negative impact on satisfaction and productivity occurred even for low to moderate levels of harassment.[42]

In addition to job-related effects, sexual harassment has significant psychological and somatic effects. Studies indicate that women experience emotional and physical problems due to the harassment. This is likely caused in part by the stress of harassing situations. Physical symptoms include stomach and appetite problems, sleep disorders, headaches, and crying spells, just to name some. There are few systematic studies on physical effects,[43] but researchers have studied psychological effects; victims experience anger, fear, depression, anxiety, helplessness, and vulnerability.[44] Among common psychological disorders associated with employment discrimination in general are "[a]nxiety disorders including panic disorder and generalized anxiety disorder; somatoform disorders, various forms of depression, and post traumatic stress disorder."[45] This has led researchers to link sexual harassment symptoms to post-traumatic stress disorder (discussed in chapter 5). Indeed, as noted earlier, targets of more severe forms of sexual harassment may experience PTSD.

Schneider and her colleagues conducted a thoughtful study on the effects of sexual harassment on women working in a private-sector organization in the Northwest and a large midwestern university. They sought to determine if experiencing sexual harassment had an impact on the women's work attitude, work behaviors, and psychological well-being. They took into consideration whether other factors, such as general job stress, affective disposition, or attitudes about harassment, might account for any relationships found. They found a relationship between women's experience of sexual harassment and job and psychological outcomes. Depending on the amount and nature of the harassment, the women's job and psychological outcomes worsened. Specifically, women who experienced high levels of harassment reported the worst job-related and psychological outcomes; women who were not sexually harassed reported the lowest negative outcomes. Women who reported moderate levels of harassment likewise had significantly worse outcomes than women who were not harassed. Even low levels of harassment increased negative outcomes. These results remained significant even considering the other factors mentioned above that might account for the negative outcomes.[46]

Dansky and Kilpatrick detail the psychological impact of sexual harassment as determined by a national study of women. The random sample included 3,006 adult women. The study considered only supervisor harassment and therefore does not address coworker harassment. From the sample, 2,941 women were grouped into four categories based on whether they had experienced (1) no harassment; (2) potential harassment; (3) potential harassment with perception that they were not harassed, but no negative job effect; and (4) sexual harassment that meets the EEOC criteria. The study looked at the incidence of PTSD and Major Depressive Disorder (MDD) in these populations. The results showed that women who experienced sexual harassment were more likely to be diagnosed with these psychological disorders. In addition, the percentage diagnosed increased from the first category to the fourth, as shown in Table 2.

TABLE 2: *Percentage Women Diagnosed with PTSD and MDD*[47]

	PTSD		MDD	
Group	Lifetime	Currently	Lifetime	Currently
No sexual harassment	9.0	3.3	12.3	7.3
Potential sexual harassment only	12.1	4.5	19.4	12.3
Potential sexual harassment and perception	20.2	7.2	20.1	14.2
EEOC definition of sexual harassment	29.7	1.3	28.8	21.9

Of significance is that 21.9% of the women who had experienced harassment that met the EEOC definition of sexual harassment were currently experiencing major depressive disorder. The researchers also found that having experienced sexual harassment independently contributed to these psychological conditions even for women who had experienced other sexual or physical assault.[48] The results also indicated the long-term effects of sexual harassment: the average time elapsed since experiencing harassment was eleven years, yet a significant number of these women were currently experiencing psychological problems.[49]

Further, there are a variety of emotional costs associated with litigating such claims that may discourage women from pursuing them. Although litigation may serve to compensate and validate the victim of harassment, it also can exacerbate psychological consequences of harassment, causing more trauma to the victim. Severe career consequences, including termination, demotion, loss of productivity, and blackballing, can follow pursuit of a claim in court.[50]

2. Sexual Harassment Targets Who Have Histories of Prior Abuse

Psychology researchers have addressed the increasing use of plaintiff's prior victimization to undercut damages as well as other aspects of sexual harassment claims. Defense lawyers are using evidence (often from psychologists or psychiatrists) of prior victimization to argue that plaintiff's psychological condition was largely a result of preexisting conditions arising from prior victimization.[51] Thus, the plaintiff is entitled to less damages and arguably, in some cases, no damages at all. Apparently, commentators made the link between prior sexual abuse and sexual harassment based on research looking at various relationships between incest and adult sexual abuse.[52] In particular, studies show that victims of childhood sexual abuse have a higher incidence of abuse as adults.[53] This has led some to speculate that such victims behave in ways that increase their chances of being abused. Although extrapolating from these studies does not seem far-fetched, it leaves open the possibility that sexual harassment might function differently than other forms of sexual abuse. And, indeed, recent studies paint a different picture from this initial assumption.

Recent studies have debunked the assertion that sexual harassment victims are hypersensitive due to past abuse, showing instead that victims of prior abuse are neither hypersensitive to sexual harassment nor more likely to experience negative psychological effects than sexual harassment targets who did not experience prior abuse. While research is still ongoing on this subject, it is clear that defense experts who make such assertions have little to no empirical support for their positions. This has led psychologist Louise Fitzgerald and her colleagues to assert that such arguments are based on "junk logic."[54]

Fitzgerald and her colleagues conducted two studies to determine whether sexual harassment targets with previous histories of abuse were somehow hypersensitive, such that they were more likely to experience psychological injury as a result of sexual harassment. They studied the reactions of 307 college women, 35% of whom had experienced sexual abuse as children. Using a fairly high-level example of sexual abuse—unwanted sexual touching—they showed their subjects four videotaped scenarios of varying levels of sexual harassment. They found that abused and nonabused women did not differ overall in their reactions to the scenarios—even those that were more extreme examples of sexual harassment. Instead, both groups' reactions varied based on the severity of the harassment. The same result held when they were asked about their likely response as a target in the same situation: "abused women did not respond differently than nonabused women."[55] Instead, the severity of the scenario affected whether they would complain. Summing up their results, Fitzgerald et al. explained, "These results suggest that there are no scientific grounds for claiming that women with a history of sexual abuse are *per se* any more reactive to sexual material than other women."[56]

Their second study attempted to determine whether childhood sexual abuse is a likely alternative cause for the psychological distress experienced by sexual harassment targets. Detailing the empirical support linking sexual harassment to a variety of psychological problems (some of which are described above), their study sought to examine links between prior sexual abuse and the negative psychological effects resulting from harassment. To do this, they interviewed and administered psychological inventories to 56 women involved in sexual harassment litigation. Although they admit that the sample is small and may not be representative, they still sought to determine whether there were any differences between those who had experienced prior sexual abuse and those who had not in terms of psychological outcomes. It is interesting that nearly 75% of the sample had experienced prior abuse.[57] They found that there was no difference between the previously abused and nonabused groups: "the most common diagnoses in this sample of sexual harassment claimants were PTSD and MDD, irrespective of whether or not they had experienced previous sexual or physical victimization."[58]

Margaret Stockdale and her colleagues performed an extensive literature review as well as a study of women who had previously been sexually harassed to determine if there was a link between prior harassment and sensitivity to harassing incidents. To begin with, their literature review "provided no evidence of a consistent bias in SH-related judgments, perceptions, or attitudes on the part of research participants who reported having experienced prior abuse."[59] In addition, using five different samples of working and student populations, they found little support for links between prior history of sexual harassment and heightened sensitivity to sexual harassment. They concluded, "[N]either the literature review nor the five empirical studies we presented found any practical support for the prior-sexual-abuse theory."[60] This has caused them to question the use of history of prior sexual abuse in such cases.

3. Juries and Damages

That sexual harassment causes plaintiffs damage does not answer the question of whether juries are particularly good at determining damage awards in these cases. Concern over purported outlandish damage awards has led to a vibrant tort reform movement in the United States. Unlike tort law, where damage caps were not initially put in place, Congress enacted Title VII's damages provision with caps. There may be cases in which the caps result in less than full compensation for victims and/or are insufficient to deter sexual harassment. If this is so, a potential solution would be for Congress to abandon the caps on damages. If such caps are lifted, will jurors go wild and award damages well above what seems reasonable in a given case? There are few studies on jury damage awards in employment discrimination cases,[61] but psychologists have studied how jurors award damages in tort cases. Some of their findings are helpful in assessing what may happen if the caps are removed.

Fortunately for purposes of discussion here, Edith Greene and Brian Bornstein sum up much of this research in their recent book *Determining Damages: The Psychology of Jury Awards*. In it, they canvass many jury studies in an effort to understand how jurors assess damages and what relationship damages have to other issues in cases, such as the blameworthiness of the defendant. There is little that is directly applicable to sexual harassment in particular and a need for more research on this issue generally; still, the trends found in the study of tort law damages are relevant to sexual harassment. Sexual harassment is essentially an employment tort and bears much resemblance to such tort claims as intentional infliction of emotional distress. Indeed, it permits damages for pain and suffering, just as intentional infliction of emotional distress does. Thus, the studies Greene and Bornstein discuss are germane to the discussion of damages in the sexual harassment context.

Several themes run throughout Greene and Bornstein's assessment of the studies of juror damage awards. The first is that jury damage awards are distorted in the public's perception by media focus on outliers, that is, on awards that are high but very infrequent. The second is that jurors actually do a pretty good job at assessing damages, and the factor that should be most significant—the severity of the victim's injury—is most predictive of the award amount.[62] As Greene and Bornstein sum up, when it comes to compensatory damage awards, jury "awards are generally modest, stable, and predictable."[63] Studies indicate that juries' final award amounts appear to reflect the award of the jurors in the moderate-damages "faction" of the jury.[64] Indeed, plaintiffs generally receive less in compensatory damages than the costs of their injuries.[65]

Noneconomic compensatory damages are the one area of compensatory damages that appears problematic. These damages include such items as emotional distress as well as pain and suffering. Unlike items of damages in which a plaintiff can point to a bill from a service provider, these damages often are left largely to the unaided discretion of the jury. Evidence suggests that there is wider variability in these damages than in other forms of compensatory relief, but there is insufficient empirical support to conclude that jurors award excessive amounts in damages of this sort.[66] The variability in awards is horizontal—i.e., plaintiffs with the same sorts of injuries receive widely varying awards. However, as a general matter, there is vertical equity, whereby those with more severe injuries tend to receive higher awards.[67]

A study by Wissler et al., detailed in Greene and Bornstein's book, found that mock jurors' perceptions of injuries in tort cases related to four factors: "(a) mental suffering, (b) physical pain, (c) visibility of injury, and (d) disability."[68] This study suggests that jurors consider pain and suffering as two distinct items. There were high correlations between suffering and the perception of the plaintiff's disability and disfigurement, as well as the injury's effect on the plaintiff's life. These correlates were much lower for pain determinations. As a result of this and other studies, Greene and Bornstein concluded that "the greater the plaintiff's disability and mental suffering, the larger the plaintiff's pain and suffering award."[69] Because emotional distress damages are a potential component of compensatory damages for sexual harassment, there is reason for some concern about this form of damages.

It is difficult to draw conclusions from the few studies that focus on employment discrimination cases and sexual harassment in particular. In a recent study of California jury verdicts in employment discrimination cases, law professor David Oppenheimer found that in the sexual harassment cases he studied (jury verdicts rendered in 1998 and 1999) the median verdict was $210,000.[70] The vast majority of the cases in his study were brought in state court, presumably under California's antidiscrimination laws, which contains no damage caps.[71] Thus, the study provides information about what damages might be without caps. Oppenheimer did not compute means (averages) of awards because he found this tended to skew results based on the occasional outlier case.[72] In addition, in only 9% of the opposite-sex sexual harassment cases he studied (7 out of 80) did the jury award more than $1 million in damages.[73]

Cass Sunstein and Judy Shih also have studied verdicts in sexual harassment cases in both state and federal courts. Although they note that their data set is small and may be skewed, they did make some preliminary findings that are troubling.[74] In particular, they "found no correlation between the size of compensatory and punitive awards."[75] In addition, they found no correlation with higher compensatory damage awards and factors that they thought might increase these awards, e.g., physical contact, forced sex, adverse employment effects, and so on.[76] Disturbingly, they found that some regressions showed that "more intimate physical contact, including touching of the plaintiffs' breasts or buttocks, significantly correlated with *lower* damage awards."[77] This is a problematic finding and runs contrary to what one would expect from the social science regarding perceptions of harassment. Sunstein and Shih did find a correlation between higher compensatory awards and quid pro quo harassment, although there was an inverse relationship between quid pro quo harassment and punitive damage awards.[78] They concluded that "[t]aken together, these findings suggest that, despite some hints of consistency, there is overall significant randomness in sexual harassment damage awards. It is possible that a larger sample of cases will reveal a more reasonable pattern of outcomes, but at least it can be said that no patterns have emerged to date.[79] Because federal cases (and state cases involving state damage caps) were not separated out from state cases (which did not have caps on damages), it is hard to make a direct comparison between jurisdictions with caps and those without caps. However, they did note that overall damage awards were low—the median award for both compensatory and punitive damages was $50,000.[80] It is difficult to come to any comprehensive conclusions about sexual harassment damages from these two studies. While more work needs to be done in this area, these studies do not suggest that sexual harassment awards are excessive.

Some studies suggest that giving jurors more guidance, in the form of jury instructions or expert testimony, in determining noneconomic damages might be helpful to lessen the variability in these awards. Although bifurcating the liability phase of a trial from the damages phase tends to result in more defense verdicts, studies indicate that when a defendant is found liable, jury awards are higher in bifurcated proceedings than when both liability and damages are decided in one proceeding.[81] As a general matter, studies show that jurors understand instructions better when they are simple and direct.[82] Perhaps a series of specific criteria in jury instructions would focus jurors on the nature of these damages, resulting in more consistent outcomes.[83]

One solution to this problem is precisely what Congress has done here—place caps on compensatory damages. However, caps tend to disproportionately affect the most severely harmed plaintiffs, and thus such plaintiffs will be undercompensated. But it is unclear that caps will have any effect on the bulk of awards, for which the jury still has little guidance in assessing damages.[84] In essence, vertical equity suffers. Indeed, studies have shown that caps (at least where jurors know about them) tend to increase damage awards that would naturally fall under the caps.[85] Other studies have suggested that courts use a schedule of pain and suffering awards to inform jurors of award amounts for similar injuries. One obvious problem with this (pointed to by commentators) is that if prior awards are plagued with the same problems, relying on them for assessing future damages awards appears equally flawed.[86] At this point, it is not clear what will lead to consistency. More empirical research is necessary, especially in employment discrimination cases.

Another alternative is expert testimony about the nature of psychological distress experienced by sexual harassment targets. Psychologists Edith Greene and her colleagues did a study of jury decision making on damages using an age discrimination fact pattern. Their intent was to assess the effects of expert testimony on the award of economic damages. They also permitted mock jurors to assess damages for pain and suffering. They set up four conditions to compare, varying who (no one; an attorney; an expert for plaintiff; and experts for both plaintiff and defendant) made recommendations for damages. Interestingly, and perhaps because of their relatively small sample size, they found little statistically significant difference in awards under these differing conditions. The one area in which they found a "marginally" significant difference (p = .08), was in predeliberation awards for lost wages between jurors who heard an expert for the plaintiff and jurors who did not receive any recommendation.[87] Between these two conditions, jurors who heard one expert awarded more than jurors who neither heard an expert nor received any recommendation. The mean awards for these two conditions were $433,000 and $575,000, respectively, for lost wages and benefits.[88] Thus, it appears that experts had little effect on the award of economic damages except in situations in which there was no recommendation made at all. Because the experts did not testify on pain and suffering, how an expert's testimony on these damages might affect such awards is unknown.

Jane Goodman-Delahunty and William Foote suggest that psychological expert testimony may be of use in a number of ways for jurors assessing damages in employment discrimination cases. They suggest that psychologists can help articulate the nature of the plaintiff's emotional suffering, interpret the plaintiff's behavior, and help avoid further anguish for the plaintiff by describing the effects of harassment. Experts can also put the target's symptoms in context and relate them to how other people have been affected by similar situations. As Goodman-Delahunty and Foote put it, experts can provide information that is "akin to 'social framework'" testimony.[89] To the extent that harassment results in diagnosable psychological disorders, psychologists and psychiatrists can explain the nature of such illnesses and how they are likely to affect the plaintiff's future functioning. Psychologists also can be helpful in aiding the jury in making the causal leap between the plaintiff's harm and the acts of the defendant.[90]

An assessment of how juries decide cases involving compensatory damages alone is insufficient because another area of damages applicable under Title VII—punitive damages—often is considered the most problematic. Unlike compensatory damages, which are designed to compensate victims for their actual losses, punitive damages are meant to deter and punish the defendant. Without caps, the fear is that jurors will become out of control in their desire to punish and will inflate awards to unreasonable levels. To begin with, it appears that punitive damages awards are rare. According to a 1995 study by the Bureau of Justice Statistics of civil trials in large U.S. counties, punitive damages were awarded in approximately 6% of the cases where the defendant was found liable. The awards were small and generally did not exceed the amount of compensatory damages.[91] Studies likewise show a high correlation between the amount of punitive damages and compensatory damages awarded, which in turn at least moderately correlates with the severity the plaintiff's injury.[92] One group of legal scholars has reached the somewhat controversial conclusion that, "Far from being randomly related, the punitive damages awards increase monotonically with compensatory damages in a statistically significant manner. The hypothesis that punitive damage awards are randomly plucked out of the air, and bear no relation to compensatory damages, can be firmly rejected."[93]

Jury decision making on damages does not seem outrageous as a general matter, but there is reason to believe that jurors may make more plaintiff-friendly decisions in employment-related cases. Although few studies look at employment discrimination in particular, studies of contract cases involving state employment reveal that a higher percentage of successful plaintiffs receive punitive damages. For example, a study of Bureau of Justice Statistics data reveals that 24% of successful plaintiffs in these cases receive punitive damages from the jury.[94] In addition, jurors more frequently award punitive damages in certain intentional tort cases.[95] To the extent sexual harassment resembles an intentional tort, they may have higher rates of punitive damages awards.

Eisenberg and his colleagues opine that punitive damages rates are higher in intentional tort and business cases because they involve "intentional or morally flawed behavior."[96] From some of the cases described above, it does appear that jurors award damages, both punitive and compensatory, that are above the cap in some cases. Defendants in those cases would certainly argue that the caps are functioning well in terms of lowering their damages, but that does not necessarily mean that caps are accomplishing the aims of compensatory and punitive damages. Indeed, it appears that jurors are acting appropriately in condemning behavior by defendants that is intentional or in some manner morally wrong.

C. *Reforming the Law to Reflect the Harm as well as to Properly Punish and Deter*

Research shows that there are various negative ramifications associated with sexual harassment experiences. Although Title VII provides compensatory damages for such injuries, the damages are capped at a relatively low level—between $50,000 and $300,000, depending on the size of the employer. Research also suggests that although caps add a degree of certainty to the risk involved in sexual harassment litigation, they do so at the expense of vertical equity. In other words, caps likely cause targets who experience the worst harassment resulting in the gravest injury to be undercompensated. Certainly in some of the cases described earlier in this chapter, jurors awarded damages that did not seem unreasonable, and yet the caps brought those damages down.

The effect of caps also is troubling because there has been little opportunity to develop a track record of damage judgments for sexual harassment under Title VII. Some state laws prohibiting sexual harassment do not impose caps, but there are few studies of these cases.[97] Congress imposed caps as a political compromise without any evidence that jury awards would be extreme. Although such compromises are a necessary part of the political process, it's time to reevaluate whether the caps are truly necessary. Soon after enactment of the Civil Rights Act of 1991, Congress attempted unavailingly to remove the caps.[98] Another aspect of damage awards that gets little press is remittitur—the process by which federal judges reduce damage awards that are too high. Indeed, remittitur might be an adequate solution to any outlier jury awards. Thus, Congress should remove the caps in these cases.[99]

One particular problem that emerges in jury damages research is the variability in emotional distress damages. These damages are now compensable under Title VII and, it can be argued, their variability in tort cases suggests that there should be an attempt to rein in jurors. The problems of horizontal equity in tort damage awards might well crop up in sexual harassment cases due to their tortlike nature,[100] but without studies showing that this has indeed been the case, it is speculative to impose caps as the solution. This is especially true, given the effect of caps on vertical equity. Looking at cases such as *Parker v. Olympus Health Care*, in which the plaintiff was raped, an award of $750,000 in compensatory damages does not seem unreasonable. Indeed, even the $1.75 million award against the employer (who had notice of prior improprieties and even of a prior rape by the same harasser) does not seem outlandish, given the facts of the case. Yet, the plaintiff received only $300,000 in that case pursuant to the cap. Likewise, in *Madison v. IBP, Inc.*, the plaintiff endured daily racial and sexual harassment in which management participated, and the plaintiff's complaints were ignored. The combined jury award of $266,750 in emotional distress damages and $2,069,000 in punitive damages was reduced to the cap of $300,000. Once again, given that the employer essentially ignored the plaintiff's complaints and allowed egregious harassment to continue, the jury's award looks appropriate. These plaintiffs are, at the least, arguably being undercompensated and undercompensated in such a manner that the employer is given little incentive to correct harassment. In addition, each of the two employers ignored either the plaintiff's harassment or prior harassment by the same harasser(s). It is reasonable to deter and punish, under such circumstances, in a significant manner. For most employers of five hundred or more employees, $300,000 amounts to little more than a slap on the wrist.

It might well be that if caps are lifted employers' worst fears will be realized: jurors will award huge damages (especially punitive damages) to sexual harassment plaintiffs. Small businesses will thereby be placed in economic peril by a single sexual harassment case. There are several reasons to believe that small business disasters of this sort would be a rarity, if they happen at all. First, Title VII applies to only employers of fifteen or more employees.[101] Thus, small mom-and-pop businesses cannot be sued under the statute. Second, the defendant must act with malice or reckless indifference to plaintiff's rights in order for punitive damages to be appropriate. Even under the lighter standard for imputing liability to employers set out in chapter 5, a defendant generally would have the opportunity to correct the harassment before punitive damages would be imposed. Finally, the legal standard for punitive damages calls for assessment of damages based in part on the defendant's wealth, at least if the defendant is impecunious.[102] The less wealthy a defendant, the less money should be awarded in punitive damages.

If the experience of tort speaks to what might happen in sexual harassment cases, the possibility of huge punitive damages verdicts is low. As a general matter, it is well documented that juries rarely award punitive damages. And, even where they do, these damages tend to be modest and reflect the amount of compensatory damages. In the few cases in which juries become extreme, there is no reason to believe that tools such as remittitur will be ineffective to restrain the occasional outlier jury. Indeed, few studies have looked at the ultimate outcome of tort suits: the amount plaintiffs actually receive after all the appeals and remittitur. The few studies that have been done suggest that courts reduce awards in most higher damages cases. For example, Ivy Broder conducted a study of 198 jury awards of more than $1 million in 1984 and 1985. She found that only slightly more than 25% (51 of 198 cases) of plaintiffs actually received the amount awarded. On average, such awards were reduced by 30% of the original judgment.[103] The aggregated total of all awards was reduced by 57%! Broder found that, on average, verdicts in intentional tort cases were reduced by 26%. The aggregated percentage reduction in these cases was 74%, which suggests that large awards were reduced significantly. Indeed, the average of the original verdicts for this subset was more than $6 million, yet, the postverdict distribution average was almost $1.8 million.[104]

More recently, Neil Vidmar and his colleagues studied medical malpractice awards in three jurisdictions. One of the things they looked at was the bottom line—i.e., what the plaintiff finally received after all attacks and postjudgment settlement negotiations were finalized. Of the 112 New York cases that qualified for this part of their study, two settled for the amount of the verdict; two settled for more; and forty-six settled for less. One case was increased by additur (a tool whereby a verdict is increased by the court; it is not available in federal court) and twenty-three were decreased through remittitur. Seventeen were reduced because of comparative negligence. The upshot was that ninety-six cases were adjusted downward, and only three were adjusted upward.[105] This suggests that in high-verdict cases, plaintiffs often receive less than the jury actually awards. Indeed, in a review of the fifty highest awards, the researchers found that twenty-five were adjusted downward and that the largest downward adjustments involved the largest awards.[106] Samples of cases from Florida and California also involved some downward adjustments, although the number adjusted downward varied.[107] The point of alluding to the Broder and Vidmar et al. studies is to emphasize that in many cases, plaintiffs do not receive the original amount a jury awards for a variety of reasons—including that the judge believes the award is too high and remits a portion of it. There is no reason to believe that judges will not do so in sexual harassment cases.

One area of research that might aid jurors in making damages assessments is jury instructions. We do know that people who are asked to complete a task do a better job when the instructions are clear. Unfortunately, jury instructions on such elements of damages as emotional distress leave it up to the jury to decide. For example, the Fifth Circuit's jury instructions for pain and suffering explicitly state: "You are not trying to determine value, but an amount that will fairly compensate the plaintiff for the damages he has suffered. There is no exact standard for fixing the compensation to be awarded for these elements of damage. Any award that you make should be fair in light of the evidence."[108] Thus, the jury is given very little guidance other than to do what is "fair in light of the evidence."

Problems with the complexity of jury instructions have led California to revise its instructions to use "plain English" constructions.[109] In particular, the instructions delineate between economic and noneconomic damages, and tell jurors that when it comes to awarding emotional distress damages, to "use your judgment to decide a reasonable amount based on the evidence and your common sense."[110] However, the instructions still do not delineate how jurors should further think about such damages. It will be interesting to see if these instructions result in greater consistency in emotional distress awards.

Research that might help courts develop instructions that would be clearer would be helpful as well. In the meantime, it would be useful to see what jury awards would look like without caps to get a sense of whether they are necessary. As it stands now, the most severely injured plaintiffs and most egregious employer behavior run the very real risk of being undercompensated and undeterred, respectively.

7

The New
Sexual Harassment Claim

Throughout this book, I have picked apart the courts' standards for evaluating sexual harassment claims, reevaluating each element through the lens of social science. Having taken a close look at certain aspects of the claim, it is fair to examine, at this point, what it all amounts to as well as to evaluate its ability to improve adjudication of such claims. Have the proffered revisions avoided many of the problems (and stereotypes) that the courts and litigants have encountered in this area of the law? Will courts still dismiss cases that look like sexual harassment to the average person? Will courts continue to fall into the trap of focusing on the target's behavior, and evaluate her actions—instead of those of the harasser—to see if she fits within the "perfect sexual harassment victim" myth? Do the modifications to the standard for imputing liability to the employer impose unrealistic burdens on the employer while requiring little of the plaintiff? Will employers continue to be able to bulletproof themselves from sexual harassment claims, while doing nothing that, as a practical matter, is likely to reduce its occurrence in their workplaces? Will plaintiffs continue to be undercompensated and defendants insufficiently deterred? All of these questions go to the heart of making Title VII really work for those it was intended to help. More fundamentally, can Title VII sexual harassment jurisprudence be modified in ways that will significantly help victims or is it some form of radical (but perhaps less realistic) change that's really called for? I will begin by considering what the claim would look like if the courts adopted the approaches set out in this book.

A. The New Sexual Harassment Claim

In the introduction, I set out the basic four elements of a sexual harassment claim. They included (1) an employee was subjected to unwelcome harassment;[1] (2) the harassment was based on the employee's sex; (3) the harassment was "sufficiently severe or pervasive" to alter a term, condition, or privilege of employment;[2] and (4) a way to impute liability to the employer.[3] In addition, I examined the reasonable woman standard, which some courts have used to evaluate whether the harassment was sufficiently severe or pervasive. I also assessed whether the current damage caps provide both adequate compensation for plaintiffs and adequate deterrence (through punishment) for defendants. The sum total of my efforts would lead to a sexual harassment claim with the following characteristics.

To begin with, I have loosened the severe or pervasive standard, asking courts to consider what survey data show about what people perceive as harassing. My focus was on the objective component of this element—the reasonable person standard—and how courts might assess situations in light of perception data from social science. What I am especially concerned with is judges granting summary judgment or overriding a jury's decision in the plaintiff's favor using judgment as a matter of law. Social science data provide useful information about what reasonable people find harassing and help substantiate the reactions of most workers as not those of the hypersensitive plaintiff but, instead, as those of the common "reasonable person." At least it should result in fewer dismissals before the case goes to the jury, as well as in fewer courts overturning jury verdicts in the plaintiff's favor. Outcomes should be more reflective of what reasonable people believe is harassing than the perceptions of individual trial judges. The solution is not perfect and is likely to leave some sexual harassment unremedied, but it is a first step—and a step that may well be palatable to the courts.

Along with this, I also proposed that fact finders might profit from focusing on the effects of harassment on the conditions of the plaintiff's employment. This is consistent with Dolkart's approach,[4] and serves to focus the fact finder on the effect the harasser's behavior has on the target's working conditions. One of the main benefits of this standard is that it takes the focus off the plaintiff and her response and properly places emphasis on the harasser's actions and their likely influence on the work environment. This approach has the added benefit of stressing the context in which the behavior occurs. The conditions of a "reasonable person's" employment may not be affected by an offhand compliment or off-color joke from a coworker. On the other hand, they might well be affected by a proposition from a supervisor. It also should help the courts avoid the trap of dividing up incidents so that the cumulative effect is not truly considered. In asking what the likely effect of the harasser's or harassers' actions is, fact finders will necessarily be required to assess all the actions— the sum total of all the harassing incidents—and their effect on the target's working conditions. Thus, the objective element would be truly contextually based, rather than only theoretically so.

This also has implications for the reasonable woman standard. Social science suggests that there may be growing agreement between men and women about what behaviors constitute sexual harassment. To the extent that there are differences in perception between men and women about some ambiguous behaviors, the differences may be decreasing. Further, gender of perceiver appears to have small effect on assessments of whether behavior is harassing. Combining this with evidence that the reasonable woman standard makes little difference in case outcomes suggests that it is time to eliminate the standard. Certainly, the reasonable woman standard is not the answer to the problems that plague the objective component of the severe or pervasive standard. Instead, it appears to act as a mere panacea, lulling advocates for sexual harassment victims into believing that courts have made a significant change in the standard when it is likely to have little effect on the outcomes of real cases. Given the reasonable woman standard's potential to further both paternalism and essentialism, as well as its limited efficacy, the standard's usefulness should be questioned.

Instead of jettisoning the reasonable woman standard, one possibility is to avoid reasonableness altogether. The perception data described in chapters 1 and 2 can act as guideposts for both judges and juries as to the types of behaviors people perceive as harassing, and the reasonableness standard can be abandoned. With guidance from the social sciences in mind, the jury could again focus on the effects of the harassment on the plaintiff's working conditions. In this manner, problems inherent in reasonableness (for example, its propensity to be based on a male norm) can be avoided while giving the jury a way to think about what level of harassment is sufficiently severe or pervasive to be actionable. The advantage to courts in adopting this approach is obvious: it is based on the plain language of the statute. Further, to the extent that some gender discrepancies persist, studies suggest that expert testimony might provide the answer. Building on the research by Kovera and her colleagues, having an expert testify about the role of gender stereotyping as well as other aspects of harassing behavior, along with an emphasis on effects of the harassment, might well be more effective than using the reasonable woman standard.

The requirement that the plaintiff show that the harassment was unwelcome should be done away with except in a narrow set of cases, and then should be available to a defendant as an affirmative defense. To begin with, unwelcomeness is irrelevant to most sexual harassment cases. Hence, it should not be an element of the plaintiff's case. Instead, a defendant can use it as an affirmative defense in the case it was designed for—where there is some evidence of a consensual relationship. Courts need to understand cases involving plaintiffs who respond in kind in self-defense or in an attempt to fit in. Although more research would be helpful to more fully understand this type of plaintiff reaction, often these cases are simple to understand, given the clearly harassing behavior involved (behavior that no person would welcome). To the extent that courts have suggested that welcomeness provides a notice function (alerting the harasser to the offensiveness of his behavior), the *Ellerth/Faragher* defense as well as the negligence standard developed for coworker harassment should provide all the notice that is necessary. Eliminating this inquiry for the vast majority of cases also will cut off intrusive discovery and the disclosure of embarrassing evidence during trial.

In order for a plaintiff to prove the third element—that the harassment was based on the sex of the plaintiff—I have suggested a multifactored analysis based on social science research on workplaces in which such discrimination thrives. These factors sweep within the concept of sexual harassment many cases that have caused the courts problems, including same-sexual harassment cases, equal opportunity harasser cases, harassing environment cases, as well as cases that involve failed consensual relationships. Included within these factors are (1) whether the workplace is gender homogeneous; (2) whether the target is isolated from others of the same gender; (3) whether the occupation is traditionally gendered female or male; (4) whether the environment is sexualized, for example, whether there are frequent sexual jokes, pinups, and the like; and (5) management's (including the immediate supervisor's) attitude toward sexual harassment.

No one factor need be present in every case in order for the fact finder to conclude that the harassment was "because of sex." Instead, the factors would focus the fact finder on the type of environment in which harassment is more likely to occur. Courts need to understand that sexual harassment is not just the result of the presence of an individual bad actor but is also highly influenced by the working environment. This approach, in effect, requires the fact finder to truly look at the totality of the circumstances at the workplace to determine if the harassment is likely because of sex. Thus, for example, it is likely that harassment of a woman in an all-male environment where she is doing a traditional masculine job is because of her sex. These factors provide concrete considerations for the fact finder to consider about the institutional circumstances that lend themselves to harassment. In this way, they make it more difficult for the fact finder to default to stereotypes. The factors could be included in jury instructions, and their ramifications set out in those instructions or be introduced through expert testimony. This allows for flexibility as well as an expansion of the types of factors that a court should consider based on increased knowledge about the functioning of sexual harassment in the workplace. These factors also would help employers assess what it is about their workplaces that makes harassment more likely.

The final element of the claim is imputing liability to the employer. My approach to this element cautions the courts against being too accepting of employers' preventive efforts, including anti–sexual harassment policies and training programs, given the little evidence available on what works. In addition, I suggest doing away with the "avoid harm otherwise" prong of the *Ellerth/Faragher* defense and to use damages more creatively. Specifically, I argue that targets of supervisor harassment should be compensated for the harm they experience regardless of the employer's preventive efforts. In this way, employers will be truly motivated to design and enforce policies that are actually effective at preventing harassment rather than simply bulletproofing themselves for a potential claim down the road. Given the high costs of sexual harassment, it is in their interest to do so. Yet, the deterrent effect is not what it could be, in part due to easy outs like this defense as well as the final issue that I address, the limitations on damages in these cases.

The last controversy takes reform out of the courtroom and into the halls of Congress. I have argued for a solution to the problem of victim undercompensation and perpetrator underdeterrence that is not based on the courts. Specifically, Congress should remove the damages caps from Title VII. Research also suggests that even though caps add a degree of certainty to the risk involved in sexual harassment litigation, they do so at the expense of vertical equity. In other words, caps likely cause targets who experience the worst harassment resulting in the worst injury to be undercompensated. Given that Title VII's twin purposes are to eliminate discrimination in the workplace and to compensate victims, caps on damages are difficult to justify, especially given that there is no history of inappropriate damages on which to base such caps.

B. The Advantages of This Approach

These series of reforms might look to observers as a bit of tweaking, although I occasionally abandon a legal element entirely for some if not all sexual harassment cases. The question remains whether they do enough to correct some of the problems with the current legal standard. This is difficult to assess without seeing my proposed standards in action. The advantages of these "tweaks" are numerous. One of the primary advantages is that aside from removing the damage caps, it is possible to argue for these changes within the current framework for sexual harassment claims. For the most part, they are consistent with the current legal standards, as set out by the Supreme Court.

The major emphasis of these reforms is the context and the environment in which sexual harassment is more (or less) likely to occur. This more contextually based approach should aid fact finders in understanding the dynamics of workplace sexual harassment without focusing as much on the action (or, in some cases, the inaction) of the victim. One advantage of this shift in focus is that it provides objective factors for the fact finder to look to, such as the gender makeup of the workplace and the masculine or feminine nature of the job. This should help fact finders and judges avoid defaulting to stereotypes regarding the manner in which women (and sometimes men) are expected to behave in the workplace. No longer will the focus be on whether the plaintiff is the perfect sexual harassment victim who behaved "appropriately" but, instead, on the job context and what it tells us about whether sexual harassment is likely to occur there.

The reforms should also promote real changes by employers, rather than perfunctory policies that are, at best, halfheartedly enforced. Making employers liable for compensatory damages in all cases of supervisor harassment would provide a major wake-up call to employers who have been relying on their antiharassment policies to avoid liability. In addition, the focus on the work environment provides a real incentive for employers to scrutinize their workplaces carefully, with an eye toward correcting workplace characteristics that are likely to lead to harassment. Increasing the potential damages by overturning the caps can only add to this incentive for employers while, at the same time, making victims truly whole. This focus on the workplace environment has the greatest chance to make real differences in the lives of working Americans.

It is my hope that using these standards will help courts and fact finders understand the dynamics of workplace sexual harassment so that they can evaluate cases based on the reality of harassment, rather than on their own notions of how people interact in the workplace. It also can help employers understand why harassment is likely to occur in their workplaces and what they can do to actually end this disturbing workplace behavior. It is in everyone's interest to eliminate sexual harassment. It is a continual drain on workplace resources in numerous ways, as detailed throughout this book. It makes work life difficult and in some cases impossible for many employed men and women. It likewise leads to inefficient workplaces. If these reforms are adopted, sexual harassment law would be based less on gender myths and more on working realities, and therefore would be more effective in eliminating discrimination in the workplace.

Notes

Notes to the Introduction

1. U.S. Merit Sys. Prot. Bd., Sexual Harassment in the Federal Workplace: Trends, Progress, Continuing Challenges viii (1995) [hereinafter USMSPB].

2. See Richard D. Arvey & Marcie A. Cavanaugh, Using Surveys to Assess the Prevalence of Sexual Harassment: Some Methodological Problems, 51 J. Soc. Issues, Spring 1995, at 39, 40.

3. In 1991, the EEOC reported that 2,003 charges of harassment based on sex and 3,223 charges of sexual harassment were filed. See U.S. Equal Employment Opportunity Comm'n, Combined Annual Report: Fiscal Years 1991 and 1992, at 28. In 1994, the EEOC reported 8,095 charges of sexual harassment and 3,978 charges of harassment based on sex. U.S. Equal Employment Opportunity Comm'n, Annual Report: Fiscal Year 1994, at 36. Looking at the statistics for sex or sexual harassment charges, this represents an increase of 250% from 1991 to 1994. One news source has stated that sexual harassment charges filed with the EEOC have increased from 6,000 in 1990 to 15,300 in 1996. See Leslie Kaufman, A Report from the Front: Why It Has Gotten Easier To Sue for Sexual Harassment, Newsweek, Jan. 13, 1997, at 32. Recently, the EEOC released data showing that sexual harassment filings have leveled off. Charge filings peaked in 1997, at 15,889. This number leveled off to 15,836 in 2000 and decreased in subsequent years. U.S. Equal Employment Opportunity Commission, Sexual Harassment Charges EEOC & FEPAs Combined: FY 1992–FY 2003, at http://www.eeoc.gov/stats/harass.html.

4. See Greg Burns, Dial Trial Pits Clean vs. Filthy Soap Plant Sexual-Harassment Case is Biggest in Years, Chicago Tribune, April 25, 2003, available at 2003 WL 19205587.

5. USMSPB, supra note 1, at 23.

6. See, e.g., Ballew v. Georgia, 435 U.S. 223, 231–33, n.10 (1978) (citing 19 studies regarding effects of smaller jury size); Brown v. Bd. of Educ., 374 U.S. 483, 692 n.11 (1954) (citing studies regarding the psychological effect of segregation).

7. Louise F. Fitzgerald et al., But Was It Really Sexual Harassment? Legal, Behavioral, and Psychological Definitions of the Workplace Victimization of Women, in Sexual Harassment: Theory, Research, and Treatment 5, 9 (William O'Donohue ed., 1997) (quoting Catharine MacKinnon); see also Catharine A. MacKinnon, Sexual Harassment of Working Women: A Case of Sex Discrimination xii (1979) (noting lack of social science studies).

8. John B. Pryor et al., A Social Psychological Model for Predicting Sexual Harassment, 51 J. Soc. Issues, Spring 1995, at 69, 70.

9. See Mia Cahill, The Social Construction of Sexual Harassment Law: The Role of the National, Organizational and Individual Context 10–11 (2001) (describing these books as having added "legitimacy and publicity" to the issue of sexual harassment); Lin Farley, Sexual Shakedown: The Sexual Harassment of Women

ON THE JOB (1978); MACKINNON, *supra* note 7; Patti A. Giuffre & Christine L. Williams, *Boundary Lines: Labeling Sexual Harassment in Restaurants*, 8 GENDER & SOC'Y 378, 379 (1994) (noting significance of MacKinnon book); Elaine Lunsford Weeks et al., *The Transformation of Sexual Harassment from Private Trouble into a Public Issue*, 56 SOCIOLOGICAL INQUIRY 432, 439, 444 (1986) (noting significance of books and EEOC guidelines); Patricia M. Hanrahan, *"How Do I Know if I'm Being Harassed or if This Is Part of My Job?" Nurses and Definitions of Harassment*, 9 NWSA J., Summer 1997, at 43, 45 (noting that MacKinnon's book, along with subsequent promulgation of EEOC guidelines, spurred research interest in sexual harassment).

10. *See, e.g.*, Rogers v. EEOC, 454 F.2d 234 (5th Cir. 1971), *cert. denied*, 406 U.S. 957 (1971) (harassment of Hispanic employee).

11. *See* Arvey & Cavanaugh, *supra* note 2, at 40.

12. *See* Patricia A. Frazier et al., *Social Science Research on Lay Definitions of Sexual Harassment*, 51 J. SOC. ISSUES, Spring 1995, at 21, 29–31 (discussing studies that sought to determine if males and females have differing perceptions of harassment).

13. *See* Louise F. Fitzgerald et al., *Why Didn't She Just Report Him? The Psychological and Legal Implications of Women's Responses to Sexual Harassment*, 51 J. SOC. ISSUES, Spring 1995, at 117, 121 (noting that the least common response to harassment is court action).

14. *See, e.g.*, Susan J. Mecca & Linda J. Rubin, *Definitional Research on African American Students and Sexual Harassment*, 23 PSYCHOL. WOMEN Q. 813 (1999); J. Nicole Shelton & Tabbye M. Chavous, *Black and White College Women's Perceptions of Sexual Harassment*, 40 SEX ROLES 593 (1999).

15. *See* Tanya Kateri Hernandez, *Sexual Harassment and Racial Disparity: The Mutual Construction of Gender and Race*, 4 J. GENDER, RACE & JUST. 183, 185 (2001).

16. *See, e.g.*, RICHARD EPSTEIN, FORBIDDEN GROUNDS: THE CASE AGAINST EMPLOYMENT DISCRIMINATION LAWS (1992); John J. Donohue, *Essay, Is Title VII Efficient?*, 134 U. PA. L. REV. 1411 (1986).

17. James R.P. Ogloff, *Two Steps Forward and One Step Backward: The Law and Psychology Movement(s) in the 20th Century*, 24 LAW & HUM. BEHAV. 457, 462 n.6 (2000) (noting that economics uses different methodologies than psychology).

18. There are notable exceptions. *See, e.g.*, Toni Lester, *Efficient but Not Equitable: The Problem with Using the Law and Economic Paradigm to Interpret Sexual Harassment in the Work Place*, 22 VT. L. REV. 519 (1998).

19. *See* Pryor et al., *supra* note 8, at 70 (citing studies reflecting that women are harassed more frequently than men); Virgil L. Sheets & Sanford L. Braver, *Organizational Status and Perceived Sexual Harassment: Detecting the Mediators of a Null Effect*, 25 PERSONALITY & SOC. PSYCHOL. BULL. 1159, 1160 (1999) (citing studies).

20. *See* Cathy L.Z. DuBois et al., *An Empirical Examination of Same- and Other-Gender Sexual Harassment in the Workplace*, 39 SEX ROLES 731, 731 (1998) (showing that more same-sexual harassment occurs between males); Craig R. Waldo et al., *Are Men Sexually Harassed? If So, By Whom?*, 22 LAW & HUM. BEHAV. 59, 60, 62 (1998) (showing that male-on-male sexual harassment is as prevalent as male-on-female sexual harassment; however, it may operate differently).

21. *See, e.g.*, Nichols v. Frank, 42 F.3d 503, 510 (9th Cir. 1994), *abrogation on other grounds recognized in* Burrell v. Star Nursery, Inc., 170 F.3d 951, 955 (9th Cir. 1999) ("there is no uniform attitude towards the role of sex nor any agreement on what is appropriate for inclusion in a code governing sexual conduct").

22. *See* Gerald L. Blakely et al., *The Effects of Training on Perceptions of Sexual Harassment Allegations*, 28 J. APPLIED SOC. PSYCHOL. 71, 72 (1998) ("what is problematic about this definition of sexual harassment is that it is vague enough to allow for different people to hold different perceptions of what sexual harassment is for them personally").

23. *See* Meritor Sav. Bank v. Vinson, 477 U.S. 57 (1986) (setting standard); Harris v.

Forklift Sys., Inc., 510 U.S. 17, 23 (1993) (totality of the circumstances must be considered in assessing whether the particular environment is sufficiently severe or pervasive to constitute harassment); Oncale v. Sundowner Offshore Servs., Inc., 523 U.S. 75, 81–82 (1998) (emphasizing context in making sexual harassment determination). I have argued elsewhere that the lower courts are ignoring the Supreme Court's directive in this regard at the expense of Title VII plaintiffs. *See* Theresa M. Beiner, *The Misuse of Summary Judgment in Hostile Environment Cases*, 34 WAKE FOREST L. REV. 71 (1999).

24. *See Meritor*, 477 U.S. at 57.

25. Ann Juliano & Stewart J. Schwab, *The Sweep of Sexual Harassment Cases*, 86 CORNELL L. REV. 548, 568, 570 (2001).

26. Peter Siegelman & John J. Donohue III, *Studying the Iceberg from Its Tip: A Comparison of Published and Unpublished Employment Discrimination Cases*, 24 L. & SOC'Y REV. 1133, 1148 (1990). They estimate that plaintiff win rates may be as low as 20% but are certainly lower than 50% when all cases are considered.

27. *Id.* at 1137–38.

28. Kevin M. Clermont & Theodore Eisenberg, *Trial by Jury or Judge: Transcending Empiricism*, 77 CORNELL L. REV. 1124, 1175 (1992).

29. Juliano & Schwab, *supra* note 25, at 574 (success for plaintiffs appealing in 27%; success for defendants appealing in 27%).

30. Theodore Eisenberg & Stewart J. Schwab, *Double Standard on Appeal: An Empirical Analysis of Employment Discrimination Cases in the U.S. Courts of Appeals* 1 *available at* http://findjustice.com/ms/pdf/double-standard.pdf, and *reprinted in* THE EMPLOYEE ADVOC., Winter 2001/2002, at 84. The figures on this point are staggering. When an employment discrimination defendant wins at trial, plaintiffs win appeals in 5.8% of cases appealed. On the other hand, when a plaintiff wins at trial, defendants are successful in 43.61% of those cases in having the judgments reversed. Kevin M. Clermont & Theodore Eisenberg, *Plaintiphobia in the Appellate Courts: Civil Rights Really Do Differ from Negotiable Instruments*, 2002 U. ILL. L. REV. 947, 954–955 tbl. 2, 958. This reversal rate for defendants is greater than any other category of federal litigation except for "other civil rights cases," which includes such cases as police misconduct and First Amendment actions. *Id.* at 958. In addition, this gap between plaintiff and defendant reversal rates is not simply a problem in one or two circuits—it "occurs in all federal circuits in all regions of the country." Eisenberg & Schwab, *supra*, at 1, 10, tbl. 4. *See also* Susan Mandel, *Equal Treatment? Study Shows a Wide Gap Between Worker, Employer Wins in Job Bias Appeals*, 87 A.B.A. J. 24 (Nov. 2001).

31. Clermont & Eisenberg, *supra* note 30, at 958.

32. *Id.* at 967, tbl. 5 (defendants appealing win 44.74% of the time, whereas plaintiffs win 11.03% of the time).

33. Juliano & Schwab, *supra* note 25, at 574, tbl. 4.

34. Kevin M. Clermont & Theodore Eisenberg, *Judge Harry Edwards: A Case in Point!*, 80 WASH. U. L. Q. 1275, 1277 (2002).

35. Nancy E. Crowe, The Effects of Judges' Sex and Race on Judicial Decision Making on the United States Courts of Appeals, 1981–1996, at 83 Fig. 3.1 (1999) (unpub. Ph.D. dissertation, University of Chicago) (on file with author).

36. Carol T. Kulik et al., *Here Comes the Judge: The Influence of Judge Personal Characteristics on Federal Sexual Harassment Case Outcomes*, 27 LAW & HUM. BEHAV. 69 (2003).

37. NINTH CIRCUIT TASK FORCE ON GENDER BIAS, EXECUTIVE SUMMARY OF THE PRELIMINARY REPORT OF THE NINTH CIRCUIT TASK FORCE ON GENDER BIAS, *available in* 45 STAN. L. REV. 2153, 2166, 2169–70 (1993); SPECIAL COMM'N. ON GENDER, DRAFT FINAL REPORT OF THE SPECIAL COMMITTEE ON GENDER TO THE D.C. CIRCUIT TASK FORCE ON GENDER, RACE AND ETHNIC BIAS 98–103 (1995); EIGHTH CIRCUIT GENDER FAIRNESS TASK FORCE, FINAL REPORT AND RECOMMENDATIONS 72–74 (1997),

reprinted in 31 CREIGHTON L. REV. 9 (1997); PRELIMINARY DRAFT REPORT OF THE SEC-
OND CIRCUIT TASK FORCE ON GENDER, RACIAL, AND ETHNIC FAIRNESS IN THE COURTS
41–42 (1997). *See also* Michael Selmi, *Why Are Employment Discrimination Cases So
Hard to Win?* 61 LA. L. REV. 555, 560 (2001); David Benjamin Oppenheimer, *Verdicts
Matter: An Empirical Study of California Employment Discrimination and Wrongful
Discharge Jury Verdicts Reveals Low Success Rates for Women and Minorities*, 37 U.C.
DAVIS L. REV. 511, 535 (2003).

38. Ogden v. Wax Works, Inc., 214 F.3d 999, 1006 (8th Cir. 2000); *see also* Burlington Indus. v. Ellerth, 524 U.S. 742, 751 (1998).

39. Harris v. Forklift Sys., Inc., 510 U.S. 17, 21 (1993) (quoting Meritor Sav. Bank v.
Vinson, 477 U.S. 57, 65, 67 (1986)).

40. *Meritor*, 477 U.S. at 68–69.

41. *Id.* at 67.

42. *See, e.g.*, Brown v. Hot, Sexy and Safer Prods., Inc., 68 F.3d 525, 540 (1st Cir.
1995), *cert. denied*, 516 U.S. 1159 (1996); Farpella-Crosby v. Horizon Health Care, 97
F.3d 803, 806 (5th Cir. 1996); Morgan v. Fellini's Pizza, Inc., 64 F. Supp. 2d 1304, 1309
(N.D. Ga. 1999).

43. *See, e.g.*, Seymore v. Shawver & Sons, Inc., 111 F.3d 794, 797 (10th Cir. 1997),
cert. denied, 522 U.S. 935 (1997); Davis v. City of Sioux City, 115 F.3d 1365, 1368 n.5
(8th Cir. 1997); *Farpella-Crosby*, 97 F.3d at 806.

44. Carter v. Chrysler Corp., 173 F.3d 693, 700 (8th Cir. 1999); *see also* Faragher v.
City of Boca Raton, 524 U.S. 775, 799 (1998); Burlington Indus., Inc. v. Ellerth, 524
U.S. 742, 759 (1998); Sharp v. City of Houston, 164 F.3d 923, 929 (5th Cir. 1999);
Williams v. Gen. Motors Corp., 187 F.3d 553, 561 (6th Cir. 1999); Curry v. D.C., 195
F.3d 654, 660 (D.C. Cir 1999) ("prompt and appropriate corrective action");
Adusumilli v. City of Chicago, 164 F.3d 353, 361 (7th Cir. 1998).

45. *See, e.g.*, David L. Faigman, *To Have and Have Not: Assessing the Value of Social Science to the Law as Science and Policy*, 38 EMORY L.J. 1005, 1008–9 (1989); An-
drew Greeley, *Debunking the Role of Social Science in Courts*, 7 HUM. RTS. 34, 34
(Spring 1978) (suggesting social science should be relegated to a "minor footnote or two
in a brief or decision"); David M. O'Brien, *The Seduction of the Judiciary: Social Science and the Courts*, 64 JUDICATURE 8 (1980); Note, *Social Science Statistics in the
Courtroom: The Debate Resurfaces in* McCleskey v. Kemp, 62 NOTRE DAME L. REV.
688 (1987). Social scientists themselves acknowledge that there are problems. *See, e.g.*,
Barbara A. Gutek et al., *The Utility of the Reasonable Woman Legal Standard in Hostile Environment Sexual Harassment Cases: A Multimethod, Multistudy Examination*, 5
PSYCHOL. PUB. POL'Y & L. 596, 604 (1999) (acknowledging that social science is "not
designed for legal use").

46. *See, e.g.*, Douglas C. Baker et al., *Perceptions of Sexual Harassment: A Re-Examination of Gender Differences*, 124 J. PSYCHOLOGY 409, 412–13 (1989) (study showing differences in perceptions of harassment between working men and women and men
and women students; "students have probably experienced less harassment simply because of their relative youth and limited work experience"); Frazier, *supra* note 12, at
34–35; Barbara A. Gutek & Mary P. Koss, *Changed Women and Changed Organizations: Consequences of and Coping with Sexual Harassment*, 42 J. VOCATIONAL BEHAV.
28, 41, 43 (1993); David E. Terpstra & Douglas D. Baker, *A Hierarchy of Sexual Harassment*, 121 J. PSYCHOLOGY 599, 604 (1987) (in a study of both undergraduates and
working women, more working women found certain behaviors harassing than did
their undergraduate counterparts); James M. Wilkerson, *The Impact of Job Level and
Prior Training on Sexual Harassment Labeling and Remedy Choice*, 29 J. APPLIED SOC.
PSYCHOL. 1605, 1605–6 (1999).

47. *See, e.g.*, Jennifer L. Hurt et al., *Situational and Individual Influences on Judgments
of Hostile Environment Sexual Harassment*, 29 J. APPLIED SOC. PSYCHOL. 1395, 1412

(1999); Louise F. Fitzgerald & J. Alayne Ormerod, *Perceptions of Sexual Harassment: The Influence of Gender and Academic Context*, 15 PSYCHOL. WOMEN Q. 281 (1991).

48. USMSPB, *supra* note 1. *See* Terri C. Fain & Douglas L. Anderton, *Sexual Harassment: Organizational Context and Diffuse Status*, 5/6 SEX ROLES 291, 296 (1987) (noting that 1981 study is "the best sample").

49. *See, e.g.*, Arvey & Cavanaugh, *supra* note 2, at 42 (noting the failure of studies to incorporate the severe or pervasive standard); Sandy Welsh, *Gender and Sexual Harassment*, 25 ANN. REV. SOC. 169, 171 (1999) (noting that early surveys had "little consensus as to how sexual harassment was defined").

50. *See* Vicki Schultz, *The Sanitized Workplace*, 112 YALE L.J. 2061, 2064–65, 2078–79 (2003).

51. *See, e.g.*, Richard L. Wiener & Linda E. Hurt, *Social Sexual Conduct at Work: How Do Workers Know When It Is Harassment and When It Is Not?*, 34 CAL. W. L. REV. 53, 70–75 (1997).

52. *See id.* at 71.

53. *See* James Gruber, *How Women Handle Sexual Harassment: A Literature Review*, 74 SOC. SCI. REP. 3, 6 (1989).

54. *See* Welsh, *supra* note 49, at 169; *see also* Barbara A. Gutek & Maureen O'Connor, *The Empirical Basis for the Reasonable Woman Standard*, 51 J. SOC. ISSUES, Spring 1995, at 151, 154–56 (describing studies that have shown a difference between men and women and studies that have shown no difference).

55. *See* Welsh, *supra* note 49, at 172–73.

56. *See id.* at 185–86; Denise H. Lach & Patricia A. Gwartney-Gibbs, *Sociological Perspectives on Sexual Harassment and Workplace Dispute Resolution*, 42 J. VOCATIONAL BEHAV. 102, 112 (1993); Aysan Sev'er, *Sexual Harassment: Where We Were, Where We Are and Prospects for the New Millennium*, 36 CANADIAN REV. SOC. & ANTHROPOLOGY 469 (1999). For examples of studies that attempt to incorporate race, see Kathleen M. Rospenda et al., *Doing Power: The Confluence of Gender, Race, and Class in Contrapower Sexual Harassment*, 12 GENDER & SOC. 40 (1998); Welsh, *supra* note 49, at 185 (citing studies).

57. *See* Beiner, *supra* note 23, at 109–12 (citing and describing examples of this from case law).

58. Gutek & O'Connor, *supra* note 54, at 157.

59. *See* James E. Gruber et al., *Sexual Harassment Types and Severity: Linking Research and Policy*, in SEXUAL HARASSMENT IN THE WORKPLACE: PERSPECTIVES, FRONTIERS, AND RESPONSE STRATEGIES at 151, 153–54 (Margaret S. Stockdale ed., 1996).

60. Juliano & Schwab, *supra* note 25, at 556 (studied cases accessible through Westlaw and Lexis).

61. *See* Oppenheimer, *supra* note 37, at 558 n. 148 (noting that 1996 sample of cases from Bureau of Justice statistics shows plaintiffs won 48% of jury trials and 20% of bench trials); *see also* Selmi, *supra* note 37, at 560 (Bureau of Justice statistics show success rates for plaintiffs in employment discrimination cases were 40% before juries and 19% before judges for years 1995–1997, including all cases decided in this period).

62. Juliano & Schwab, *supra* note 25, at 570, tbl. 2b.

63. Used like this, social science becomes relevant to "adjudicative facts," or facts that bear on a factual issue between the parties. *See* Kenneth Culp Davis, *Judicial Notice*, 55 COLUM. L. REV. 945, 957–58 (1955). This is in contrast to legislative facts, or facts that are used to develop a general legal rule that would be applicable to all cases. *See id.*

64. *See id.* at 952–53; Faigman, *supra* note 45, at 1086–87.

65. *See* Kumho Tire Co., Ltd. v. Carmichael, 526 U.S. 137 (1999); Gen. Elec. Co. v. Joiner, 118 S. Ct. 512 (1997); Daubert v. Merrell Dow Pharm., Inc., 509 U.S. 579 (1993).

66. *See* Faigman, *supra* note 45, at 1086–87, 1089. Much of Professor Faigman's criticism is a result of the era in which he was writing, during which the test established in *Frye v. United States*, 293 F. 1013 (D.C. Cir. 1923), was the main way in which testimony was evaluated. Under *Frye*, if "the proffered evidence—including the conclusions reached—was generally accepted in a relevant community of experts," that testimony would be admissible at trial. Erica Beecher-Monas, *Blinded by Science: How Judges Avoid the Science in Scientific Evidence*, 71 TEMP. L. REV. 55, 59 (1998). In *Daubert*, the Court required "the trial judge to conduct an independent inquiry into the scientific validity, scientific reliability, and relevance of the proposed testimony." *See id.* at 62.

67. *See* Faigman, *supra* note 45, at 1089 (stating that if judges make a good threshold determination regarding validity, social science poses fewer problems for the jury).

68. *See id.* at 1088 ("However sensible an expert's conclusion might appear as a matter of policy, the proper forum for changing legal rules remains in the legislature or before judges, not on a case-by-case basis before juries."); Davis, *supra* note 63, at 953. *But see* Kenneth Culp Davis, *Facts in Lawmaking*, 80 COLUM. L. REV. 931, 934 (1980).

69. *See* Frederick Schauer & Virginia J. Wise, *Legal Positivism as Legal Information*, 82 CORNELL L. REV. 1080, 1108 & app. (1997) (describing increased use of nonlegal materials in Supreme Court cases).

70. Davis, *supra* note 63, at 953. Worse yet, the Court will assume facts that are capable of empirical validation. *See* Davis, *supra* note 68, at 934–35. *See also* Ronald Dworkin, *Hard Cases*, 88 HARV. L. REV. 1057, 1061 (1975) (criticizing judges as policy makers).

NOTES TO CHAPTER 1

1. Jennifer J. Laabs, *HR Puts Its Sexual Harassment Questions on the Line*, 74 PERSONNEL J. 36 (1995).

2. Meritor Sav. Bank v. Vinson, 477 U.S. 57, 67 (1986) (quoting Henson v. Dundee, 682 F.2d 897, 904 (11th Cir. 1982)).

3. *See* Theresa M. Beiner, *The Misuse of Summary Judgment in Hostile Environment Cases*, 34 WAKE FOREST L. REV. 71, 83–115 (1999) (and cases cited and described therein).

4. *See Meritor*, 477 U.S. at 64.

5. 510 U.S. 17, 21 (1993) (quoting *Meritor*, 477 U.S. at 65, 67).

6. *Id.* at 21.

7. *Id.*

8. *See, e.g.*, Burns v. McGregor Elec. Indus., Inc., 989 F.2d 959, 962 n.3 (8th Cir. 1993); Ellison v. Brady, 924 F.2d 872 (9th Cir. 1991); Andrews v. City of Philadelphia, 895 F.2d 1469, 1482 (3d Cir. 1990); Yates v. Avco Corp., 819 F.2d 630, 637 (6th Cir. 1987); Harris v. Int'l Paper Co., 765 F. Supp. 1509, 1515 (D. Me. 1991).

9. *Harris*, 510 U.S. at 21.

10. *Id.* at 21–22.

11. *Id.* at 23.

12. *Id.* at 22.

13. 523 U.S. 75, 81–82 (1998) (citation omitted).

14. *See id.* at 79–80.

15. *See, e.g.*, Stacks v. Southwestern Bell Yellow Pages, Inc., 27 F.3d 1316, 1326 (8th Cir. 1994); Andrews v. City of Philadelphia, 895 F.2d 1469, 1485 (3d Cir. 1990); Hicks v. Gates Rubber Co., 833 F.2d 1406, 1415 (10th Cir. 1987); *see also* Joshua F. Thorpe, Note, *Gender-Based Harassment and the Hostile Work Environment*, 1990 DUKE L.J. 1361, 1364–65 (arguing in favor of such a standard). *See generally* Vicki Schultz, *Reconceptualizing Sexual Harassment*, 107 YALE L.J. 1683 (1998).

16. *Oncale*, 523 U.S. at 80.

17. Clark County Sch. Dist. v. Breeden, 532 U.S. 268, 269 (2001) (per curiam) (citations omitted).

18. *Id.* at 270. The court also held that she failed to show that her protected activity was causally connected to the adverse employment action alleged in the case, another element of a retaliation claim. *Id.* at 272.

19. *Id.* at 271 (quoting Faragher v. Boca Raton, 524 U.S. 775, 787–88 (1998)).

20. *Id.* (quoting *Faragher*, 524 U.S. at 788).

21. See Beiner, *supra* note 3, at 126–30 (recounting findings of studies).

22. See Kevin M. Clermont & Theodore Eisenberg, *Trial by Jury or Judge: Transcending Empiricism*, 77 CORNELL L. REV. 1124, 1174 (1992) (study of cases between 1979 and 1989 showed plaintiff win rates of 20% in bench trials and 39% in jury trials); Michael Selmi, *Why Are Employment Discrimination Cases Hard to Win?*, 61 LA. L. REV. 555, 560 (2001) (employment discrimination plaintiff win rates as 40% for jury trials and 19% for bench trials).

23. Jane Goodman-Delahunty, *Pragmatic Support for the Reasonable Victim Standard in Hostile Workplace Sexual Harassment Cases*, 5 PSYCHOL., PUB. POL'Y & L. 519, 531–32 (1999) (quoting Oncale v. Sundowner Offshore Servs., Inc., 523 U.S. 75, 81 (1998)). *See also* Harris v Forklift Sys., Inc., 510 U.S. 17, 21 (1993) ("As we pointed out in *Meritor*, 'mere utterance of an . . . epithet which engenders offensive feelings in a [*sic*] employee,' ibid. (internal quotation marks omitted) does not sufficiently affect the conditions of employment to implicate Title VII."); Meritor, 447 U.S., at 67 ("not all workplace conduct that may be described as 'harassment' affects a 'term, condition, or privilege' of employment within the meaning of Title VII").

24. See Schultz, *supra* note 15.

25. No. AW-95-196, 1996 WL 414057, at *1 (D. Md. May 17, 1996), *aff'd*, 113 F.3d 1232 (4th Cir. 1997).

26. Although plaintiff testified that there were ten such incidents, the court could account for only three or more incidents, given the number of times plaintiff worked with the alleged harasser. *See id.* at *3. However, the court considered that there might be as many as ten such incidents for purposes of summary judgment. *Id.* at *1, *3 n.3 (citing Weiss v. Coca-Cola Bottling Co., 900 F.2d 333, 335–37 (1993)); *see also* Peinado v. Norwegian Am. Hosps., Inc., 2001 WL 726993, at *8 (N.D. Ill. 2001) (referring to repeated use of profanity, sexually explicit jokes and innuendo around lower-ranking employees as "sophomoric behavior" that did not provide a basis for a sexual harassment claim).

27. *Hosey*, No. AW-95-196, 1996 WL 414057, at *2.

28. Saidu-Kamara v. Parkway Corp., 155 F. Supp. 2d 436, 439–40 (E.D. Pa. 2001).

29. *Id.* at 440.

30. *See, e.g.*, Bowman v. Shawnee State Univ., 220 F.3d 456, 463–65 (6th Cir. 2000) (upholding summary judgment where, among other things, supervisor grabbed plaintiff's buttocks and rubbed plaintiff's shoulders); Adusumilli v. City of Chicago, 164 F.3d 353, 361–63 (7th Cir. 1998), *cert. denied*, 528 U.S. 988 (1999) (upholding summary judgment where, among other things, harasser touched plaintiff's buttocks and arms); McGraw v. Wyeth-Ayerst Labs., Inc., No. Civ. A 96-5780, *available at* 1997 WL 799437, at *6 (E.D. Pa. Dec. 30, 1997) (granting summary judgment where plaintiff's supervisor constantly requested dates and kissed her without consent, "forcing his tongue into her mouth").

31. EEOC v. Champion Int'l Corp., No. 93 C 20279, 1995 WL 488333, at *2 (N.D. Ill. Aug. 1, 1995).

32. *See id.* at *4.

33. *Id.* at *6.

34. *Id.* at *8.

35. *Id.* at *10.

36. Gregory v. Daly, 243 F.3d 687, 690 (2d Cir. 2001).
37. Gregory v. Daly, 78 F. Supp. 2d 48, 49 (N.D.N.Y. 1999).
38. Duncan v. Gen. Motors Corp., 300 F.3d 928, 931–32 (8th Cir. 2002).
39. *Id.* at 934.
40. *Id.* at 935.
41. *See* Madison v. IBP, Inc., 2001 WL 704432, at *10 (8th Cir. 2001); Conner v. Schrader-Bridgeport Int'l, Inc., 227 F.3d 179, 193–94 (4th Cir. 2000) (noting that the district court had "improperly disaggregat[ed] the incidents from the whole" in granting judgment as a matter of law).
42. Saxton v. AT&T Co., 10 F.3d 526, 529 (7th Cir. 1993).
43. *Id.* at 534.
44. *Id.* at 534–35 (quoting Harris v. Forklift Sys., Inc., 510 U.S. 17, 21 (1993), and Meritor Sav. Bank, FSB v. Vinson, 477 U.S. 57, 67 (1986) (citation omitted)).
45. *See id.* at 535. Saxton's claim also failed on the independent basis that the employer had taken sufficient remedial measures. *See id.*
46. *Champion*, 1995 WL 488333, at *10 (citing Daniels v. Essex Group, Inc., 937 F.2d 1264, 1274 (7th Cir. 1991)).
47. *See also* Rocha Vigil v. City of Las Cruces, 113 F.3d 1247 (10th Cir. 1997), *available at* 1997 WL 265095, *reh'g denied*, 119 F.3d 871 (10th Cir. 1997). *But see* Hicks v. Gates Rubber Co., 833 F.2d 1025 (10th Cir. 1987) (allowing aggregation of both sexually and racially hostile incidents); Jefferies v. Harris County Cmty. Action Ass'n, 615 F.2d 1025 (5th Cir. 1980). Forell and Matthews argue that victims of harassment should be permitted to choose how they characterize cases involving harassment based on more than one protected status. *See* Caroline A. Forell & Donna M. Matthews, A Law of Her Own: The Reasonable Woman as a Measure of Man 92–93 (2000). *But see* Tam B. Tran, *Title VII Hostile Work Environment: A Different Perspective*, 9 J. Contemp. Legal Issues 357, 373–76 (1998) (detailing cases and arguing in favor of considering both statuses at once and describing cases in which this was done).
48. For cases relying on *Saxton*, see, e.g., Zelinskii v. Pennsylvania State Police, 282 F. Supp. 2d 251 (M.D. Pa. 2003); Hosey v. McDonald's Corp., No. AW-95-196, 1996 WL 414057 (D. Md. May 17, 1996), *aff'd*, 113 F.3d 1232 (4th Cir. 1997). For cases questioning *Saxton*, see Cooke v. Stefani Mgmt. Servs., Inc., 250 F.3d 564, 568 (7th Cir. 2001); Butta-Brinkman v. FCA Int'l, Ltd., 950 F. Supp. 230, 233 (N.D. Ill. 1996).
49. 81 F.3d 48, 49 (6th Cir. 1996).
50. 2001 WL 345793, at *1 (6th Cir. 2001).
51. *See id.* at *4.
52. *Id.*
53. 510 U.S. 17, 20 (1993). For cases suggesting that *Rabidue v. Osceola Refinery Co., Division of Texas-American Petrochemicals, Inc.*, 805 F.2d 611 (6th Cir. 1986), *cert. denied*, 481 U.S. 1041 (1987), has been overruled, see *Scheske v. Kirsch Division of Cooper Industries, Inc.*, 30 F.3d 134 (tbl.), 1994 WL 276892 (6th Cir. 1996), and *Bartholomew v. Delahaye Group, Inc.*, 1995 WL 907797, at *4 (D.N.H. 1995).
54. *See, e.g.,* Carlisle v. Ohio Dep't of Rehabilitation and Correction, 2002 WL 1583272 at *4–*5 (S.D. Ohio 2002); *Gwen*, 2001 WL 345793 at *3; Blankenship v. Parke Care Centers, Inc., 123 F.3d 868, 872 (6th Cir. 1997). All of these cases use the standard from *Rabidue* that the plaintiff must show that the harassment "unreasonably interfered with her work performance." Given that this standard was developed in a case in which the court also held that the harassment had to cause severe psychological damage to be actionable, this heightened standard reasonably can be questioned.
55. *See* Steven Hetcher, *Non-Utilitarian Negligence Norms and the Reasonable Woman Standard*, 54 Vand. L. Rev. 863, 864 (2001) ("The reasonable person standard is an empty vessel that jurors fill with community norms.").
56. *See* Christopher M. Alexander, *Crushing Equality: Gender Equal Sentencing in*

America, 6 AM. U.J. GENDER & L. 199, n.181 (1997); Amy E. Black & Stanley Roth-man, *Shall We Kill All the Lawyers First?: Insider and Outsider Views of the Legal Pro-fession*, 21 HARV. J.L. & PUB. POL'Y 835, 839, 842 n.14 (1998). *See generally* Goodman-Delahunty, *supra* note 23, at 541 ("[a]bsent guidance on how the objective standard is to be applied, courts may substitute their own judgment for that of the harasser. Nu-merous commentators have expressed concern that judges are too untrustworthy to per-form this task.") (citations omitted); Irene Padavic & James D. Orcutt, *Perceptions of Sexual Harassment in the Florida Legal System: A Comparison of Dominance and Spillover Explanations*, 11 GENDER & SOC'Y 682, 688–89, 693 (1997) (study of Florida judiciary found that awareness of gender-typing forms of behavior was less for male judges than female judges, and decreased for male judges based on age; "nearly half of the female judges reported that male judges have made jokes or demeaning remarks about women, and one-third of them indicated that male judges have subjected female attorneys to verbal sexual advances"); Daniel R. Pinello, *Linking Party to Judicial Ide-ology in American Courts: A Meta-Analysis*, 20 JUST. SYS. J. 219, 243 (1999) (examin-ing relationship between judges' voting records and political affiliation). For current de-mographics of the federal judiciary, see Sheldon Goldman et al., *W. Bush Remaking the Judiciary: Like Father Like Son?*, 86 JUDICATURE 282, 309 tbl. 2, tbl. 4 (2003).

57. *See, e.g.*, Louise F. Fitzgerald et al., *The Incidence and Dimensions of Sexual Ha-rassment in Academia and the Workplace*, 32 J. VOCATIONAL BEHAV. 152, 171 (1988); Patricia M. Hanrahan, *"How Do I Know if I'm Being Harassed or if This Is Part of My Job?" Nurses and Definitions of Sexual Harasment*, NAT'L WOMEN'S STUD. ASS'N J. 43 (Summer 1997).

58. Richard D. Arvey & Marcie A. Cavanaugh, *Using Surveys to Assess the Preva-lence of Sexual Harassment: Some Methodological Problems*, 51 J. SOC. ISSUES 39, 43 (Spring 1995).

59. Barbara A. Gutek et al., *The Utility of the Reasonable Woman Legal Standard in Hostile Environment Sexual Harassment Cases: A Multimethod, Multistudy Examina-tion*, 5 PSYCHOL. PUB. POL'Y & L. 596, 604–5 (1999).

60. *Id.* at 606; *see also* Barbara K. Burian et al., *Group Gender Composition Effects on Judgments of Sexual Harassment*, 22 PSYCHOL. WOMEN Q. 465, 467 (1998) (noting studies do not present perceivers with competing perspectives in scenarios).

61. *See, e.g.*, James E. Gruber & Michael D. Smith, *Women's Responses to Sexual Harassment: A Mutivariate Analysis*, 17 BASIC & APPLIED PSYCHOL. 543, 549 (1995); Gutek et al., *supra* note 59, at 607 (noting this).

62. Louise F. Fitzgerald et al., *But Was It Really Sexual Harassment? Legal, Behav-ioral, and Psychological Definitions of Workplace Victimization of Women*, in SEXUAL HARASSMENT: THEORY, RESEARCH AND TREATMENT 5, 15–18 (William O'Donohue ed., 1997).

63. *See, e.g.*, Dara A. Charney & Ruth C. Russell, *An Overview of Sexual Harass-ment*, 151 AM. J. PSYCHIATRY 10, 11 (1994) (citing studies); Terri C. Fain & Douglas L. Anderton, *Sexual Harassment: Organizational Context and Diffuse Status*, 5/6 SEX ROLES 291, 301–3 (1987) (examining impact of education and age based on 1981 U.S. Merit Systems Protection Board study; marital status of target effects likelihood of being harassed); Fitzgerald et al., *supra* note 62, at 18–19 (citing studies of feminist ideology); Carol A. Ford & Francisco J. Donis, *The Relationship Between Age and Gender in Workers' Attitudes Toward Sexual Harassment*, 130 J. PSYCHOLOGY 627 (1996) (exam-ining age); Patti A. Giuffre & Christine L. Williams, *Boundary Lines: Labeling Sexual Harassment in Restaurants*, 8 GENDER & SOC'Y 378, 384, 387–92 (1994) (sexual orien-tation; race); Mary A. Gowan & Raymond A. Zimmerman, *Impact of Ethnicity, Gen-der, and Previous Experience on Juror Judgments in Sexual Harassment Cases*, 26 J. AP-PLIED SOC. PSYCHOL. 596, 610 (1996) (ethnicity); James E. Gruber & Lars Bjorn, *Women's Responses to Sexual Harassment: An Analysis of Sociocultural, Organiza-*

tional, and Personal Resource Models, 67 Soc. Sci. Q. 814, 815 (citing studies of un-married women); Inger W. Jensen & Barbara A. Gutek, *Attributions and Assignment of Responsibility in Sexual Harassment*, 38 J. Soc. Issues, Winter 1982, at 121, 126 (personal experience with sexual harassment); Tricia S. Jones et al., *Effects of Employment Relationship, Response of Recipient and Sex of Rater on Perceptions of Sexual Harassment*, 65 Perception and Motor Skills 55, 56, 59 (1987) (effect of target response on perceptions of harassment); Michael A. Plater & Robert E. Thomas, *The Impact of Job Performance, Gender, and Ethnicity on the Managerial Review of Sexual Harassment Allegations*, 28 J. Applied Soc. Psychol. 52, 64–67 (1998) (ethnicity); Gary N. Powell, *Effects of Sex Role Identity and Sex on Definitions of Sexual Harassment*, 14 Sex Roles 9 (1986) (sex role identity); John B. Pryor, *A Lay Person's Understanding of Sexual Harassment*, 13 Sex Roles 273, 276 (1985) (citing studies involving marital status of harasser); Richard C. Sorenson et al., *Solving the Chronic Problem of Sexual Harassment in the Workplace: An Empirical Study of Factors Affecting Employee Perceptions and Consequences of Sexual Harassment*, 34 Cal. W. L. Rev. 457, 490 (1998) (evaluating effect of "attitudes towards sexual harassment" as predictor of perceived seriousness); Daniel A. Thomann & Richard L. Wiener, *Physical and Psychological Causality as Determinants of Culpability in Sexual Harassment Cases*, 17 Sex Roles 573, 575 (1987) (citing studies of feminist ideology); Gail E. Wyatt & Monika Riederle, *The Prevalence and Context of Sexual Harassment Among African American and White Women*, 10 J. Interpersonal Violence 309, 310–17 (1995) (race). Race is a factor that has been overlooked by researchers in this area. *See* Sorenson et al., *supra*, at 462–63. For the potential impact of race on sexual harassment, see Jann H. Adams, *Sexual Harassment and Black Women: A Historical Perspective*, *in* Sexual Harassment: Theory, Research and Treatment at 213 (William O'Donohue ed., 1997).

64. *See* Fitzgerald et al., *supra* note 62, at 9 ("there is a considerable variance in the range of behaviors assessed by harassment surveys, a state of affairs yielding conflicting frequency estimates and fluctuating prevalence rates"). Differences in definition will cause problems in determining the frequency of harassment but should not cause too much difficulty for assessing what people find harassing.

65. James E. Gruber, *A Typology of Personal and Environmental Sexual Harassment: Research and Policy Implications for the 1990s*, 26 Sex Roles 447, 451 tbl. III (1992).

66. Fitzgerald et al., *supra* note 62, at 11, 12 tbl. 2-2, 13 (arguing that the SEQ is the "most conceptually and technically sophisticated available"); *see also* Craig R. Waldo et al., *Are Men Sexually Harassed? If So, By Whom?*, 22 Law & Hum. Behav. 59, 60 (1998).

67. Jasmine Tata, *The Structure and Phenomenon of Sexual Harassment: Impact of Category of Sexually Harassing Behavior, Gender, and Hierarchical Level*, 23 J. Applied Soc. Psychol. 199, 200–201 (1993) (citing F.J. Till, *Sexual Harassment: A Report on the Sexual Harassment of Students* (National Advisory Council on Women's Educational Programs) (1980)).

68. United States Merit Sys. Prot. Bd., Sexual Harassment in the Federal Workplace: Trends, Progress, Continuing Challenges 5 (1995) [hereinafter USMSPB].

69. Margaret S. Stockdale & Kathryn G. Hope, *Confirmatory Factor Analysis of U.S. Merit System Protection Board's Survey of Sexual Harassment: The Fit of the Three-Factor Model*, 51 J. Vocational Behav. Spring (1997), at 338, 345, 352. They had several caveats about this fit, however. *See id.* at 352–54.

70. *Id.* at 354.

71. *See, e.g.*, Douglas D. Baker et al., *The Influence of Individual Characteristics and Severity of Harassing Behavior on Reactions to Sexual Harassment*, 22 Sex Roles 305, 313 tbl. I (1990) (study of undergraduate students showed 98% perceived proposition

tied to job threat or enhancement as harassment); Bonnie S. Dansky et al., *Sexual Harassment: I Can't Define It but I Know It When I See It*, at tbl. 1 (1992) (paper presented at annual meeting of American Psychological Association, Washington, D.C.; on file with the author) (1989 national study of 4,009 women; 85.8% of those who experience proposition tied to job threat found it harassing; 83.0% of women experiencing subtle proposition tied to job enhancement found it harassing); Alison M. Konrad & Barbara A. Gutek, *Impact of Work Experiences on Attitudes Toward Sexual Harassment*, 31 ADMIN. SCI. Q. 422, 429 tbl.1 (1986) (1980 telephone survey of more than 1,200 working men and women in the Los Angeles area: 94.5% of men and 98% of women perceived request for sexual relations accompanied by job threat for refusing as sexual harassment; 91.9% of men and 95.8% of women perceived request for date accompanied by job threat for not complying as sexual harassment); Tata, *supra* note 67, at 207 (showing no gender effects for sexual bribery, sexual coercion, and sexual assault); David E. Terpstra & Douglas D. Baker, *A Hierarchy of Sexual Harassment*, 121 J. PSYCHOLOGY 599, 602 (1987) (99% agreed proposition tied to job threat sexually harassing; 98% agreed proposition tied to job enhancement was sexually harassing). *See generally* Louise F. Fitzgerald & Alayne J. Ormerod, *Breaking the Silence: The Sexual Harassment of Women in Academia and the Workplace*, in PSYCHOLOGY OF WOMEN 553, 559–60 (Florence L. Denmark & Michele A. Paludi eds., 1993) (recounting studies).

72. *See* MIA CAHILL, THE SOCIAL CONSTRUCTION OF SEXUAL HARASSMENT LAW 58 (2001) (in survey of five firms in the U.S. and Austria, 91% of employees surveyed believed a vignette that included grabbing a woman's breast was "absolutely illegal" and 7% believed it "probably illegal"); Baker et al., *supra* note 71, at 313 tbl. 1 (99% of undergraduates studied believed fingers straying to breast scenario constituted sexual harassment; 96% of undergraduates studied perceived rape as sexual harassment); Dansky et al., *supra* note 71, at tbl. 1 (90.2% of women perceived unencouraged sexual touching as harassing); Tata, *supra* note 67, at 207; Terpstra & Baker, *supra* note 71, at 602 (98% agreed that physical contact of a sexual nature constituted harassment; 96% of undergraduates perceived rape as sexual harassment); Thomann & Wiener, *supra* note 63, at 574 (citing studies); Timothy Reilly et al., *The Factorial Survey: An Approach to Defining Sexual Harassment on Campus*, 38 J. SOC. ISSUES, Winter 1982, at 99, 107 (finding high amount of consensus at the "extremes").

73. *See* USMSPB, *supra* note 68, at 2, 7 & tbl. 1.

74. *See, e.g.*, Gruber, *supra* note 65.

75. Terpstra & Baker, *supra* note 71, at 602 & tbl. 1.

76. Masoud Hemmasi et al., *Gender-Related Jokes in the Workplace: Sexual Humor or Sexual Harassment?* 24 J. APPLIED SOC. PSYCHOL. 1114, 1122 (1994). Interestingly, sexist jokes that had females as their subjects were considered most offensive. *Id.* However, men were more likely to tell such jokes than women. *Id.*

77. Denise Haunani Solomon & Mary Lynn Miller Williams, *Perceptions of Social-Sexual Communications at Work: The Effects of Message, Situation, and Observer Characteristics on Judgments of Sexual Harassment*, 25 J. APPLIED COMMUN. RES. 196, 205 (1997).

78. *See* USMSPB, *supra* note 68, at vii, 7 & tbl. 1.

79. *See id.* at viii.

80. *Id.* at 8–9.

81. For studies involving frequency, intensity, and duration, see Fitzgerald et al., *supra* note 62, at 11; James E. Gruber et al., *Sexual Harassment Types and Severity: Linking Research and Policy*, in SEXUAL HARASSMENT IN THE WORKPLACE: PERSPECTIVES, FRONTIERS, AND RESPONSE STRATEGIES 151, 164 (Margaret S. Stockdale ed., 1996) (targeted behavior); Thomann & Wiener, *supra* note 63, at 585 (repeated behavior; severity).

82. *See, e.g.*, Thomann & Wiener, *supra* note 63, at 585.

83. Jennifer L. Hurt et al., *Situational and Individual Influences on Judgments in*

Hostile Environment Sexual Harassment, 7 J. Applied Soc. Psychol. 1395, 1396–1400, 1403, 1406 (1999).

84. Thomann & Wiener, *supra* note 63, at 585; *see also* Dansky et al., *supra* note 71, at tbl. 3 (survey of sexually harassed women indicating that 72.4% of those described "worst" epsiode of harassment as a series of incidents); Fitzgerald et al., *supra* note 62, at 15 (citing studies linking frequency of incidents to perceptions of severity).

85. Jane L. Dolkart, *Hostile Environment Harassment: Equality, Objectivity, and the Shaping of Legal Standards*, 43 Emory L.J. 151, 198–223 (1994).

86. *See, e.g., id.* at 153 (reasonable victim); Eileen M. Blackwood, *The Reasonable Woman in Sexual Harassment Law and the Case for Subjectivity*, 16 Vt. L. Rev. 1005, 1026 (1992) (subjective approach).

87. *See* Margaret S. Stockdale et al., *The Relationship between Prior Sexual Abuse and Reactions to Sexual Harassment*, 8 Psychol. Pub. Pol'y & L. 64, 88 (2002).

88. Concrete Pipe and Prods. of Cal., Inc., v. Constr. Laborers Pension Trust for S. Cal., 508 U.S. 602, 622 (1993) (quoting *In re* Winship, 397 U.S. 358, 371–72 (1970) (Harlan, J., concurring)). *See also* Charles B. Mueller & Laird C. Kirkpatrick, 1 Federal Evidence §65, at 319 (2d ed. 1994); John W. Strong, 2 McCormick on Evidence §339, at 438 (4th ed. 1992).

89. *See* United States v. Shonubi, 895 F.Supp. 460, 471 (E.D.N.Y. 1995), *sentence vacated by*, 103 F.3d 1085 (2d Cir. 1997) (citing United States v. Fatico, 458 F. Supp. 388, 410 (E.D.N.Y. 1978), *aff'd on other grounds*, 603 F.3d 1053 (2d Cir. 1979), *cert. denied*, 444 U.S. 1073 (1980) (containing chart summarizing survey results) ("A survey of judges in the Eastern District of New York found general agreement that 'a preponderance of the evidence' translates into 50+ percent probability."). Judge Weinstein, the author of the opinion in *Shonubi*, also explained that "there is a consensus among judges that burdens of proof can be stated in numerical terms. Moreover, with some variation, there is agreement as to what those numbers are." 895 F. Supp. at 471.

90. USMSPB, *supra* note 68, at 2 (noting a 61% return rate resulting in more than 8,000 questionnaires being returned).

91. *See* Lipsett v. Univ. of Puerto Rico, 740 F. Supp. 921, 925 (D.P.R. 199); Dolkart, *supra* note 85, at 200 ("without guidance concerning how to interpret the evidence, any form of reasonableness standard is vulnerable to the incorporating of the trier of fact's own perception of what is reasonable"); Donna Shestowsky, Note, *Where Is the Common Knowledge? Empirical Support for Requiring Expert Testimony in Sexual Harassment Trials*, 51 Stan. L. Rev. 357, 358–59 (1999) (noting that judges assume that what constitutes sexual harassment is "common knowledge").

92. *See* Dolkart, *supra* note 85, at 210–16 (arguing for an individualized standard).

93. *See* Vicki Schultz, *The Sanitized Workplace*, 112 Yale L.J. 2061 (2003).

94. *See* Ann Juliano & Stewart J. Schwab, *The Sweep of Sexual Harassment Cases*, 86 Cornell L. Rev. 548, 567 tbl. 1 (2001). In addition, physical harassment of a nonsexual nature (i.e., hitting) occurred in 8.6% of cases. Plaintiffs in these cases fared slightly better—winning 62.8% of the time. *See id.*

95. *Id.* at 570.

96. Dolkart, *supra* note 85, at 210.

97. *Meritor*, 477 U.S. at 67.

Notes to Chapter 2

1. *See, e.g.*, Azy Barak, *Cross-Cultural Perspectives on Sexual Harassment, in* Sexual Harassment: Theory, Research, and Treatment 263, 280 (William O'Donohue ed., 1997) (citing studies); Barbara A. Gutek, *How Subjective Is Sexual Harassment? An Examination of Rater Effects*, 17 Basic & Applied Soc. Psychol. 447, 454–59 (1995)

(both reviewing early studies showing gender differences); John B. Pryor, *The Lay Person's Understanding of Sexual Harassment*, 13 SEX ROLES 273, 276 (1985); Daniel A. Thomann & Richard L. Wiener, *Physical and Psychological Causality as Determinants of Culpability in Sexual Harassment Cases*, 17 SEX ROLES 573, 574 (1987) (citing studies).

2. *See* Barbara A. Gutek et al., *The Utility of the Reasonable Woman Legal Standard in Hostile Environment Sexual Harassment Cases: A Multimethod, Multistudy Examination*, 5 PSYCHOL. PUB. POL'Y & L. 596, 607 (1999) (noting that it is likely that the Ninth Circuit in *Ellison v. Brady* developed the "reasonable woman" standard in response to this research).

3. *See, e.g.*, Carol L. Baird et al., *Gender Influence on Perceptions of Hostile Environment Sexual Harassment*, 77 PSYCHOL. REP. 79, 82 (1995) (noting that the debate over the reasonable woman standard has yet to be resolved); Sharon J. Bittner, Note, *The Reasonable Woman Standard after Harris v. Forklift Systems, Inc.: The Debate Rages On*, 16 WOMEN'S RTS. L. REP. 127 (1994). *See generally* CAROLINE A. FORELL & DONNA M. MATTHEWS, A LAW OF HER OWN: THE REASONABLE WOMAN AS A MEASURE OF MAN 23–119 (2000).

4. *See, e.g.*, Jennifer L. Hurt et al., *Situational and Individual Influences on Judgments of Hostile Environment Sexual Harassment*, 29 J. APPLIED SOC. PSYCHOL. 1395, 1399 (1999) (citing studies that showed no effect based on gender of rater); Thomann & Wiener, *supra* note 1, at 589 (finding that "sex of the observer does not play a significant role in sexual harassment ratings"); David E. Terpstra & Douglas D. Baker, *A Hierarchy of Sexual Harassment*, 12 J. PSYCHOLOGY 599, 602–604 (1987) (finding rank order of severity very similar in samples of male and female students and working women; distinctions appeared more based on working and nonworking groups); Kenneth M. York, *Defining Sexual Harassment in Workplaces: A Policy-Capturing Approach*, 32 ACAD. OF MGMT. J. 830, 844 (1989) (in study of EEO officers, "gender was not a significant factor affecting the officers' consistency, mean judgments, and weightings of cues.").

5. *See, e.g.*, Mary A. Gowan & Raymond A. Zimmerman, *Impact of Ethnicity, Gender, and Previous Experience on Juror Judgments in Sexual Harassment Cases*, 26 J. APPLIED SOC. PSYCHOL. 596, 608 (1996) (in study of students and workers, women were more likely to perceive ambiguous behaviors as harassment than men); Michael A. Plater & Robert E. Thomas, *The Impact of Job Performance, Gender, and Ethnicity on the Managerial Review of Sexual Harassment Allegations*, 28 J. APPLIED SOC. PSYCHOL. 52, 64–65 (1998) (in study of university employees using ambiguous scenario, women were more likely to believe company should compensate victim for incident than men; however, there were no gender effects with respect to the perception that the alleged harasser behaved inappropriately); Jasmine Tata, *The Structure and Phenomenon of Sexual Harassment: Impact of Category of Sexually Harassing Behavior, Gender, and Hierarchical Level*, 23 J. APPLIED SOC. PSYCHOL. 199, 207 (1993) (showing gender effects for only gender harassment and seductive behavior).

6. *See, e.g.*, Andrews v. City of Philadelphia, 895 F.2d 1469, 1482 (3d Cir. 1990); Yates v. Avco, Corp., 819 F.2d 630, 637 (6th Cir. 1987).

7. Ellison v. Brady, 924 F.2d 872, 878 (9th Cir. 1991).

8. *Id.* at 879.

9. *Id.*

10. *See* Elizabeth L. Shoenfelt et al., *Reasonable Person versus Reasonable Woman: Does It Matter?*, 10 AM. U. J. GENDER SOC. POL'Y & L. 633, 637–38 (2002) (describing cases); Muzzy v. Cahillane Motors, Inc., 434 Mass. 409, 413 n.3 (2001) (citing cases from the federal courts).

11. 180 F.3d 426, 436 n.3 (2d Cir. 1999).

12. *Id.*

13. *See, e.g.*, Charles R. Calleros, *Title VII and the First Amendment: Content-Neu-*

tral Regulation, Disparate Impact, and the "Reasonable Person," 58 OHIO ST. L.J. 1217, 1258–59 (1997); George Rutherglen, *Sexual Harassment: Ideology or Law?*, 18 HARV. J. L. & PUB. POL'Y 487, 496 (1995) (noting that "the Supreme Court has resolved the question without directly confronting it" in *Harris*).

14. Gillming v. Simmons Indus., 91 F.3d 1168, 1172 (8th Cir. 1996). Previously, the Eighth Circuit had embraced the standard. *See* Burns v. McGregor Elec. Indus., Inc., 989 F.2d 959, 965 (8th Cir. 1993).

15. Harris v. Forklift Sys., Inc., 510 U.S. 17, 21 (1993).

16. Oncale v. Sundowner Offshore Servs., Inc., 523 U.S. 75, 81 (1998) (quoting *Harris*, 510 U.S. at 23).

17. Virgil L. Sheets & Sanford L. Braver, *Organizational Status and Perceived Sexual Harassment: Detecting the Mediators of a Null Effect*, 25 PERSONALITY AND SOC. PSYCHOL. BULL. 1159, 1160 (1999) (citations omitted).

18. *See* Shoenfelt et al., *supra* note 10, at 649–50 & nn.119–22 (citing studies).

19. *See* Patricia A. Frazier et al., *Social Science Research on Lay Definitions of Sexual Harassment*, 51 J. SOC. ISSUES, Spring 1995, at 21, 23 (discussing studies). *See also* Douglas D. Baker et al., *The Influence of Individual Characteristics and Severity of Harassing Behavior on Reactions to Sexual Harassment*, 22 SEX ROLES 305, 311–13 (1990) (study showing that 98% of students surveyed believed sexual proposition with job threat was harassment); Diana Burgess & Eugene Borgida, *Sexual Harassment: An Experimental Test of Sex-Role Spillover Theory*, 23 PERSONALITY SOC. PSYCHOL. BULL. 63, 70–71 (1997) (later study supporting this as well); Christopher W. Williams et al., *An Attributional (Causal Dimensional) Analysis of Perceptions of Sexual Harassment*, 25 J. APPLIED SOC. PSYCHOL. 1169, 1174 (1995) (in study of students, finding no gender effects for perceptions of harassment in scenario where coworker presses woman against the wall and grabs her buttocks).

20. U.S. MERIT SYS. PROT. BD., SEXUAL HARASSMENT IN THE FEDERAL WORKPLACE: TRENDS, PROGRESS, CONTINUING CHALLENGES 7, tbl. 1 (1995) [hereinafter USMSPB].

21. *See* Burgess & Borgida, *supra* note 19, at 72; James D. Johnson et al., *Perceptual Ambiguity, Gender and Target Intoxication: Assessing the Effects of Factors that Moderate Perceptions of Sexual Harassment*, 27 J. APPLIED SOC. PSYCHOL. 1209, 1212, 1215 (1997) (in study of undergraduates, certainty that incident of physical touching—grabbing victim's buttocks and winking—constitutes sexual harassment did not vary based on gender).

22. Frazier et al., *supra* note 19, at 29–30; *see also, e.g.*, Gowan & Zimmerman, *supra* 5, at 608 (study of students and workers showing gender differences in perceptions of ambiguous behaviors); Johnson et al., *supra* note 21, at 1214–15 (finding gender differences in perception for more ambiguous behaviors in a study of undergraduates); Kimberly A. Lonsway, *Sexual Harassment Mythology: An Emerging Framework*, ABF Working Paper #9719, at 6–7 (1998) (citing studies supporting this); Williams et al., *supra* note 19, at 1174–75 (study of students showing gender effects in least severe and most ambiguous scenarios).

23. Barbara A. Gutek & Maureen O'Connor, *The Empirical Basis for the Reasonable Woman Standard*, 51 J. SOC. ISSUES, Spring 1995, at 151, 156. *See also* Richard L. Wiener & Linda E. Hurt, *Social Sexual Conduct at Work: How Do Workers Know When It Is Harassment and When It Is Not?*, 34 CAL. W. L. REV. 53 (1997) (study of 50 individuals showing significant variance in agreement among women as to what constitutes sexual harassment but less variance—although still a significant amount—among men).

24. *See, e.g.*, Baird et al., *supra* note 3, at 82 (noting that, in study of undergraduates, the full range of the 7-point scale—ranging from strongly disagree to strongly agree that scenario was harassment—was used by respondents for all 68 scenarios); Douglas D. Baker et al., *Perceptions of Sexual Harassment: A Re-Examination of Gender Differ-*

ences, 124 J. PSYCHOLOGY 409, 415 (1989) ("[t]he findings of the current study indicate that the major differences in perceptions of sexual harassment may occur between individuals with different organizational backgrounds"). *But see* Jennifer Berdahl et al., *The Sexual Harassment of Men? Exploring the Concept with Theory and Data*, 20 PSYCHOL. WOMEN Q. 527, 535 (1996) (in study of undergraduates, within-sex variance found only for men; women showed high level of agreement).

25. USMSPB, *supra* note 20, at 7, tbl. 1.

26. *Id.* at ix (37% of women and 14% of men reported such incidents).

27. *Id.* at 7 & tbl. 1. The numbers are as follows: 94% of women and 87% of men "probably" or "definitely" would consider suggestive letters, calls, materials sexually harassing if directed by a supervisor; 92% of women and 81% of men "probably" or "definitely" would find them harassing if directed by a coworker. Of women, 91% and of men, 86% would find pressure for dates from a supervisor sexually harassing; 85% of women and 76% of men "probably" or "definitely" would find pressure for dates from a coworker sexually harassing. Of women, 91% and of men, 76% "probably" or "definitely" would find suggestive looks, gestures sexually harassing when directed from a supervisor; 88% of women and 70% of men "probably" or "definitely" would find them so when directed from a coworker. Of women, 83% and of men, 73% "probably" or "definitely" find sexual teasing, jokes, remarks from a supervisor sexual harassment; 77% of women and 64% of men "probably" or "definitely" find such behavior from a coworker sexual harassment. The percentages indicated include both those who responded "definitely" and "probably" to the question of whether they would consider such behavior harassment. *Id.* at 7 & tbl. 1. *But see* Barbara K. Burian et al., *Group Gender Composition Effects on Judgments of Sexual Harassment*, 22 PSYCHOL. WOMEN Q. 465, 474 (1998) (finding a "big difference" in perceptions based on gender in a rather recent study of undergraduates using an ambiguous scenario—58.4% of women stated the situation was sexual harassment, whereas only 35.3% of men did).

28. Gutek et al, *supra* note 2, at 625.

29. *See id.* at 620. The short scenario was a five-sentence description of an ambiguous harassment scenario. *Id.* at 609. The multimedia study consisted of the subjects listening to a male or female narrate a long scenario, along with seeing a picture of the defendant, plaintiff, both parties, or neither party, at random. *See id.* Students were used as subjects in both these scenarios. *See id.* at 610–11. Finally, the adult scenario appears to refer to the perceptions of 344 jury pool members after they had read the long scenario. *See id.* at 610, 615, tbl. 1.

30. Sex was also predictive in some samples of whether the subject would personally identify with the plaintiff as well as whether the subject would view the plaintiff as credible. *See id.* Again, the effects were not great (3% to 7% for personally identify and 1% to 9% for plaintiff credibility). In addition, sex differences were found for assessments of plaintiff responsibility in the picture sample and multimedia sample as well as on the issue of damages in the scenario adult sample. In all, the difference was as predicted; women were more likely to find the plaintiff less responsible and to give the plaintiff higher damages. *See id.*

31. Jeremy Blumenthal, *The Reasonable Woman Standard: A Meta-Analytic Review of Gender Differences in Perceptions of Sexual Harassment*, 22 LAW & HUM. BEHAV. 33, 43 (1998).

32. *Id.*

33. *Id.*

34. *Id.* at 46.

35. Maria Rotundo et al., *A Meta-Analytic Review of Gender Differences in Perceptions of Sexual Harassment*, 86 J. APPLIED PSYCHOL. 914, 918, 919 (2001).

36. *Id.* at 918 tbl. 2, 919.

37. *Id.* at 919.

38. Gutek & O'Connor, *supra* note 23, at 156. *See also* Baker et al., *supra* note 19, at 318 ("the perceived severity of sexual harassment had a relatively strong effect on individuals' reactions").

39. Gutek & O'Connor, *supra* note 23, at 159. *See also* Blumenthal, *supra* note 31, at 51–52 (suggesting that other variables correlated with gender may be causing the small gender effects found in his meta-analysis). Gutek and O'Connor are cautious in their criticism: "Nothing in our analysis suggests that this belief [in the efficacy of the reasonable woman standard] does not have a basis in both common sense and empirical fact. Rather, our concern is whether the empirical evidence used to demonstrate that gap is sufficiently strong, consistent, and meaningful to justify a sex-based legal standard." Gutek & O'Connor, *supra*, at 159.

40. *See* Hurt et al., *supra* note 4, at 1408. Thus, they argue that men are more tolerant of sexual harassment, which leads them to judge situations as less harassing. *See id.*; *see also, e.g.*, Masoud Hemmasi et al., *Gender-Related Jokes in the Workplace: Sexual Humor or Sexual Harassment*, 24 J. APPLIED SOC. PSYCHOL. 1114, 1126 (1994) (finding, in a study of perceptions of workplace humor, "sensitivity to sexist issues is a better predictor of attitudes towards sexual harassment than is biological sex"); Danielle Foulis & Marita P. McCabe, *Sexual Harassment: Factors Affecting Attitudes and Perceptions*, 37 SEX ROLES 773 (1997) (finding attitudes toward sexual harassment and gender role predictive of perceptions of sexual harassment in a study of Australian high school students, university students, and workers); Gowan & Zimmerman, *supra* note 5, at 611–12 (finding prior experience of sexual harassment overcomes gender differences in how a potential juror would vote on ambiguous behavior).

41. Hurt et al., *supra* note 4, at 1410.

42. Denise Haunani Solomon & Mary Lynn Miller Williams, *Perceptions of Social-Sexual Communications at Work: The Effects of Message, Situation, and Observer Characteristics on Judgments of Sexual Harassment*, 25 J. APPLIED COMMUN. RES. 196, 205 (1997).

43. *See id.* at 207.

44. Baker et al., *supra* note 24, at 413.

45. *See id.*

46. Jeanne Henry & Julian Meltzoff, *Perceptions of Sexual Harassment as a Function of Target's Response Type and Observer's Sex*, 39 SEX ROLES 253, 265 (1998).

47. *See* Plater & Thomas, *supra* note 5, at 58, 66.

48. James E. Gruber et al., *Sexual Harassment Types and Severity: Linking Research and Policy, in* SEXUAL HARASSMENT IN THE WORKPLACE: PERSPECTIVES, FRONTIERS, AND RESPONSE STRATEGIES 170 (Margaret S. Stockdale ed., 1996) (emphasis in original). They note, however, that "it appears that men who are asked to evaluate the severity or harm of harassment may need to be provided with information that informs them of the differential impact of similar types of sexual harassment on women." *Id.*

49. *See, e.g.*, Louise F. Fitzgerald et al., *Why Didn't She Just Report Him? The Psychological and Legal Implications of Women's Responses to Sexual Harassment*, 51 J. SOC. ISSUES, Spring 1995, at 117, 125 (describing generally the many studies that support the gender difference in evaluation of harassing incidents).

50. Richard L. Wiener, *Social Analytic Jurisprudence in Sexual Harassment Litigation: The Role of Social Framework and Social Fact*, 51 J. SOC. ISSUES, Spring 1995, at 167, 169 (detailing studies) (citations omitted). For a recent study that supports it, see Baird et al., *supra* note 3, at 82 (in a study of 198 undergraduates, "[o]ver-all, women rated the scenarios as more harassing than men regardless of how many male or female perpetrator items were in the questionnaire").

51. Wiener, *supra* note 50, at 169.

52. Gutek & O'Connor, *supra* note 23, at 160. As they explain, "The myth of the

manipulative seductress and innocent male victim die hard and women may be held more accountable than men for 'provoking' sexual harassment." *Id.* (citations omitted).

53. Wiener, *supra* note 50, at 170.

54. *See, e.g.*, David Shultz, *From Reasonable Man to Unreasonable Victim?: Assessing Harris Forklift Systems and Shifting Standards of Proof and Perspective in Title VII Sexual Harassment Law*, 27 SUFFOLK U. L. REV. 717, 734–35 (1993); Calleros, *supra* note 13, at 1258; Toni Lester, *The Reasonable Woman Test in Sexual Harassment Law—Will It Really Make a Difference?*, 26 IND. L. REV. 227, 247–60 (1993). *But see* Eileen M. Blackwood, *The Reasonable Woman in Sexual Harassment Law and the Case for Subjectivity*, 16 VT. L. REV. 1005, 1021 (1992) (suggesting that judges and jurors would substitute their own perspective "irrespective of whether they are told to analyze it from a male or female perspective").

55. Gutek et al., *supra* note 2, at 623.

56. *Id.*

57. *Id. But see* John B. Pryor & Jeanne D. Day, *Interpretations of Sexual Harassment: An Attributional Analysis*, 18 SEX ROLES 405 (1988) (finding that assigning an assessor with a point of view—either that of the victim or perpetrator—could alter interpretation of the event to make it more or less harassing).

58. *See* Richard L. Wiener et al., *Social Analytic Investigation of Hostile Work Environments: A Test of the Reasonable Woman Standard*, 19 LAW & HUM. BEHAVIOR 263, 276 (1995) [hereinafter Wiener et al., *Test*]. *See also* Richard L. Wiener et al., *Perceptions of Sexual Harassment: The Effects of Gender, Legal Standard, and Ambivalent Sexism*, 21 LAW & HUM. BEHAVIOR 71 (1997) [hereinafter Wiener et al., *Effects*].

59. *See* Wiener et al., *Test, supra* note 58, at 278. They suggest using expert witnesses to explain to jurors how a reasonable woman would perceive alleged harassing acts. *Id.* at 279. *But see* Pryor & Day, *supra* note 57, at 414 (in a study of college students designed to assess the shift in perspective between victim and harasser, they found that "males shifted between the male and female perspective with the same ease as females"). Wiener et al. did note that the legal standard appeared to have some effect on the manner in which the judgment of harassment was reached, i.e., on which factors the subjects used in their assessment (i.e., severity, pervasiveness, unwelcomeness). *See* Wiener et al., *Test, supra* note 58, at 276.

60. Shoenfelt et al., *supra* note 10, at 666.

61. *See id.*

62. *Id.* at 669.

63. Gutek et al., *supra* note 2, at 625.

64. *Id.* at 626.

65. Ann Juliano & Stewart J. Schwab, *The Sweep of Sexual Harassment Cases*, 86 CORNELL L. REV. 548, 584 (2001).

66. *Id.* at 584–85.

67. Blumenthal, *supra* note 31, at 43; Gutek et al., *supra* note 2, at 620.

68. *See, e.g.*, FORELL & MATTHEWS, *supra* note 3.

69. *See* Stephanie M. Wildman, Book Review, *Ending Male Privilege: Beyond the Reasonable Woman*, 98 MICH. L. REV. 1797, 1809–10 (2000) (discussing the "sameness/difference" debate that "produced a serious schism in the feminist legal community").

70. *See, e.g.*, Blackwood, *supra* note 54, at 1021 (describing the reasonable person as a "middle-class man in his shirtsleeves pushing (or perhaps, riding) his lawnmower"); Andre Douglas Pond Cummings, *"Lions and Tigers and Bears, Oh My" or "Redskins and Braves and Oh Why": Reuminations on McBride v. Utah State Tax Commission, Political Correctness, and the Reasonable Person*, 36 CAL. W.L. REV. 11, 26 (1999); Nancy S. Ehrenreich, *Pluralist Myths and Powerless Men: The Ideology of Reasonableness in Sexual Harassment Law* 99 YALE L.J. 1177, 1213 (1994); Deborah B. Goldberg,

The Road to Equality: The Application of the Reasonable Woman Standard in Sexual Harassment Cases, 2 CARDOZO WOMEN'S L.J. 195, 212 (1995); Gutek et al., *supra* note 2, at 599; Shultz, *supra* note 54, at 736.

71. *See, e.g.*, Radtke v. Everett, 501 N.W. 2d 167 (Mich. 1993); Bittner, *supra* note 3, at 136; Zanita E. Fenton, Caroline A. Forrell & Donna M. Matthews, *A Law of Her Own: The Reasonable Woman as a Measure of Man (New York University Press, New York, NY 2000)*, 37 CRIM. L. BULL. 119, 120–21 (2001); Katherine M. Franke, *What's Wrong with Sexual Harassment?*, 48 STAN. L. REV. 677, 691 (1997); Kellie A. Kalbac, *Through the Eye of the Beholder: Sexual Harassment Under the Reasonable Person Standard*, 3 KAN. J. L. & PUB. POL'Y 160 (1994); Kathleen A. Kenealy, *Sexual Harassment and the Reasonable Woman Standard*, 8 LAB. LAW. 203, 204 (1992); Melanie A. Meads, *Applying the Reasonable Woman Standard in Evaluating Sexual Harassment Claims: Is It Justified?*, 17 LAW & PSYCHOL. REV. 209, 219 (1993); Shultz, *supra* note 54, at 743–44; Deborah Zalesne, *The Intersection of Socioeconomic Class and Gender in Hostile Environment Claims Under Title VIII: Who Is the Reasonable Person?*, 38 B.C. L. REV. 861, 865 (1997).

72. *See* Jane L. Dolkart, *Hostile Environment Harassment: Equality, Objectivity, and the Shaping of Legal Standards*, 43 EMORY L.J. 151, 200–206 (1994) (arguing that the reasonable woman standard marginalizes women, reducing them to stereotyped characteristics); Angela P. Harris, *Race and Essentialism in Feminist Legal Theory*, 42 STAN. L. REV. 581, 585 (1990); Pamela L. Hemminger, *Sexual Harassment and the Reasonable Woman Standard*, 20 PEPP. L. REV. 1148, 1154 (1993); Zalesne, *supra* note 71, at 864, 878–80; Tracy L. Treger, Note, *The Reasonable Woman? Unreasonable!!!* Ellison v. Brady, 14 WHITTIER L. REV. 675, 689–93 (1993); Wildman, *supra* note 69, at 1812.

73. *See* Zalesne, *supra* note 71, at 864.

74. *See, e.g.*, Wildman, *supra* note 69, at 1806.

75. *See, e.g.*, Fenton, *supra* note 71, at 121 ("to the extent we accept that these crimes are essentially ones of power and control, it is the perspective of the powerless which should determine the reasonableness of actions within that situation"); Jeremy D. Pasternak, Comment, *Sexual Harassment and Expertise: The Admissibility of Expert Witness Testimony in Cases Utilizing the Reasonable Woman Standard*, 35 SANTA CLARA L. REV. 651, 684 (1995); Shultz, *supra* note 54, at 736–37.

76. *See, e.g.*, Robert S. Adler & Ellen R. Pierce, *The Legal, Ethical, and Social Implications of the "Reasonable Woman" Standard in Sexual Harassment Cases*, 61 FORDHAM L. REV. 773, 825–27 (1993); Liesa L. Bernardin, Note, *Does the Reasonable Woman Exist and Does She Have Any Place in Hostile Environment Sexual Harassment Claims Under Title VII After Harris*, 46 FLA. L. REV. 291, 318 (1994); Bittner, *supra* note 3, at 136–37 (arguing that it will lead male jurors to stereotype); Kalbac, *supra* note 71, at 169.

77. *See, e.g.*, Paul B. Johnson, *The Reasonable Woman in Sexual Harassment Law: Progress or Illusion?*, 28 WAKE FOREST L. REV. 619, 645–48 (1993); Shultz, *supra* note 54, at 738–40; Robert Unikel, Comment, *"Reasonable" Doubts: A Critique of the Reasonable Woman Standard in American Jurisprudence*, 87 NW. U. L. REV. 326, 367 (1992).

78. *See, e.g.*, Adler & Peirce, *supra* note 76, at 822–24; Lynn Dennison, Note, *An Argument for the Reasonable Woman Standard in Hostile Environment Claims*, 54 OHIO ST. L.J. 473, 493–94 (1993); Kalbac, *supra* note 71, at 166, 167; Kenealy, *supra* note 71, at 208; Shultz, *supra* note 54, at 740–42.

79. The amount of scholarly debate on the subject has been great. *See, e.g.*, Theresa M. Beiner, *Sex, Science and Social Knowledge: The Implications of Social Science Research on Imputing Liability to Employers for Sexual Harassment*, 7 WM. & MARY J. WOMEN & L. 273, 328–29 n. 369 (2001) (citing numerous articles discussing the issue); Theresa M. Beiner & John M.A. DiPippa, *Hostile Environments and the Religious Employee*, 19 U. ARK. LITTLE ROCK L.J. 577, 631 n.355 (1997) (same).

80. *See, e.g.*, Tindle v. Caudell, 56 F.3d 966, 971 (8th Cir. 1995); Jenson v. Eveleth Taconite Co., 824 F. Supp. 847, 884 n.89 (D. Minn. 1993); Robinson v. Jacksonville Shipyards, Inc., 760 F. Supp. 1486, 1534–37 (M.D. Fla. 1991) (all rejecting First Amendment arguments). There are, of course, exceptions, but they are few. *See, e.g.*, DeAngelis v. El Paso Mun. Police Officers Ass'n, 51 F.3d 591, 596–97 (5th Cir. 1995) (acknowledging potential First Amendment problems when the harassing behavior took the form of a column in a newsletter); Johnson v. County of L.A. Fire Dep't, 865 F. Supp. 1430, 1438 (C.D. Cal. 1994) (reading *Playboy* in private at the workplace is protected by the First Amendment; employer was a public entity). George Rutherglen has noted that there are no cases that appear to hold employers liable for speech that is protected by the First Amendment. *See* Rutherglen, *supra* note 13, at 492 & n.22 (arguing that there is no impermissible chilling effect).

81. Juliano & Schwab, *supra* note 65, at 567 (footnote omitted).

82. Gutek et al. acknowledge that there are several explanations as to why their studies showed no effect. However, the standard might still be valuable for the effect it has on how employers develop policies and practices related to workplace harassment. Gutek et al., *supra* note 2, at 625. It may be that jurors already look at it from the perspective of the victim—in this case a woman. Finally, people may not know what content to give the "reasonable woman" standard. Thus, expert testimony may be necessary to describe this "reasonable woman" before the standard will make a difference in outcomes. *Id.*

83. *See* Wiener & Hurt, *supra* note 23, at 74 (noting "the most important impact of the reasonable woman person vs. reasonable woman standard lies not in how the actual language influences resolution of conflicts at trial, but rather in the manner in which the promulgated rules influence the behavior of men and women in the workplace").

84. Margaret Bull Kovera et al., *Reasoning About Scientific Evidence: Effects of Juror Gender and Evidence Quality on Juror Decisions in a Hostile Work Environment Case*, 84 J. APPLIED PSYCHOL. 362, 369 fig.1 (1999).

85. *Id.* at 369–70.

86. The judges in the case were Judges Kozinski, Stephens, and Beezer, who wrote the decision. Beezer and Kozinksi were appointed by President Reagan. Stephens was appointed by President Kennedy. *See* BIOGRAPHICAL DIRECTORY OF THE FEDERAL JUDICIARY 1789–2000 at 372, 607, 777 (2001).

87. As one source has pointed out, "In fact, prior to 1986, neither Title VII nor Title VIII sex or race discrimination cases required proof that a plaintiff had acted in accord with 'someone else's notion of reasonable behavior.'" Zalesne, *supra* note 71, at 888 (quoting BARBARA A. BABCOCK ET AL., SEX DISCRIMINATION AND THE LAW: HISTORY, PRACTICE AND THEORY 617 (2d ed. 1996)). *See also* Kenealy, *supra* note 71, at 209 (noting that the reasonable woman standard focuses on the conduct of the victim rather than that of the harasser).

88. Davis v. U.S. Postal Serv., 142 F.3d 1334, 1341 (10th Cir. 1998) (quoting Dey v. Colt Constr. & Dev. Co., 28 F.3d 1446, 1455 (7th Cir. 1994) (quoting King v. Hillen, 21 F.3d 1572, 1583 (Fed. Cir. 1994))).

89. *Id.* at 1341.

90. King, 21 F.3d at 1581.

NOTES TO CHAPTER 3

1. Else K. Bolotin, *Understanding the Emotional Reactions to Treatment of Sexual Harassment*, in SEX AND POWER ISSUES IN THE WORKPLACE at 53, 54 (1992); *see generally* Adrienne D. Davis & Stephanie M. Wildman, *The Legacy of Doubt: Treatment of Sex and Race in the Hill-Thomas Hearings*, 65 S. CAL. L. REV. 1367, 1375–78 (1992).

As commentators have pointed out, Professor Hill's case involved more than sexual harassment; instead, it involved sexual harassment of an African-American woman, a phenomenon that requires its own study. *See* Kimberle Crenshaw, *Demargenalizing the Intersection of Race and Sex: A Black Feminist Critique of Antidiscrimination Doctrine, Feminist Theory and Antiracist Politics*, 1989 U. CHI. LEGAL F. 139; Davis & Wildman, *supra*, at 1385–86.

2. Meritor Sav. Bank v. Vinson, 477 U.S. 57, 68 (1986).

3. *See, e.g.*, Janine Benedet, *Hostile Environment Sexual Harassment Claims and the Unwelcome Influence of Rape Law*, 3 MICH. J. GENDER & L. 125 (1995); Susan Estrich, *Sex at Work*, 43 STAN. L. REV. 813 (1991).

4. *Meritor*, 477 U.S. at 68.

5. *See* Delaria v. Am. Gen. Fin., Inc., 998 F. Supp. 1050, 1059 (S.D. Iowa 1998); EQUAL EMPLOYMENT OPPORTUNITY COMM'N, POLICY GUIDANCE ON CURRENT ISSUES OF SEXUAL HARASSMENT, EEOC Notice N-915-050, at 7 (March 19, 1990).

6. *See* Estrich, *supra* note 3; Ann C. Juliano, *Did She Ask for It?: The "Unwelcome" Requirement in Sexual Harassment Cases*, 77 CORNELL L. REV. 1558 (1992); Miranda Oshige, Note, *What's Sex Got to Do with It?* 47 STAN. L. REV. 565, 579–80 (1995); Mary F. Radford, *By Invitation Only: The Proof of Welcomeness in Sexual Harassment Cases*, 72 N.C. L. REV. 499 (1994); Joan S. Weiner, Note, *Understanding Welcomeness in Sexual Harassment Law: Its History and a Proposal for Reform*, 72 NOTRE DAME L. REV. 621 (1997); Casey J. Wood, *"Inviting Sexual Harassment": The Absurdity of the Welcomeness Requirement in Sexual Harassment Law*, 38 BRANDEIS L.J. 423 (2000).

7. Carr v. Allison Gas Turbine Div., Gen. Motors Corp., 32 F.3d 1007, 1008–9 (7th Cir. 1994) (Posner, J.).

8. *See, e.g.*, Wood, *supra* note 6, at 428–29.

9. *See* Oshige, *supra* note 6, at 581.

10. *See, e.g.*, U. S. MERIT SYS. PROT. BD., SEXUAL HARASSMENT IN THE FEDERAL WORKPLACE: TRENDS, PROGRESS, AND CONTINUING CHALLENGES x (1995) [hereinafter USMSPB]; Caroline C. Cochran et al., *Predictors of Responses to Unwanted Sexual Attention*, 21 PSYCHOL. WOMEN Q. 207, 217 (1997) (in study of university students, faculty, and staff, majority of those experiencing harassing behavior chose to ignore it; only 2% made formal reports); Kimberly T. Schneider et al., *Job-Related and Psychological Effects of Sexual Harassment in the Workplace: Empirical Evidence from Two Organizations*, 82 J. APPLIED PSYCHOL. 401, 403 (1997).

11. Meritor Sav. Bank v. Vinson, 477 U.S. 57, 68 (1986) (citing 29 C.F.R. §1604.11(a)).

12. *Id.*

13. *Id.* at 68–69 (quoting Vinson v. Taylor, 753 F.2d 141, 146 n.36 (D.C. Cir. 1985)).

14. *Id.* at 69.

15. *Id.* (quoting 29 C.F.R. §1604.11(b) (1985)).

16. *See* Juliano, *supra* note 6, at 1576; Estrich, *supra* note 3, at 827.

17. *See generally* Jacqueline H. Sloan, Comment, *Extending Rape Shield Protection to Sexual Harassment Actions: New Federal Rule of Evidence 412 Undermines* Meritor Sav. Bank v. Vinson, 25 SW. U. L. REV. 363 (1996).

18. FED. R. EVID. 412 (1984).

19. *Id.* 412(a) and advisory committee's notes.

20. *Id.* 412(b)(2). In addition, evidence of the plaintiff's reputation is admissible if placed in controversy by the plaintiff. *Id.*

21. *Id.* 412, advisory committee's notes. The advisory committee suggests rule modifications to the Judicial Conference, which develops federal court rules. 1 JAMES WM. MOORE ET AL., MOORE'S FEDERAL PRACTICE §1.04 [3] [b] (3d ed. 1997).

22. *But see* Sloan, *supra* note 17, at 391 (noting that while the rule makes it appear

that this portion of *Meritor* is no longer good law, courts are hesitant to exclude evidence when it is used for the welcomeness inquiry).

23. FED. R. EVID. 412, advisory committee notes.

24. *See, e.g.*, P.J. Herchenroeder v. John Hopkins University Applied Physics Lab., 171 F.R.D. 179, 181–82 (D. Md. 1997); Sanchez v. Zabihi, 166 F.R.D. 500, 501 (D.N.M. 1996); Barta v. City & County of Honolulu, 169 F.R.D. 132, 135 (D. Hawaii 1996).

25. Harris v. Forklift Sys., Inc., 510 U.S. 17, 21 (1993).

26. 998 F. Supp. 1050, 1058–59 (S.D. Iowa 1998).

27. *See generally* Jane Goodman-Delahunty, *Pragmatic Support for the Reasonable Victim Standard in Hostile Workplace Sexual Harassment Cases*, 5 PSYCHOL. PUB. POL'Y & L. 519, 538, 539 (1999) (noting confusion between welcomeness inquiry and subjective component of severe or pervasive standard; noting that claims where the subjective test, but not the objective test, is met are more common).

28. Ann C. Juliano & Stewart J. Schwab, *The Sweep of Sexual Harassment Cases*, 86 CORNELL L. REV. 548, 565 (2001) ("The bulk of sexual harassment cases involve hostile environment claims. Almost 70% of the cases only include a hostile environment claim, while another 22.5% combine a hostile environment claim with a quid pro quo claim.").

29. 909 F. Supp. 1539, 1546 (S.D. Fla. 1995).

30. *See* Meritor Sav. Bank v. Vinson, 477 U.S. 57, 68 (1986); *see generally* Radford, *supra* note 6, at 514–15 (noting that lower courts have conceded that unwelcomeness is a difficult question of fact).

31. 940 F. Supp. 1344, 1361 (S.D. Ind. 1996).

32. *See* Weiner, *supra* note 6, at 628–32 (describing such cases).

33. Hocevar v. Purdue Frederick Co., 223 F.3d 721, 736 (8th Cir. 2000).

34. *Id.* at 724 (Lay, J., dissenting) (emphasis in original; citations omitted).

35. *Id.* at 725.

36. *Id.* at 736.

37. *Id.* at 729–30 (Lay, J., dissenting). Judge Gibson agreed with the result reached by Judge Beam on the summary judgment motion, but concurred separately. *See id.* at 739–41 (Gibson, J., concurring specially in affirmance of grant of summary judgment on hostile environment claim).

38. 909 F. Supp. 1539, 1542 (S.D. Fla. 1995).

39. *Id.* at 1546–47.

40. *Id.* at 1545.

41. *Id.* at 1547–48.

42. *Id.* at 1548.

43. *Id.* at 1548 n.6.

44. *See, e.g.*, Reed v. Shepard, 939 F.2d 484, 485 (7th Cir. 1991); Weinsheimer v. Rockwell Int'l Corp. 754 F. Supp. 1559, 1567 (M.D. Fla. 1990); Perkins v. Gen. Motors Corp. 709 F. Supp. 1487, 1489 (W.D. Mo. 1989); Loftin-Boggs v. City of Meridian, Miss., 633 F. Supp. 1323, 1324 (S.D. Miss. 1986); Gan v. Kepro Circuit Sys., Inc., 28 Fair Empl. Prac. Cases (BNA) 639 (E.D. Mo. 1982).

45. *See, e.g.*, *Weinsheimer*, 754 F. Supp. at 1564 n.12; *Loftin-Boggs*, 633 F. Supp. at 1327 n.8.

46. *See, e.g.*, *Balletti*, 909 F. Supp. at 1547; *Reed*, 939 F.2d at 486; *Weinsheimer*, 754 F. Supp. at 1563; *Loftin-Boggs*, 633 F. Supp. at 1327; *Gan*, 28 Fair Empl. Prac. Cases (BNA) 639.

47. 32 F.3d 1007, 1009–10 (7th Cir. 1994).

48. *Id.* at 1010.

49. *Id.*

50. *Id.* at 1011 (emphasis in original, citations omitted).

51. *Id.* at 1011.

52. 830 F.2d 552, 557 (4th Cir. 1987) (quoting Katz v. Dole, 709 F.2d 251, 254 n.3 (4th Cir. 1983)), *abrogation on other grounds recognized in* Mikels v. City of Durham, N.C., 193 F.3d 323, 329 n.4 (4th Cir. 1999).

53. *See, e.g.,* Kouri v. Liberian Servs., 55 Fair Empl. Prac. Cas. (BNA) 124 (E.D. Va. 1991), *aff'd,* Kouri v. Todd, 960 F.2d 146 (4th Cir. 1992), *cert. denied,* 173 S. Ct. 189 (1992).

54. 915 F.2d 777, 784 (1st Cir. 1990).

55. *See, e.g.,* Walker v. AMR Servs. Corp., 971 F. Supp. 110, 114 (E.D.N.Y. 1997) (summary judgment denied on unwelcomeness where plaintiff accepted rides home from harasser); Cuesta v. Tex. Dep't of Crim. Justice, 805 F. Supp. 451, 457 (W.D. Tex. 1991) (plaintiff's brief shoulder rub of boss did not prove welcomeness where supervisor engaged in clearly inappropriate behavior).

56. 170 F. Supp. 2d 219, 231 (D. Conn. 2001).

57. *Id.* The alleged harasser claimed the plaintiff initiated the sexual exchanges, sending e-mails and sexually erotic voicemails. *Id.* at 232.

58. *Id.* at 232–33.

59. *Id.* at 231 n.17.

60. *Id.* at 234.

61. *Id.* at 235.

62. A motion in limine is a pretrial motion to determine the admissibility of evidence.

63. 177 F.R.D. 48, 51 (D.D.C. 1997). For courts that have decided similarly, see Jaros v. Lodgenet Entm't Corp., 171 F. Supp. 2d 992, 1003 (D.S.D. 2001); Socks-Brunot v. Hirschvogel, Inc., 184 F.R.D. 113 (S.D. Ohio 1999).

64. *Howard,* 177 F.R.D. at 52.

65. *Id.*

66. *Id.*

67. 276 F.3d 1091, 1105 (9th Cir. 2002).

68. *Lodgenet,* 171 F. Supp. 2d 992, 1003 (D. S. Dakota 2001).

69. *Id.*

70. *Id.*

71. 132 F.3d 848, 855–56 (1st Cir. 1998).

72. *Id.* at 856 & n.2. The court did permit admission of evidence of plaintiff's alleged flirtatious behavior directed at the alleged harasser as well as evidence related to a relationship plaintiff had that allegedly distracted her from work, resulting in her termination.

73. Fedio v. Circuit City Stores, No. CIV. A 97-5851, 1998 WL 966000, at *5 (E.D. Pa. Nov. 4, 1998).

74. *Id.* at *2.

75. *Id.* at *6. *See also* FED. R. EVID. 412, advisory committee notes.

76. 166 F.R.D. 500, 501 (D.N.M. 1996).

77. *See, e.g.,* Frank E. Saal et al., *Friendly or Sexy? It May Depend on Whom You Ask,* 13 PSYCHOL. WOMEN Q. 263 (1989).

78. USMSPB, *supra* note 10, at 29. Interestingly, of the 44% of women and 19% of men who reported being harassed, only 12% had reported such behavior. *Id.* at 30.

79. *Id.* at 30.

80. *See* Sharyn A. Lenhart & Diane K. Shrier, *Potential Costs and Benefits of Sexual Harassment Litigation,* 26 PSYCHIATRIC ANNALS 132, 132–33, 134–37 (1996) (noting that "substantially less than 10% of the women who are harassed file a formal complaint or seek legal help" and describing ramifications of litigating sexual harassment cases).

81. *See* James Gruber, *How Women Handle Sexual Harassment: A Literature Review,* 74 SOC. SCI. REV. 3, 5, 8 (tbl.) (1989).

82. In particular, he is concerned about the lack of data regarding the relationship between the severity of the harassment, the atmosphere at the target's workplace, and the target's response. *See id.* at 5–6.

83. *See* Aysan Sev'er, *Sexual Harassment: Where We Were, Where We Are and Prospects for the New Millennium*, 36 CANADIAN REV. SOC. & ANTHROPOLOGY 469, 478 (1999).

84. *See* Louise F. Fitzgerald, *Examining (and Eliminating) the Consequences of Sexual Harassment: An Integrated Model, in* SEX AND POWER ISSUES IN THE WORKPLACE, A CONFERENCE TO PROMOTE MEN AND WOMEN WORKING PRODUCTIVELY TOGETHER 61, 63 (1992) (citing studies); Barbara A. Gutek & Mary P. Koss, *Changed Women and Changed Organizations: Consequences of and Coping with Sexual Harassment*, 42 J. VOCATIONAL BEHAV. 28, 31 (1993) (indicating that 10% of women harassed leave their jobs either by quitting, or by being fired or transferred); Rebecca A. Thacker, *A Descriptive Study of Situational and Individual Influences upon Individuals' Responses to Sexual Harassment*, 49 HUM. REL. 1105, 1116 (1996).

85. *See* Sev'er, *supra* note 83, at 478. In a study of military personnel, DuBois et al. found that men likewise do not report harassment. Of the men surveyed who experienced same-sexual harassment, only 7.8% took formal action. *See* Cathy L.Z. DuBois et al., *An Empirical Examination of Same- and Other-Gender Sexual Harassment in the Workplace*, 39 SEX ROLES 731, 740 (tbl. III) (1998). Of the men who experienced other-sexual harassment, only 3% took formal action. *See id.* By far the most prevalent reason given for not reporting other-gender harassment was that the target "saw no need to report it." *See id.*

86. *See* Cochran et al., *supra* note 10, at 223.

87. *See* Douglas D. Baker et al., *The Influence of Individual Characteristics and Severity of Harassing Behavior on Reactions to Sexual Harassment*, 22 SEX ROLES 305, 318 (1990); *but see* James E. Gruber & Lars Bjorn, *Women's Responses to Sexual Harassment: An Analysis of Sociocultural, Organizational, and Personal Resource Models*, 67 SOC. SCI. Q. 814, 822 (1986).

88. USMSPB, *supra* note 10, at 35.

89. Baker et al., *supra* note 87, at 318. They also opined that "it seems that the more individuals perceived incidents to be harassment, the more assertive were the reactions." *Id.*

90. *See, e.g.*, Linda Brooks & Annette R. Perot, *Reporting Sexual Harassment*, 15 PSYCHOL. WOMEN Q. 31, 42–43, 45 (1991) ("Feminist ideology and frequency of behavior showed direct effects on perceived offensiveness, which in turn directly predicted reporting.").

91. Margaret S. Stockdale, *The Direct and Moderating Influences of Sexual-Harassment Pervasiveness, Coping Strategies, and Gender on Work-Related Outcomes*, 22 PSYCHOL. WOMEN Q. 521, 531 (1998).

92. USMSPB, *supra* note 10, at 30.

93. *See, e.g.*, Hocevar v. Purdue Frederick Co., 223 F.3d 721 (8th Cir. 2000). For an interesting account of sexual harassment and discrimination in the brokerage industry, see SUSAN ANTILLA, TALES FROM THE BOOM-BOOM ROOM: WOMEN VS. WALL STREET (2002).

94. *See, e.g.*, KERRY SEAGRAVE, THE SEXUAL HARASSMENT OF WOMEN IN THE WORK-PLACE, 1600 TO 1993 (McFarland & Co. 1994); SUSAN EISENBERG, WE'LL CALL YOU IF WE NEED YOU: EXPERIENCES OF WOMEN WORKING CONSTRUCTION 69–85 (Cornell University Press 1998); Janice D. Yoder & Patricia Aniakudo, *When Pranks Become Harassment: The Case of African American Women Firefighters*, 35 SEX ROLES 253 (1996).

95. James E. Gruber & Lars Bjorn, *Blue-Collar Blues: The Sexual Harassment of Women Autoworkers*, 9 WORK & OCCUPATIONS 271, 282 (1981); *see also* Jane L.

Dolkart, *Hostile Environment Harassment: Equality, Objectivity, and the Shaping of Legal Standards*, 43 EMORY L.J. 151, 184–85 n.127 (1994) (citing study in which 75% of nontraditional female workers reported experiencing harassment); Phyllis Kernoff Mansfield, *The Job Climate for Women in Traditionally Male Blue-Collar Occupations*, 25 SEX ROLES 63, 71 (1991) (finding that 60% of tradeswomen studied reported experiencing harassment and 36.2% of female transit workers reported experiencing harassment, whereas only 6.4% of clerical workers reported experiencing harassment).

96. Gruber & Bjorn, *supra* note 95, at tbl. 3.

97. EISENBERG, *supra* note 94, at 82–83.

98. *Id.* at 83. Eisenberg noted that women of color, specifically African American women, were "doubly vulnerable" to acts of harassment.

99. Suzanne E. Tallichet, *Gendered Relations in the Mines and the Division of Labor Underground*, 9 GENDER & SOC'Y 697, 702 (1995).

100. *Id.*

101. *Id.* at 703.

102. Kristen R. Yount, *Ladies, Flirts, and Tomboys: Strategies for Managing Sexual Harassment in an Underground Coal Mine*, 19 J. CONTEMP. ETHNOGRAPHY 396, 400 (1991); Tallichet, *supra* note 99, at 703.

103. Yount, *supra* note 102, at 400.

104. *Id.* at 403–4.

105. *Id.* at 407–9, 411–12.

106. *Id.* at 414.

107. *Id.* at 416.

108. *Id.*

109. MARY LINDENSTEIN WALSHOK, BLUE-COLLAR WOMEN: PIONEERS ON THE MALE FRONTIER 230 (1981).

110. *Id.* at 231.

111. *Id.* at 232.

112. *Id.* at 239–40.

113. *See* Robin M. Kowalski, *Inferring Sexual Interest from Behavioral Cues: Effects of Gender and Sexually Relevant Attitudes*, 29 SEX ROLES 13, 14 (1992) (citing studies).

114. *See, e.g.*, Antonia Abbey, *Sex Differences in Attributions for Friendly Behavior: Do Males Misperceive Females' Friendliness?*, 42 J. PERSONALITY & SOC. PSYCHOL. 830, 836 (1982); Antonia Abbey et al., *Misperceptions of Friendly Behavior as Sexual Interest: A Survey of Naturally Occurring Incidents*, 11 PSYCHOL. WOMEN Q. 173, 178 (1987).

115. Catherine B. Johnson et al., *Persistence of Men's Misperceptions of Friendly Cues across a Variety of Interpersonal Encounters*, 15 PSYCHOL. WOMEN Q. 463, 466 (1991).

116. *Id.* at 473.

117. Margaret S. Stockdale, *The Role of Sexual Misperceptions of Women's Friendliness in an Emerging Theory of Sexual Harassment*, 42 J. VOCATIONAL BEHAV. 84, 87 (1993).

118. Frank E. Saal, *Men's Misperceptions of Women's Interpersonal Behaviors and Sexual Harassment, in* SEXUAL HARASSMENT IN THE WORKPLACE: PERSPECTIVES, FRONTIERS, AND RESPONSE STRATEGIES at 67, 81 (Margaret S. Stockdale ed., 1996).

119. *See, e.g.*, Estrich, *supra* note 3.

120. *See generally* Linda Burnham, *Welfare Reform, Family Hardship and Women of Color*, 577 ANNALS 38, 39 (2001).

121. *See* Wood, *supra* note 6, at 429.

122. Carr v. Allison Gas Turbine Div., Gen. Motors Corp., 32 F.3d 1007, 1008–9 (7th Cir. 1994) (Posner, J.).

123. EIGHTH CIRCUIT GENDER FAIRNESS TASK FORCE, FINAL REPORT & RECOMMEN-

DATIONS OF THE EIGHTH CIRCUIT GENDER FAIRNESS TASK FORCE, *reprinted in* 31 CREIGHTON L. REV. 9, 15, 73 (1997).

124. *See id.* at 74–75.

125. *See* Andrea A. Curcio, *Rule 412 Laid Bare: A Procedural Rule That Cannot Adequately Protect Sexual Harassment Plaintiffs from Embarrassing Exposure*, 67 U. CIN. L. REV. 125, 140 (1998).

126. *See, e.g.*, Ramirez v. Nabil's Inc., 1995 WL 609415 (D. Kan. Oct. 5, 1995); Bottomly v. Leucadia Nat'l, 163 F.R.D. 617 (D. Utah 1995).

127. *Howard*, 177 F.R.D. 48, 52 (D.D.C. 1997).

128. *See, e.g.*, RICHARD EPSTEIN, FORBIDDEN GROUNDS: THE CASE AGAINST EMPLOYMENT DISCRIMINATION LAWS 350 (1992); Michael J. Frank, *The Social Context Variable in Hostile Environment Litigation*, 77 NOTRE DAME L. REV. 437, 459 n.102 (2002); Mark McLaughlin Hager, *Harassment as a Tort: Why Title VII Hostile Environment Liability Should be Curtailed*, 30 CONN. L. REV. 375, 380 n.8 (1988).

129. *See* Estrich, *supra* note 3, at 833–34 (discussing "serious disincentives" to filing a sexual harassment suit); Oshige, *supra* note 6, at 582–83.

130. Hager, *supra* note 128, at 380 n.8 (citing study).

131. Freada Klein, *The 1988 Working Woman Sexual Harassment Survey: Executive Report* 20, 23 (1988). Even in that category, the 27% figure referred to reporting rates in cases in which the employer had no reporting mechanism. *Id.* at 23. *See also* Ronni Sandroff, *Sexual Harassment in the Fortune 500*, WORKING WOMAN 69, 72 (Dec. 1988) (talking generally about soured relationships, while providing no statistics).

132. SOC'Y FOR HUMAN RES. MGMT., WORKPLACE ROMANCE SURVEY 2 (Alexandria, VA, Public Affairs Dept. 1998), *cited in* Charles A. Pierce & Herman Aguinis, *A Framework for Investigating the Link between Workplace Romance and Sexual Harassment*, 26 GROUP & ORGANIZATIONAL MGMT. 206, 208 (2001).

133. Pierce & Aguinis, *supra* note 132, at 221.

134. Studies have found that prior romance between the harasser and target does have an effect on raters' evaluations of the scenarios. *See, e.g.*, Charles A. Pierce et al., *Effects of a Dissolved Workplace Romance and Rater Characteristics on Responses to a Sexual Harassment Accusation*, 43 ACAD. MGMT. J. 869, 875, 877 (2000); Russel J. Summers & Karin Myklebust, *The Influence of a History of Romance on Judgments and Response to a Complaint of Sexual Harassment*, 27 SEX ROLES 345, 352 (1992).

135. *See* Keppler v. Hinsdale Township High School Dist., 715 F. Supp. 862, 864–65 (N.D. Ill. 1989) (allegations that former paramour engineered plaintiff's termination because she refused to continue their relationship); Frank, *supra* note 128, at 459 nn.102–3. *See also* EPSTEIN, *supra* note 128, at 350. In one case cited, the female employee was fired at the request of the supervisor's spouse. Mauro v. Orville, 259 A.D.2d. 89, 92 (N.Y. App. Div. 1999) (under New York law).

136. *See, e.g., Mauro*, 259 A.2d at 92; *Keppler*, 715 F. Supp. at 869–70; Freeman v. Continental Technical Serv., Inc., 710 F. Supp. 328, 331 (N.D. Ga. 1988) (discriminatory termination case); *see also* Frank, *supra* note 128, at 459 n.102.

137. *See, e.g.*, Mosher v. Dollar Tree Stores, Inc., 240 F.3d 662 (7th Cir. 2001) (summary judgment for employer upheld); Place v. Abbott Lab., 215 F.3d 803 (7th Cir. 2000) (judgment in favor of plaintiff reversed); Huebschen v. Dep't of Health & Soc. Serv., 716 F.2d 1167 (7th Cir. 1983) (reversed after verdict in male plaintiff's favor); Smith v. Nat'l R.R. Passenger Corp. 25 F. Supp.2d 578 (E.D. Pa. 1998) (motion to dismiss granted).

138. *See* B. Glenn George, *The Back Door: Legitimizing Sexual Harassment Claims*, 73 B.U. L. REV. 1, 29–30 (1993) (suggesting use as an affirmative defense); Radford, *supra* note 6, at 526 (same).

139. *See* Benedet, *supra* note 3, at 145–46 (noting notice approach used by some courts).

140. At least one court has recognized this. *See* Williams v. General Motors Corp., 187 F. 3d 553, 566 (6th Cir. 1999) (noting that a plaintiff's failure to report harassment is not relevant to whether she experienced it or not but may "be relevant to the affirmative defense to employer liability in cases of harassment by a supervisor recently adopted by the Supreme Court in *Faragher* and *Burlington Industries*").

NOTES TO CHAPTER 4

1. *See* William E. Foote & Jane Goodman-Delahunty, *Same-sexual harassment: Implications of the* Oncale *Decision for Forensic Evaluation of Plaintiffs*, 17 BEHAV. SCI. & L. 123, 125 (1999); Margaret S. Stockdale et al., *Sexual Harassment of Men: Evidence for a Broader Theory of Sexual Harassment and Sex Discrimination*, 5 PSYCHOL. PUB. POL'Y & L. 630, 660 (1999).

2. 110 CONG. REC. 2581 (1964) (statements of Rep. St. George).

3. *See* Hilary S. Axam & Deborah Zalesne, *Simulated Sodomy and Other Forms of Heterosexual "Horseplay:" Same Sex Sexual Harassment, Workplace Gender Hierarchies, and the Myth of the Gender Monolith Before and After* Oncale, 11 YALE J.L. & FEMINISM 155, 176 (1999); Mary Anne C. Case, *Disaggregating Gender from Sex and Sexual Orientation: The Effeminate Man and Feminist Jurisprudence*, 105 YALE L.J. 1, 2 (1995).

4. Meritor Sav. Bank v. Vinson, 477 U.S. 57, 66 (1986) (quoting Rogers v. EEOC, 454 F.2d 234, 238 (5th Cir. 1971), *cert denied*, 406 U.S. 957 (1972)).

5. *Id.* at 67.

6. Price Waterhouse v. Hopkins, 490 U.S. 228, 251 (1989) (Brennan, J.) (citations omitted).

7. *Id.* at 272–73 (O'Connor, J., concurring in judgment).

8. *See* Vicki Schultz, *Reconceptualizing Sexual Harassment*, 107 YALE L.J. 1683, 1762 (1998) (arguing for a broadening of the theory to include gender harassment).

9. Oncale v. Sundowner Offshore Servs., Inc., 523 U.S. 75, 80–81 (1998).

10. *Id.* at 81.

11. David S. Schwartz, *When Is Sex Because of Sex? The Causation Problem in Sexual Harassment Law*, 150 U. PA. L. REV. 1697, 1729 (2002); *see also* L. Camille Hebert, *Sexual Harassment as Discrimination "Because of . . . Sex": Have We Come Full Circle?*, 27 OHIO N.U. L. REV. 439, 448 (2001) (noting that *Oncale* "resurrected" the issue of when harassment is "because of sex").

12. *See, e.g.*, Shepherd v. Slater Steels Corp., 168 F.3d 998, 1009 (7th Cir. 1999) (*Oncale* list meant to be "instructive," not "exhaustive").

13. Rene v. MGM Grand Hotel, Inc., 305 F.3d 1061, 1066 (9th Cir. 2002) (en banc).

14. *Id.* at 1068 (Pregerson, J., concurring).

15. *Id.* at 1076–77 (Hug, J., dissenting).

16. Nichols v. Azteca Rest. Enter., Inc., 256 F.3d 864, 870 (9th Cir. 2001).

17. *Id.* at 874.

18. *See, e.g.*, Doe v. City of Belleville, Illinois, 119 F.3d 563 (7th Cir. 1997), *cert. granted, j'ment vacated by* City of Belleville v. Doe, 523 U.S. 1001 (1998) (reversing trial court's grant of summary judgment); Ianetta v. Putnam Invs., Inc., 142 F. Supp. 2d 131 (D. Mass. 2001) (motion to dismiss).

19. Bibby v. Philadelphia Coca Cola Bottling Co., 260 F.3d 257, 259–60 (3d Cir. 2001).

20. *Id.* at 260.

21. Johnson v. Hondo, Inc., 125 F.3d 408, 410–11 (7th Cir. 1997).

22. *Id.* at 412.

23. *Id.*

24. *See, e.g.,* Davis v. Coastal Int'l Sec., Inc., 275 F.3d 1119 (D.C. Cir. 2002) (sexually oriented harassment based on personal animosity); EEOC v. Harbert-Yeargin, Inc., 266 F.3d 498 (6th Cir. 2001) (sexually oriented acts dismissed as horseplay, upholding trial court's granting of judgment as a matter of law after jury verdict for plaintiff).

25. *Harbert-Yeargin, Inc.,* 266 F.3d at 520 (Guy, J.).

26. *Id.* at 522.

27. Davis, 275 F.3d at 1121–22, 1124–25.

28. LaDay v. Catalyst Tech., Inc., 302 F.3d 474, 476 (5th Cir. 2002).

29. *Id.*

30. *Id.* at 477.

31. *Id.* at 480 (emphasis in original).

32. *See also* Shepherd v. Slater Steels Corp., 168 F.3d 998, 1009–10 (7th Cir. 1999) (holding similarly).

33. Ocheltree v. Scollon Prods., Inc., 308 F.3d 351 (4th Cir. 2002), *aff'd in part, rev'd in part,* 335 F.3d 325 (4th Cir. 2003) (en banc). The en banc Fourth Circuit upheld the jury's decision with respect to compensatory damages but held there was no basis for the punitive damages award. 335 F.3d at 327.

34. *Ocheltree,* 308 F.3d at 353.

35. *Id.* at 357–58.

36. *Id.* at 359.

37. *Id.* at 376 (Michael, J., dissenting in part and concurring in part).

38. *Id.* at 378.

39. *See* 335 F.3d at 332–33.

40. Holman v. Indiana, 211 F.3d 399, 401 (7th Cir. 2000).

41. *Id.* at 403 (emphasis in original).

42. *Id.* at 404.

43. Brown v. Henderson, 257 F.3d 246, 249–50 (2d Cir. 2001).

44. *Id.* at 253–54 (citing Carson v. Bethlehem Steel Corp., 82 F.3d at 157, 158 (7th Circ. 1996) (emphasis in original).

45. *Id.* at 254.

46. Beard v. Flying J, Inc., 266 F.3d 792, 798 (8th Cir. 2001).

47. *Id.* at 798 (citing Quick v. Donaldson Co., 90 F.3d 678 (7th Cir. 2001)).

48. EEOC v. R&R Ventures, 244 F.3d 334, 338–39 (4th Cir. 2001).

49. Gross v. Burggraf Constr. Co., 53 F.3d 1531, 1536 (10th Cir. 1995).

50. *Id.* at 1537–38.

51. Robinson v. Jacksonville Shipyards, Inc., 760 F. Supp. 1486, 1493–1502 (M.D. Fla. 1991).

52. *Id.* at 1523.

53. *See also, e.g.,* Hurley v. Atlantic City Police Dep't, 174 F.3d 95 (3d Cir. 1999); Jenson v. Eveleth Taconite Co., 130 F.3d 1287 (8th Cir. 1997); Christopher Massaro, *The Role of Workplace Culture Evidence in Hostile Workplace Environment Sexual Harassment Litigation: Does Title VII Mean New Management or Just Business as Usual?,* 46 N.Y. L. SCH. L. REV. 349, 359–65 (2002–3) (discussing cases).

54. Succar v. Dade County Sch. Bd., 229 F.3d 1343, 1344 (11th Cir. 2000) (per curiam).

55. *Id.* at 1345 (quoting McCollum v. Bolger, 794 F.2d 602, 610 (11th Cir. 1986)).

56. *Id.*

57. *See* Pipkins v. City of Temple Terrace, Florida, 267 F.3d 1197, 1200 (11th Cir. 2001).

58. 78 F.3d 1164 (7th Cir. 1996). The *Galloway* case has been compared to similar racial harassment cases in Robert J. Gregory, *You Can Call Me a "Bitch" Just Don't Use the "N-Word": Some Thoughts on* Galloway v. General Motors Service Parts Opera-

tions *and* Rogers v. Western Southern Life Insurance Co., 46 DePaul L. Rev. 741 (1997).

59. *Galloway*, 78 F.3d at 1165.

60. *Id.*

61. *Id.* at 1167.

62. *Id.* at 1168.

63. Green v. Adm's of the Tulane Educ. Fund, 284 F.3d 642, 657 (5th Cir. 2002), *as amended on denial of rehearing and rehearing en banc* (April 26, 2002).

64. *See* Catharine MacKinnon, Sexual Harassment of Working Women 1, 55 (1979).

65. *See* John A. Bargh & Paula Raymond, *The Naive Misuse of Power: Nonconscious Sources of Sexual Harassment*, 51 J. Soc. Issues, Spring 1995, at 85; Cathy L.Z. DuBois et al., *An Empirical Examination of Same- and Other-Gender Sexual Harassment in the Workplace*, 39 Sex Roles 731, 733 (1998); John B. Pryor & L.M. Stoller, *Sexual Cognition Processes in Men Who Are High in Likelihood to Sexually Harass*, 20 Personality & Soc. Psychol. Bull. 163 (1994).

66. *See* Pryor & Stoller, *supra* note 65, at 164.

67. *See* MacKinnon, *supra* note 64, at 1–7.

68. *See* Louise F. Fitzgerald & Alayne J. Ormerod, *Breaking Silence: The Sexual Harassment of Women in Academia and the Workplace*, in Psychology of Women: A Handbook of Issues and Theories at 553, 561–63 (Florence L. Denmark & Michele A. Paludi eds., 1993); Frank E. Saal et al., *Friendly or Sexy? It May Depend on Whom You Ask*, 13 Psychol. Women Q. 263, 264–65 (1989); Margaret S. Stockdale, *The Role of Sexual Misperceptions of Women's Friendliness in an Emerging Theory of Sexual Harassment*, 42 J. Vocational Behav. 84, 94–97 (1993).

69. Sandra S. Tangri et al., *Sexual Harassment at Work: Three Explanatory Models*, 38 J. Soc. Issues, Winter 1982, at 33, 40 (citation omitted).

70. *Id.* at 47–49.

71. Stacy DeCoster et al., *Routine Activities and Sexual Harassment in the Workplace*, 26 Work & Occupations 21, 29, 42 (1999).

72. *See* Stockdale, *supra* note 68, at 96.

73. Jennifer L. Berdahl et al., *The Sexual Harassment of Men? Exploring the Concept with Theory and Data*, 20 Psychol. Women Q. 527, 543 (1996).

74. *See id.* at 537.

75. Katherine M. Franke, *What's Wrong with Sexual Harassment?*, 49 Stan. L. Rev. 691, 745 (1997).

76. Margaret S. Stockdale, *The Sexual Harassment of Men: Articulating the Approach-Rejection Theory of Sexual Harassment* at 6, *to be published in* In the Company of Men: Re-Discovering the Links between Sexual Harassment and Male Domination (James E. Gruber & Phoebe Morgan eds., forthcoming) (manuscript on file with author).

77. *Id.* at 10.

78. *Id.* at 11.

79. *Id.*

80. *Id.* at 22.

81. *See id.* (discussing Laura L. Miller, *Not Just Weapons of the Weak: Gender Harassment as a Form of Protest for Army Men*, 60 Soc. Psychol. Q. 32 (1997)).

82. Margaret S. Stockdale et al., *Perceptions of Sexual Harassment of Men*, at 26, *in* Psychol. Men & Masculinities (forthcoming) (manuscript on file with author).

83. *See, e.g.*, Craig R. Waldo et al., *Are Men Sexually Harassed? If so, by Whom?*, 22 Law & Human Behav. 59 (1998); Berdahl, *supra* note 73.

84. *See, e.g.*, Tangri et al., *supra* note 69.

85. *See* Stockdale, *supra* note 76, at 95.

86. *See* Barbara A. Gutek & Bruce Morasch, *Sex-Ratios, Sex-Role Spillover and Sexual Harassment of Women at Work*, 38 J. SOC. ISSUES, Winter 1982, at 55, 57.

87. *Id.*

88. *Id.* at 58.

89. *Id.* at 57. Others have argued that coworkers may not have supervisory power over one another, but they still may have situational or physical power over others. Thus, power might still function as a factor in coworker harassment. *See* Miller, *supra* note 81, at 36–39, 50.

90. Gutek & Morasch, *supra* note 86, at 58.

91. *See id.* at 63. The USMSPB survey findings are consistent with the impact of sex-ratio posited by Gutek and Morasch. That study found that "[v]ictims are more likely than nonvictims to work exclusively or mostly with individuals of the opposite sex." U.S. MERIT SYS. PROT. BD., SEXUAL HARASSMENT IN THE FEDERAL WORKPLACE: TRENDS, PROGRESS, CONTINUING CHALLENGES 17 (1995). *See also* Diana Burgess & Eugene Borgida, *Sexual Harassment: An Experimental Test of Sex-Role Spillover Theory*, 23 PERSONALITY & SOC. PSYCHOL. BULL. 63, 65 (1997).

92. *See* Burgess & Borgida, *supra* note 91, at 73.

93. *Id.* at 64, 68 (citing study that supports this theory); Susan Sheffey & R. Scott Tinsdale, *Perceptions of Sexual Harassment in the Workplace*, 22 J. APPLIED SOC. PSYCHOL. 1502, 1514 (1992) (study of undergraduates that supports this).

94. Eugene Borgida et al., *On the Courtroom Use and Misuse of Gender Stereotyping Research*, 51 J. SOC. ISSUES, Spring 1995, at 181; Kay Deaux, *How Basic Can You Be? The Evolution of Research on Gender Stereotypes*, 51 J. SOC. ISSUES, Spring 1995, at 11, 13; Susan T. Fiske & Peter Glick, *Ambivalence and Stereotypes Cause Sexual Harassment: A Theory with Implications for Organizational Changes*, 51 J. SOC. ISSUES, Spring 1995, at 97.

95. Deaux, *supra* note 94, at 15.

96. Fiske & Glick, *supra* note 94, at 102–3. Others have identified four general stereotypes of women, namely, "sex object, career woman, housewife, and athlete." Kay Deaux & Mary Kite, *Gender Stereotypes, in* PSYCHOLOGY OF WOMEN: A HANDBOOK OF ISSUES AND THEORIES 107, 115 (Florence L. Denmark & Michele A. Paludi, eds. 1993) (citing studies).

97. Fiske & Glick, *supra* note 94, at 103.

98. *Id.* at 106.

99. *Id.* at 105.

100. *Id.* at 103.

101. Gutek & Morasch, *supra* note 86, at 65.

102. Borgida et al., *supra* note 94, at 182. Their fourth point, regarding the lack of individuating information, refers to a phenomenon that occurs when information about an individual in unavailable. In such instances, people will fill gaps by using stereotypes. *Id.* at 183.

103. Susan T. Fiske, *Controlling Other People: The Impact of Power on Stereotyping*, 48 AM. PSYCHOL. 621, 623 (1993).

104. *See* Waldo et al., *supra* note 83, at 61.

105. Stockdale et al., *supra* note 1, at 636.

106. *Id.* at 637.

107. *Id.* at 639.

108. *See id.* at 651, 658 (relying on data from 1995 Department of Defense survey).

109. *See* Katherine K. Baker, *Gender, Genes, and Choice: A Comparative Look at Feminism, Evolution and Economics*, 80 N.C. L. REV. 465, 467, 471–74 (2002); Owen D. Jones, *Realities of Rape: Of Science and Politics, Causes and Meanings*, 86 CORNELL L. REV. 1386, 1391–92 (2001).

110. Michael V. Studd & Urs E. Gattiker, *The Evolutionary Psychology of Sexual Harassment in Organizations*, 12 ETHOLOGY & SOCIOBIOLOGY 249, 286 (1991).

111. KINGSLEY R. BROWNE, BIOLOGY AT WORK: RETHINKING SEXUAL EQUALITY 194–96 (2002).

112. *Id.*

113. Stockdale, *supra* note 68, at 89 (citing Antonia Abbey, *Misperceptions of Friendly Behavior as Sexual Interest: A Survey of Naturally Occurring Incidents*, 11 PSYCHOL. WOMEN Q. 173, 182–84 (1987)).

114. *See* BROWNE, *supra* note 111, at 199–201.

115. *See* Cindy Struckman-Johnson & David Struckman-Johnson, *College Men's and Women's Reactions to Hypothetical Sexual Touch Varied by Initiator Gender and Coercion Level*, 29 SEX ROLES 371, 379–80 (1993) (study of undergraduate student perceptions). *But see* Joshua A. Raines, Same-Sex Sexual Harassment: Factors Affecting the Perception of an Evaluative Third Party/2002/(unpublished master's thesis, Ball State University) (study of undergraduate students found evaluations as sexual harassment more likely in heterosexual than homosexual scenario where harassing incident was ambiguous).

116. *See* BROWNE, *supra* note 111, at 199 (citing Fox v. Sierra Dev. Co., 876 F. Supp. 1169 (D. Nev. 1995)).

117. *See* Hebert, *supra* note 11, at 457 (noting that courts are "receptive" to same-sexual harassment cases where the conduct might be motivated by sexual interest). *But see* Franke, *supra* note 75, at 766–67 (arguing that making such conduct actionable conflicts with her antisubordination theory of sexual harassment).

118. *See* Baker, *supra* note 109, at 489, 494, 513; RUTH BLEIER, SCIENCE AND GENDER: A CRITIQUE OF BIOLOGY AND ITS THEORIES ON WOMEN 115–37 (1984).

119. *See* Baker, *supra* note 109, at 484; Douglas A. Terry, *Don't Forget About Reciprocal Altruism: Critical Review of the Evolutionary Jurisprudence Movement*, 34 CONN. L. REV. 477, 483–84 (2002) (noting that biological tendencies "can be overcome by environmental, cultural, and social factors").

120. *See* Jones, *supra* note 109, at 1398.

121. *See* Terry, *supra* note 119, at 484.

122. *See, e.g.*, Nguyen v. Immigration & Naturalization Serv., 533 U.S. 33 (2001) (justifying an assumption of citizenship for children of American mothers but not American fathers); Michael M. v. Sonoma County Superior Court, 450 U.S. 464 (1981) (justifying application of statutory rape laws only to underage males—but not females—based on differences in biology); Muller v. Oregon, 208 U.S. 412 (1908) (justifying based on biology laws limiting the hours women work); Bradwell v. Illinois, 83 U.S. (16 Wall.) 130 (1873) (prohibiting women from practicing law based on their "nature"); *see generally* DEBORAH L. RHODE, JUSTICE AND GENDER 14, 101–3 (1989); Baker, *supra* note 109, at 515–16.

123. *See* John B. Pryor, *The Social Psychology of Sexual Harassment: Person and Situation Factors Which Give Rise to Sexual Harassment*, *in* SEX AND POWER ISSUES IN THE WORKPLACE 90 (1992).

124. Jackie Krasas Rogers & Kevin D. Hanson, *"Hey, Why Don't You Wear a Shorter Skirt?" Structural Vulnerability and the Organization of Sexual Harassment in Temporary Clerical Employment*, 11 GENDER & SOC'Y 215, 226 (1997).

125. John B. Pryor et al., *A Social Psychological Model for Predicting Sexual Harassment*, 51 J. SOC. ISSUES, Spring 1995, at 69, 73 [hereinafter Pryor, *Model*]; *see also* Eugene Borgida et al., *supra* note 94, at 182–83; Deaux, *supra* note 94, at 15–16; Juanita M. Firestone & Richard J. Harris, *Changes in Patterns of Sexual Harassment in the U.S. Military: A Comparison of the 1988 and 1995 DoD Surveys*, 25 ARMED FORCES & SOC'Y 613, 623 (1999); Fiske & Glick, *supra* note 94, at 110–11; Louise F. Fitzgerald et al., *Why Didn't She Just Report Him? The Psychological and*

Legal Implications of Women's Responses to Sexual Harassment, 51 J. Soc. Issues, Spring 1995, at 117, 127; Audrey J. Murrell et al., *Sexual Harassment and Gender Discrimination: A Longitudinal Study of Women Managers,* 51 J. Soc. Issues, Spring 1995, at 139, 140–41; John B. Pryor et al., *A Social Psychological Analysis of Sexual Harassment: The Person/Situation Interaction,* 42 J. Vocational Behav. 68, 69–73 (1993) [hereinafter Pryor, *Analysis*].

126. They noted that it would be impossible to show cause/effect without manipulating the social norm—a difficult thing to do. *See* Pryor, *Model, supra* note 125, at 74.

127. Deaux, *supra* note 94, at 15–16; *see also* Borgida et al., *supra* note 94, at 183 (citing studies).

128. *See* Fiske & Glick, *supra* note 94, at 111.

129. Laurie A. Rudman & Eugene Borgida, *The Afterglow of Construct Accessibility: The Behavioral Consequences of Priming Men to View Women as Sexual Objects,* 31 J. Experimental Soc. Psychol. 493, 503 (1995).

130. *See id.* at 497, 498–99, 503–4.

131. Doug McKenzie-Mohr & Mark P. Zanna, *Treating Women as Sexual Objects: Look to the (Gender Schematic) Male Who Has Viewed Pornography,* 16 Personality & Soc. Psychol. Bull. 296, 305 (1990).

132. *See id.* at 299, 305. Bem's theory is that "[s]ome persons, termed gender schematic, are believed to have a generalized readiness to process information on the basis of sex-linked categories and will use this dimension in preference to all other possible bases of categorization." Deaux & Kite, *supra* note 96, at 119.

133. *See* Pryor, *Model, supra* note 125, at 70 ("Potential harassers may perceive that they are free to harass if management tolerates or condones such behavior"); Pryor, *supra* note 123, at 91 (describing study he conducted in 1991 that revealed that female employees' ratings of managers' attitudes toward sexual harassment correlated with the incidence of certain types of sexual harassment on the job).

134. For an example of this in a real case, see Burns v. McGregor Elec. Indus., 989 F.2d 959 (8th Cir. 1993).

135. Pryor, *Model, supra* note 125, at 79. In that study, college students were asked to train a female to use a word processing program. They were "trained" by observing a graduate student who engaged in harassing conduct, e.g., flirting, touching the woman's hair and shoulders, and leering at her. Those men with high LSH (likely to sexually harass) engaged in more sexually harassing conduct than low LSH men. *See id.* Interestingly, men with high LSH who observed a more professional role model, i.e., one who did not engage in any sexually harassment conduct, did not engage in such behaviors. "Thus, individual predispositions to sexually harass were acted upon only when the local social norms permitted." *Id.*

136. *See* James M. Wilkerson, *The Impact of Job Level and Prior Training on Sexual Harassment Labeling and Remedy Choice,* 29 J. Applied Soc. Psychol. 1605, 1606–7 (1999).

137. Barbara A. Gutek et al., *Predicting Social-Sexual Behavior at Work: A Contact Hypothesis,* 33 Acad. of Mgmt. J. 560, 565 (1990).

138. *See* Wilkerson, *supra* note 136, at 1607.

139. Pryor, *Model, supra* note 125, at 72.

140. *Id.* at 73.

141. *Id.* (emphasis in original).

142. Murrell et al., *supra* note 125, at 141 (citing Barbara A. Gutek & Aaron Groff Cohen, *Sex Ratios, Sex Role Spillover, and Sex at Work: A Comparison of Men's and Women's Experiences,* 40 Human Relations 97 (1987)); *see also* Gutek & Morasch, *supra* note 86, at 70–71 (noting in their study that none of the women in integrated work environments responded that sexual harassment was a "major problem at work").

143. James F. Gruber, *The Impact of Male Work Environments and Organizational*

Policies on Women's Experiences of Sexual Harassment, 12 GENDER & SOC'Y 301, 302, 311–12 (1998) (citing studies; this study as well shows the same). Gruber found that having a predominantly male work environment was a "significant predictor" of harassment in the form of physical threats or sexual materials. *Id.* at 314. However, for other forms of harassing behaviors frequency of contact with men, rather than actual gender composition of the workplace, was a better predictor of the incidence of workplace harassment. *See id.* at 312.

144. USMSPB, *supra* note 91, at 17.

145. *See* John B. Pryor, *Sexual Harassment Proclivities in Men*, 17 SEX ROLES 269 (1987); *see also* Pryor, *Model, supra* note 125, at 70.

146. Pryor, *supra* note 145; *see also* Pryor, *Model, supra* note 125, at 74.

147. *See* Pryor, *Effects, supra* note 125, at 74–75. This tends to support the theory that sexual harassment is about power, rather than sex.

148. *See* Pryor, *Model, supra* note 125, at 75 (citing numerous studies).

149. *Id.* at 76.

150. *Id.* at 76. There was no correlation between a "Love and Affection" scale developed by Nelson and LSH, which suggests this conclusion. *See id.*

151. *Id.* at 78.

152. *See id.*

153. *See* Bargh & Raymond, *supra* note 65.

154. *See* Denise M. Driscoll et al., *Can Perceivers Identify Likelihood to Sexually Harass?*, 38 SEX ROLES 557, 559 (1998) (citing unpublished study by A. Barak & N. Kaplan, *Relationships Between Men's Admitted Sexual Harassment Behaviors and Personal Characteristics* (1996)).

155. *See, e.g.*, Rudman & Borgida, *supra* note 129.

156. *See* Pryor, *Analysis, supra* note 125, at 77 (citing Christine LaVite, The Interaction between Situational Factors and Individual Predispositions in the Likelihood to Sexually Harass (1991) (unpublished master's thesis, Illinois State University)). LaVite also found that when the role model was a nonharasser, low LSH men touched the trainee more often than high LSH men. *See id.* (55% of low LSH versus 22% of high LSH).

157. *See* Pryor & Stoller, *supra* note 65, at 168.

158. *See* Rudman & Borgida, *supra* note 129.

159. Louise F. Fitzgerald et al., *Antecedents and Consequences of Sexual Harassment in Organizations: A Test of an Integrated Model*, 82 J. APPLIED PSYCHOL. 578, 578–79 (1997).

160. *Id.* at 580–81.

161. *Id.* at 586–88.

162. Matthew S. Hesson-McInnis & Louise F. Fitzgerald, *Sexual Harassment: A Preliminary Test of an Integrative Model*, 27 J. APPLIED SOC. PSYCH. 877, 882 tbl. 1 (1997).

163. *Id.* at 895.

164. *Id.* They specifically cite the work of Studd and Gattiker discussed earlier in this chapter.

165. *See* Kathryn Abrams, *The New Jurisprudence of Sexual Harassment*, 83 CORNELL L. REV. 1169 (1998); Franke, *supra* note 75; Schultz, *supra* note 8.

166. *See, e.g.*, Schwartz, *supra* note 11.

167. *See, e.g.*, Helen Lafferty, *Is Sexual Harassment Sex Discrimination? Still an Open Question*, BUFF. WOMEN'S L.J. 21 (1999); Ellen Frankel Paul, *Sexual Harassment as Sex Discrimination: A Defective Paradigm*, 8 YALE L. & POL'Y REV. 333 (1990).

168. *See* Schwartz, *supra* note 11, at 1769–72 (criticizing Schultz, Franke, and Abrams for not coming up with practical solutions in light of the statute's text).

169. *See* Foote & Goodman-Delahunty, *supra* note 1, at 124, 127–28; Stockdale et al., *supra* note 1, at 632–33.
170. *See* Stockdale, *supra* note 76.
171. *See* Foote & Goodman-Delahunty, *supra* note 1, at 129 (citing study).
172. Linda Hamilton Krieger, *The Content of Our Categories: A Cognitive Bias Approach to Discrimination and Equal Employment Opportunity*, 47 Stan. L. Rev. 1161, 1174 (1995).
173. *See* Schwartz, *supra* note 11, at 1748–58.
174. Johnson v. Hondo, Inc., 125 F.3d 408, 410–11 (7th Cir. 1997).
175. Vicki Schultz, *The Sanitized Workplace*, 112 Yale L.J. 2061, 2064 (2003).
176. Axam & Zalesne, *supra* note 3, at 192.
177. *See* Case, *supra* note 3, at 33.
178. *See* Schultz, *supra* note 175.
179. Studies indicate that it may be impossible to avoid all sexual expression in the workplace even if it were desirable to do so. *See* Sharon A. Lobel, *Sexuality at Work: Where Do We Go from Here?*, 42 J. Vocational Behav. 136 (1993).
180. Brown v. Henderson, 257 F.3d 246, 253–54 (2d Cir. 2001).
181. Ocheltree v. Scollon Prods., Inc., 308 F.3d 351, 378 (4th Cir. 2002), *aff'd in part, rev'd in part*, 335 F.3d 325 (4th Cir. 2003) (en banc) (Michael, J., dissenting in part and concurring in judgment in part).
182. Galloway v. Gen. Motors Serv. Parts Operations, 78 F.3d 1164, 1167 (7th Cir. 1996).
183. Deaux & Kite, *supra* note 96, at 130 (citations omitted).
184. *See* Schultz, *supra* note 175, at 2192.
185. *See generally* Susan Bisom-Rapp, *Bulletproofing the Workplace: Symbol and Substance in Employment Discrimination Law*, 26 Fla. St. U. L. Rev. 959 (1999).
186. Fiske & Glick, *supra* note 94, at 110. Sex segregation still persists in many jobs throughout American businesses. *See* Thomas L. Steiger & Mark Wardell, *Gender and Employment in the Service Sector*, 42 Soc. Probs. 91, 93 (1995) (studies cited).
187. Fiske & Glick, *supra* note 94, at 110.
188. *Id.* at 111. Studies show that simply hiring one woman is not enough. Such a person is seen as a "token," and is imbued with every stereotype of the group she represents. As Fiske & Glick point out, "the solution to solo structures [tokenism] is to achieve a critical mass of 20% or more, and not fewer than two individuals." *Id. See also* Theresa M. Beiner, *Do Reindeer Games Count as Terms, Conditions or Privileges of Employment under Title VII*, 37 B.C. L. Rev. 643, 652 & n.48 (1996); Nadine Taub, *Keeping Women in Their Place: Stereotyping Per Se as a Form of Employment Discrimination*, 21 B.C. L. Rev. 345, 358–59 (1980).
189. By "affirmative action stereotyping," I (and Fiske and Glick) refer to the supposition that someone who is a nontraditional hire, for example, a female into an all-male work area, is being hired based not on her qualifications but instead on her status as "female"—for diversity purposes.
190. Fiske & Glick, *supra* note 94, at 112.

Notes to Chapter 5

1. *See, e.g.*, Fenton v. Hisan, Inc., 174 F.3d 827, 829–30 (6th Cir. 1999); Carter v. Chrysler Corp., 173 F.3d 693, 700 (8th Cir. 1999) (racial harassment context); Baty v. Willamette Indus., Inc., 172 F.3d 1232, 1241–42 (10th Cir. 1999); Burrell v. Star Nursery, Inc., 170 F.3d 951, 955 (9th Cir. 1999).
2. *See* Faragher v. City of Boca Raton, 524 U.S. 775 (1998); Burlington Indus., Inc. v. Ellerth, 524 U.S. 742, 759, 760–61 (1998).

3. Meritor Savings Bank v. Vinson, 477 U.S. 57, 72 (1986).

4. *Id.*

5. *See Faragher*, 524 U.S. at 785 (acknowledging the lower courts' difficulties); *see* David Benjamin Oppenheimer, *Exacerbating the Exasperating: Title VII Liability of Employers for Sexual Harassment Committed by Their Supervisors*, 81 CORNELL L. REV. 66 (1995); J. Hoult Verkerke, *Notice Liability in Employment Discrimination Law*, 81 VA. L. REV. 273 (1995).

6. *Faragher*, 524 U.S. at 804.

7. *Id.* at 807; *Ellerth*, 524 U.S. at 765.

8. *See Faragher*, 524 U.S. at 808; *Ellerth*, 524 U.S. at 765.

9. *Faragher*, 524 U.S. at 797–99.

10. *Id.* at 798, 807.

11. *See, e.g.*, Robinson v. City of Pittsburgh, 120 F.3d 1286, 1297 (3d Cir. 1997); Jansen v. Packaging Corp. of Am., 123 F.3d 490 (7th Cir. 1997); Savino v. C.P. Hall. Co., 988 F. Supp. 1171, 1181–83 (N.D. Ill. 1997). *But see* Gary v. Long, 59 F.3d 1391, 1396 (D.C. Cir. 1995) (threats that were not carried out were not actionable as quid pro quo harassment).

12. *See* Pennsylvania State Police v. Suders, 124 S. Ct. 2342 (2004).

13. *See Ellerth*, 524 U.S. at 753–54, 764–65 (acknowledging that holding is the same); *see also id.* at 766 (Ginsburg, J., concurring in judgment) (noting that the standard adopted in *Ellerth* was "substantively identical" to that of *Faragher*).

14. *Id.* at 765.

15. *Id.*

16. Watkins v. Prof'l Sec. Bureau, Ltd., 201 F.3d 439 (table), 1999 WL 1032614 at **4 (4th Cir. 1999) (per curiam) (quoting Brown v. Perry, 184 F.3d 388, 396 (4th Cir. 1999) (internal quotations omitted)). *See also* Caridad v. Metro-North Commuter R.R., 191 F.3d 283, 295 (2d Cir. 1999) (existence of policy and employer's endeavors to investigate and remedy problems reported by employees sufficient); Shaw v. AutoZone, Inc., 180 F.3d 806, 811 (7th Cir. 1999) ("the existence of an appropriate anti-harassment policy will often satisfy this first prong").

17. *See* Joanna L. Grossman, *The Culture of Compliance: The Final Triumph of Form over Substance in Sexual Harassment Law*, 26 HARV. WOMEN'S L.J. 3, 9–14 (2003) (describing cases).

18. *Caridad*, 191 F.3d at 295. *See also* Savino v. C.P. Hall Co., 199 F.3d 925, 929, 933–34 (7th Cir. 1999) (defendant still may take advantage of defense even though corrective measures, "a stern warning," did not end harassment).

19. *Watkins*, 1999 WL 1032614, at **5 (quoting *Ellerth*, 118 S. Ct. at 2270).

20. *Id.* at **1.

21. *Caridad*, 191 F.3d at 290.

22. 199 F.3d at 933. As the court explained, "unreasonable foot-dragging will result in at least a practical reduction in damages, and may completely foreclose liability." *Id.* at 935. The court also held that the employer took prompt remedial action once it learned of the harassment. *Id.*

23. 191 F.3d at 295. *See also* Shaw v. Autozone, Inc., 180 F.3d 806, 813 (7th Cir. 1999) (plaintiff's excuse for not reporting that she did not feel "comfortable enough" with anyone at the employer to discuss the harassment with them was not reasonable).

24. 191 F.3d at 290.

25. *Id.*

26. This "less severe" incident included a supervisor's fondling her breasts and putting his hands down her pants as she was changing clothes in the uniform room. Watkins v. Prof'l Sec. Bureau, Ltd., 201 F.3d 439 (tbl.), 1999 WL 1032614, at **1 (4th Cir. 1999).

27. *Shaw*, 180 F.3d at 813.

28. 1999 WL 1032614 at **5 n.15. Interestingly enough, that is not what the actual jury found in this case. Instead, it had ruled in favor of Watkins on her hostile environment claim and awarded her $63,000 in damages. The district court refused to submit the issue of punitive damages to the jury. *Id.* at **2. The district court ultimately granted a motion for judgment as a matter of law or in the alternative a new trial on the hostile environment claim. *Id. See also Shaw*, 180 F.3d at 811 (because plaintiff had signed acknowledgment that stated, "I understand it is my responsibility to read and learn the policies and procedures contained in the AutoZone Handbook and Safety Booklet," which contained antiharassment policy, court held that plaintiff had "constructive knowledge" of such policy).

29. 184 F.3d 388, 397 (4th Cir. 1999).

30. *Shaw*, 180 F.3d at 813 (quoting Parkins v. Civil Constructors of Illinois, Inc., 163 F.3d 1027, 1038 (7th Cir. 1998) (quoting Perry v. Harris Chernin, Inc., 126 F.3d 1010, 1014 (7th Cir. 1997))).

31. *Brown*, 184 F.3d at 396. *But see* Distasio v. Perkin Elmer Corp., 157 F.3d 55, 64 (2d Cir. 1998) (employer may be held accountable for knowledge of harassment where employee with duty to report it to employer pursuant to company policy possessed knowledge of the harassment).

32. 1999 WL 1032614 at **5 (citations omitted).

33. *See* Equal Employment Opportunity Comm'n, Enforcement Guidance: Vicarious Employer Liability for Unlawful Harassment by Supervisors 13–14 (1999).

34. 170 F.3d 505, 510–11 (5th Cir. 1999).

35. *See* 199 F.3d 925, 929 (7th Cir. 1999). *See also* Caridad v. Metro-North Commuter R.R., 191 F.3d 283, 296 (2d Cir. 1999) (summary judgment granted on affirmative defense); *Watkins*, 1999 WL 1032614, at **5 (judgment as a matter of law upheld based on defense); *Brown*, 184 F.3d at 397–98 (summary judgment on affirmative defense affirmed).

36. *See, e.g.*, Douglas D. Baker et al., *The Influence of Individual Characteristics and Severity of Harassing Behavior on Reactions to Sexual Harassment*, 22 Sex Roles 305, 313 tbl. I (1990) (study of undergraduate students showed 98% perceived proposition tied to job threat or enhancement as harassment); Bonnie S. Dansky et al., *Sexual Harassment: I Can't Define It but I Know It When I See It*, at tbl. 1 (1992) (paper presented at annual meeting of American Psychological Association, Washington, D.C.; on file with the author) (1989 national study of 4,009 women; 85.8% of those who experience proposition tied to job threat found it harassing; 83.0% of women experiencing proposition tied to job enhancement found it harassing); Alison M. Konrad & Barbara A. Gutek, *Impact of Work Experiences on Attitudes toward Sexual Harassment*, 31 Admin. Sci. Q. 422, 429 tbl.1 (1986) (1980 telephone survey of more than 1,200 working men and women in the Los Angeles area: 94.5% of men and 98% of women perceived request for sexual relations accompanied by job threat for not complying as sexual harassment; 91.9% of men and 95.8% of women perceived request for date accompanied by job threat for not complying as sexual harassment); David E. Terpstra & Douglas D. Baker, *A Hierarchy of Sexual Harassment*, 121 J. Psychology 599, 602 (1987) (99% agreed proposition tied to job threat sexually harassing; 98% agreed proposition tied to job enhancement was sexually harassing). *See generally* Louise F. Fitzgerald & Alayne J. Ormerod, *Breaking the Silence: The Sexual Harassment of Women in Academia and the Workplace, in* Psychology of Women 553, 559–60 (Florence L. Denmark & Michele A. Paludi eds., 1993) (recounting studies).

37. Elissa L. Perry et al., *Individual Differences in the Effectiveness of Sexual Harassment Awareness Training*, 28 J. Applied Soc. Psychol. 698, 699 (1998). *See also* Robert S. Moyer & Anjan Nath, *Some Effects of Brief Training Interventions on Perceptions of Sexual Harassment*, 28 J. Applied Soc. Psychol. 333, 334 (1998).

38. Susan Bisom-Rapp, *An Ounce of Prevention Is a Poor Substitute for a Pound of Cure: Confronting the Developing Jurisprudence of Education and Prevention in Employment Discrimination Law*, 22 BERKELEY J. EMPLOYMENT & LAB. L. 1, 44–47 (2001).

39. Perry et al., *supra* note 37, at 716.

40. *Id.* at 716. Perry et al. suggest that more experience-based teaching methods, such as role playing and group discussion would be more effective.

41. *See* Moyer & Nath, *supra* note 37, at 344. *See also* James M. Wilkerson, *The Impact of Job Level and Prior Training on Sexual Harassment Labeling and Remedy Choice*, 29 J. APPLIED SOC. PSYCHOL. 1605, 1611–12, 1617 (1999) (In a study of managers of a janitorial business, prior sexual harassment training did not correlate with managers labeling "weaker" factual scenario as sexual harassment more than those who did not receive training. They did, however, identify sexual harassment more frequently in a strong sexual harassment scenario. Trained employees also endorsed directly confronting the harasser and formal complaint remedies more than untrained managers did in the "weaker" factual scenario.).

42. *See* Moyer & Nath, *supra* note 37, at 341 (84 participants; 42 subjects and controls).

43. Bisom-Rapp, *supra* note 38, at 44–47.

44. *Id.*

45. *See, e.g.*, James E. Gruber, *The Sexual Harassment Experiences of Women in Nontraditional Jobs: Results from Cross-National Research*, in SEX AND POWER ISSUES IN THE WORKPLACE 123 (1992); Wendy Pollack, *Expanding the Legal Definition of Sexual Harassment*, in SEX AND POWER ISSUES IN THE WORKPLACE 143, 146–47 (1992) (describing the difference between harassment experienced by women in traditional female jobs and those in traditional male jobs).

46. *See* Gerald L. Blakely et al., *The Effects of Training on Perceptions of Sexual Harassment Allegations*, 28 J. APPLIED SOC. PSYCHOL. 71, 73, 77 (1998) (male students who had not seen a sexual harassment training video "rated the ambiguous sexually oriented work behaviors as significantly less harassing" than those who did).

47. Grossman, *supra* note 17, at 49.

48. Lauren B. Edelman et al., *The Endogeneity of Legal Regulation: Grievance Procedures as Rational Myth*, 105 AM. J. SOCIOLOGY 406 (1999); *see also* Bisom-Rapp, *supra* note 38, at 14.

49. *See* James F. Gruber, *The Impact of Male Work Environments and Organizational Policies on Women's Experiences of Sexual Harassment*, 12 GENDER & SOC'Y 301, 304 (1998) (citing study by J. Gruber & M. Smith, *Women's Responses to Sexual Harassment: A Multivariate Analysis*, 17 BASIC & APPLIED SOC. PSYCHOL. 543 (1995)).

50. *Id.* at 312 (describing "proactive" methods).

51. *Id.* at 314. Sexual categorical remarks refer to remarks made about other women—not the target. *Id.* at 308.

52. *See id.* at 316.

53. *See* Louise F. Fitzgerald, *Examining (and Eliminating) the Consequences of Sexual Harassment: An Integrated Model*, in SEX AND POWER ISSUES IN THE WORKPLACE at 61, 63 (1992); Rebecca A. Thacker, *A Descriptive Study of Situational and Individual Influences upon Individuals' Response to Sexual Harassment*, 49 HUM. REL. 1105, 1106 (1996); Rebecca A. Thacker & Stephan F. Gohmann, *Emotional and Psychological Consequences of Sexual Harassment: A Descriptive Study*, 30 J. PSYCHOLOGY 429, 429–30 (1996).

54. *See* Thacker, *supra* note 53, at 1106–7. It certainly seems logical that a target of harassment would have more to fear in reporting harassment by a supervisor than in reporting harassment by a coworker.

55. *See* Barbara A. Gutek & Mary P. Koss, *Changed Women and Changed Organi-*

zations: Consequences of and Coping with Sexual Harassment, 42 J. VOCATIONAL BEHAV. 28, 36 (1993).

56. *See* Grossman, *supra* note 17, at 57–64.

57. AM. PSYCHIATRIC ASS'N, DIAGNOSTIC AND STATISTICAL MANUAL OF MENTAL DISORDERS 424 (4th ed. 1994) [hereinafter DSM-IV].

58. *See* Jessica Wolfe et al., *Sexual Harassment and Assault as Predictors of PTSD Symptomatology among U.S. Female Persian Gulf War Military Personnel*, 13 J. INTERPERSONAL VIOLENCE 40, 54 (1998) (study of female Gulf War veterans the results of which "suggest that the frequency of less severe events (i.e., physical sexual harassment) has the greatest impact on women who also experience more severe forms of sexual victimization"). Prior exposure to traumatic events that create PTSD is high among women in the United States. *See* Ronald C. Kessler, *Posttraumatic Stress Disorder; The Burden to the Individual and to Society*, 61 J. CLINICAL PSYCHIATRY 4, 6 (2000) (studies have shown a range of 7.8% to 12.3% (study of women) of the U.S. population have experienced PTSD under the DSM-III standard).

59. *See* Edgar Garcia-Rill & Erica Beecher-Monas, *Gatekeeping Stress: The Science and Admissibility of Post-traumatic Stress Disorder*, 24 U. ARK. LITTLE ROCK L. REV. 9, 17 (2001) (citing studies).

60. *See, e.g.*, Baty v. Willamette Indus., Inc., 172 F.3d 1232, 1240 (10th Cir. 1999); Gotthardt v. Nat'l R.R. Passenger Corp., 191 F.3d 1148, 1152 (9th Cir. 1999); Reinhold v. Virginia, 135 F.3d 920, 928 (4th Cir. 1998), *vacated on reh'g*, 151 F.3d 172 (4th Cir. 1998); Nichols v. Frank, 42 F.3d 503, 507 (9th Cir. 1994); Townsend v. Ind. Univ., 995 F.2d 691, 692 (7th Cir. 1993).

61. DSM-IV, *supra* note 57.

62. *Id.* at 424. PTSD also can be experienced in response to other forms of stress. However, this seems to be the scenario likely experienced by sexual harassment victims.

63. *Id.* at 424–25.

64. Watkins v Prof'l Sec. Bureau, Ltd., 201 F.3d 439 (table), 1999 WL 1032614, at **5 (4th Cir. 1999).

65. *See, e.g.*, Lisa Bloom, *Gretel Fights Back: Representing Sexual Harassment Plaintiffs Who Were Sexually Abused as Children*, 12 BERK. WOMEN'S L.J. 1 (1997); Kent D. Streseman, *Headshrinkers, Manmunchers, Moneygrubbers, Nuts & Sluts: Reexamining Compelled Mental Examinations in Sexual Harassment Actions under the Civil Rights Act of 1991*, 80 CORNELL L. REV. 1268 (1995).

66. *See* Margaret S. Stockdale et al., *Acknowledging Sexual Harassment: A Test of Alternative Models*, 17 BASIC & APPLIED SOC. PSYCHOL. 469, 493 (1995).

67. Louise F. Fitzgerald et al., *The Incidence of Sexual Harassment in Academia and the Workplace*, 32 J. VOCATIONAL BEHAV. 152, 171 (1988). *See also* Caroline C. Cochran et al., *Predictors of Responses to Unwanted Sexual Attention*, 21 PSYCHOL. WOMEN Q. 207, 217 (1997) (study of university faculty, students, and staff that showed 37% did not report harassing conduct because they did not know it was harassment); Kimberly T. Schneider et al., *Job-Related and Psychological Effects of Sexual Harassment in the Workplace: Empirical Evidence from Two Organizations*, 82 J. APPLIED PSYCHOL. 401, 406–7 (1997) (findings similar in a study of employees of northwestern employer and midwestern university).

68. Louise H. Kidder et al., *Recalling Harassment, Reconstructing Experience*, 51 J. SOC. ISSUES, Spring 1995, at 53, 56, 62.

69. Louise F. Fitzgerald et al., *Why Didn't She Just Report Him? The Psychological and Legal Implications of Women's Responses to Sexual Harassment*, 51 J. SOC. ISSUES, Spring 1995, at 117, 122 (citing study by James E. Gruber & Lars Bjorn, *Women's Responses to Sexual Harassment: An Analysis of Socio-Cultural Organizational, and Personal Resource Models*, 67 SOC. SCIENCE Q. 814 (1986)).

70. *Id.* at 121 (citing Ellen J. Wagner, SEXUAL HARASSMENT IN THE WORKPLACE:

HOW TO PREVENT, INVESTIGATE AND RESOLVE COMPLAINTS IN YOUR ORGANIZATION (1992)).

71. *See* Stephanie Riger, *Gender Dilemmas in Sexual Harassment Policies and Procedures*, in SEX AND POWER ISSUES IN THE WORKPLACE 43, 44 (1992).

72. *See* Stockdale et al., *supra* note 66, at 493.

73. *See id.* at 492.

74. *See* Cochran et al., *supra* note 67, at 223.

75. *See* Barbara A. Gutek & Bruce Morasch, *Sex-Rations, Sex-Role Spillover and Sexual Harassment of Women at Work*, 38 J. SOC. ISSUES, Winter 1982, at 55, 71.

76. *See* Ingebjorg S. Folgero & Ingrid H. Fjeldstad, *On Duty–Off Guard: Cultural Norms and Sexual Harassment in Service Organizations*, 16 ORG. STUD. 299, 311 (1995) ("[I]n a cultural setting where sexual harassment is generally accepted as part of the job, feelings of harassment may be suppressed to a degree where the victim actively denies that the problem exists."); Sandy Welsh, *Gender and Sexual Harassment*, 25 ANN. REV. SOC. 169, 174–75 (1999) (recounting a variety of studies suggesting this phenomenon).

77. *See* Patti A. Giuffre & Christine L. Williams, *Boundary Lines: Labeling Sexual Harassment in Restaurants*, 8 GENDER & SOCIETY 378, 397 (1994).

78. *See id.* at 384, 389–96.

79. *See* Fitzgerald et al., *supra* note 69, at 119.

80. *See id.*

81. *Id.* at 122 (citing studies by Gutek & Koss, *supra* note 55; M. Martindale, *Sexual Harassment in the Military: 1988*, Defense Manpower Data Center (1990); U.S. MERIT SYS. PROT. BD., SEXUAL HARASSMENT OF FEDERAL WORKERS: IS IT A PROBLEM? (1981); BARBARA A. GUTEK, SEX AND THE WORKPLACE (1985); Inger Jensen & Barbara A. Gutek, *Attributions and Assignment of Responsibility for Sexual Harassment*, 38 J. SOC. ISSUES, Winter 1982, at 121; James E. Gruber & Lars Bjorn, *Blue-Collar Blues: The Sexual Harassment of Women Autoworkers*, 9 WORK & OCCUPATIONS 271 (1982); C. M. PHILLIPS ET AL., THE RISKS OF GOING TO WORK (1989); B.E. Saunders, *Sexual Harassment of Women in the Workplace: Results from the National Women's Study*, presented at 8th Annual NC/SC labor Law Seminar, Ashville, NC (1992); U.S. MERIT SYS. PROT. BD., SEXUAL HARASSMENT IN THE FEDERAL WORKPLACE: AN UPDATE (1988)).

82. James E. Gruber, *How Women Handle Sexual Harassment: A Literature Review*, 74 SOC. SCI. RES. 3, 4 (1989).

83. *See* U.S. MERIT SYS. PROT. BD., SEXUAL HARASSMENT IN THE FEDERAL WORKPLACE: TRENDS, PROGRESS, CONTINUING CHALLENGES viii (1995) (87% of federal supervisors and 77% of nonsupervisory employees were trained in sexual harassment; 78% of employees reported knowing the channels to follow in order to report harassment; 92% of federal employees surveyed were aware that there was a sexual harassment policy).

84. *Id.* at 35. This table is essentially reproduced from the United States Merit Systems Protection Board Report.

85. *See* Inger W. Jensen & Barbara A. Gutek, *Attributions and Assignment of Responsibility in Sexual Harassment*, 38 J. SOC. ISSUES, Winter 1982, at 121, 127, 128, 132.

86. USMSPB, *supra* note 83, at 35.

87. Matthew S. Hesson-McInnis & Louise F. Fitzgerald, *Sexual Harassment: A Preliminary Test of an Integrative Model*, 27 J. APPLIED SOC. PSYCHOL. 877, 896 (2002).

88. *Id.*

89. *Id.*

90. Fitzgerald et al., *supra* note 69, at 126 (citing and describing Alayne J. Ormerod, The Effect of Self-Efficacy and Outcome Expectations on Responses to Sexual Harass-

ment (1991) (unpub. master's equivalency thesis, Dep't of Educ. Psychol., University of Illinois, Champaign)).

91. *Id.* (citing and describing Ormerod, *supra* note 90; *see also* Gutek & Koss, *supra* note 55, at 34 (citing study indicating that among a group of 488 women who had been sexually harassed, 57% "thought their career would be hurt if they complained about the harassment")); Fitzgerald et al., *supra* note 69, at 126.

92. Gutek & Koss, *supra* note 55, at 30.

93. Audrey Murrell et al., *Sexual Harassment and Gender Discrimination: A Longitudinal Study of Women Managers*, 51 J. Soc. Issues, Spring 1995, at 139, 141 (citations omitted).

94. *See* Gutek & Koss, *supra* note 55, at 31–32.

95. Frances S. Coles, *Forced to Quit: Sexual Harassment Complaints and Agency Response*, 14 Sex Roles 81 (1986). *But see* Gutek & Koss, *supra* note 55 (noting the percentage of women who quit, transfer, or are fired at 10% for those sexually harassed).

96. *See* Coles, *supra* note 95, at 133.

97. USMSPB, *supra* note 83, at 23, 26. These numbers have gone down in most categories since the government's 1987 study, with the exception of decreased productivity, which has risen from 14 percent to 21 percent. *See id. See* Gutek & Koss, *supra* note 55, at 34 (citing study).

98. Mindy E. Bergman et al., *The (Un)reasonableness of Reporting: Antecedents and Consequences of Reporting Sexual Harassment*, 87 J. Applied Psych. 230, 232 (2002).

99. *Id.*

100. *Id.* at 237.

101. *Id.* at 237.

102. *Id.* at 241.

103. Holly D. v. California Inst. of Tech., 339 F.3d 1158, 1162 (9th Cir. 2003).

104. Jin v. Metro Life Ins. Co., 310 F.3d 84, 94 (2d Cir. 2002).

105. In Hurley v. Atlantic City Police Dep't, 174 F.3d 95 (3d Cir. 1998), the third circuit approved admission of such evidence by the plaintiff in spite of a challenge under Federal Rules of Evidence 401 and 403. Evidence of sexual harassment of other female police officers as well as evidence of comments made between only male officers was held admissible in part to determine whether the sexual harassment policy was effective. *Id.* at 111. The plaintiff was unaware of the statements of the male officers admitted as well as of the other women harassed until discovery in the case.

106. *See* Martha S. West, *Preventing Sexual Harassment: The Federal Courts' Wake-Up Call for Women*, 68 Brook. L. Rev. 457, 505, 519–22 (2002).

107. *See* Faragher v. City of Boca Raton, 524 U.S. 775, 807 (1998).

108. *See* Theresa M. Beiner & John M.A. DiPippa, *Hostile Environments and the Religious Employee*, 19 U. Ark. Little Rock L.J. 571, 631–32 (1997) (discussing debate and citing sources). For examples from the case law, see, e.g., Orthodox Presbyterian Church v. Florio, 902 F. Supp. 492 (D.N.J. 1995) (constitutionality of New Jersey statute), *aff'd on other grounds*, 1996 WL 617418 (3d Cir. 1996); Tindle v. Caudell, 56 F.3d 966, 971 (8th Cir. 1995); Jenson v. Eveleth Taconite Co., 824 F. Supp. 847, 884 n.89 (D. Minn. 1993); Robinson v. Jacksonville Shipyards, 760 F. Supp. 1486 (M.D. Fla. 1991); Aguilar v. Avis Rent A Car Sys., 21 Cal. 4th 121 (Cal. 1999) (holding that a remedial injunction prohibiting the use of racial epithets in the workplace does not violate the First Amendment). *But see* DeAngelis v. El Paso Officers Ass'n, 51 F.3d 591, 596–97 (5th Cir. 1995), *cert. denied*, 116 S. Ct. 473 (1995) (acknowledging potential First Amendment problems); Johnson v. Los Angeles County Fire Dept., 865 F. Supp. 1430 (C.D. Cal. 1994) (reading of *Playboy* in private at workplace protected by First Amendment).

109. R.A.V. v. St. Paul, 505 U.S. 377, 389 (1992) (fighting words); Jules B. Gerard,

The First Amendment in Hostile Environment: A Primer on Free Speech Sexual Harassment, 68 NOTRE DAME L. REV. 1003, 1006–7, 1015–16 (1993) (discussing fighting words); David Benjamin Oppenheimer, *Workplace Harassment and the First Amendment: A Reply to Professor Volokh*, 17 BERKELEY J. EMPLOY. & LAB. L. 321, 322–25 (1996) (arguing that harassment often constitutes fighting words, is directed at a captive audience, or constitutes a tort).

110. *See* Kingsley R. Browne, *Title VII as Censorship: Hostile-Environment Harassment and the First Amendment*, 52 OHIO ST. L.J. 481, 483–84, 513–31 (1991) (admitting that "with only one apparent exception no reported harassment decision has imposed liability solely on the basis of arguably protected expression"; detailing other First Amendment exceptions potentially applicable here) (citation omitted).

111. 760 F. Supp. 1486, 1534–36 (M.D. Fla. 1991).

112. *See* Beiner & DiPippa, *supra* note 108, at 631, 632 (directed speech); Eugene Volokh, *Comment, Freedom of Speech and Workplace Harassment*, 39 UCLA L. REV. (1992) (directed speech).

113. *See* Cynthia L. Estlund, *The Architecture of the First Amendment and the Case of Workplace Harassment*, 72 NOTRE DAME L. REV. 1361, 1381 (1997) (suggesting new category of unprotected speech); Mari J. Matsuda, *Public Response to Racist Speech: Considering the Victim's Story*, 87 MICH. L. REV. 2320 (1989) (same).

114. However, the EEOC suggests another possible way out for employees faced with this defense using the second prong. If the employee has complained and the harassment continues, the EEOC has suggested that the employer will be unable to show that the employee failed to avoid harm otherwise, an aspect of the second prong of the defense.

115. *See, e.g.*, Brown v. Perry, 184 F.3d 288, 297 (4th Cir. 1999).

116. U.S.C. §1981a(b)(1) (2003). These damages are capped, depending on the size of the employer. *See id.* at §1981a(b)(3).

117. *See* EEOC v. Shell Oil Co., 466 U.S. 54, 77–78 (1984) (describing encouraging voluntary compliance as a latent objective, whereas the "more general objective" was to "root out discrimination in employment").

118. *See* McKennon v. Nashville Banner Publ'g Co., 513 U.S. 879, 883 (1995).

119. Burlington Indus., Inc. v. Ellerth, 524 U.S. 742, 764 (1998).

120. Faragher v. Boca Raton, 524 U.S. 775, 805–6 (1998) (quoting Albemarle Paper Co. v. Moody, 422 U.S. 405, 418 (1975)).

121. *McKennon*, 513 U.S. at 884 (ADEA context).

122. *See, e.g.*, EIGHTH CIRCUIT GENDER FAIRNESS TASK FORCE, FINAL REPORT AND RECOMMENDATIONS (1997), *reprinted in* 31 CREIGHTON L. REV. 9, 74–75 (1997).

123. *See Faragher*, 524 U.S. at 804 n.4.

124. H. Rep. No. 102-40(I), at 64–65, *reprinted in* 1991 U.S.C.C.A.N. 602–3 (emphasis in original).

125. *See id.* at 69 (quoting William C. Burns, testifying on behalf of Pacific Bell & Electric Company), *reprinted in* 1991 U.S.C.C.A.N. at 607.

126. *See id.* at 73–74, *reprinted in* 1991 U.S.C.C.A.N. at 611–12.

127. 527 U.S. 526, 535 (1999).

128. 524 U.S. at 798.

129. 527 U.S. at 545 (quoting Am. Dental Ass'n v. Kolstad, 139 F.3d 958, 974 (Tatel, J., dissenting)).

NOTES TO CHAPTER 6

1. *See, e.g.*, Pollard v. E. I. DuPont de Nemours & Co., 532 U.S. 843, 848, 850–51 (2001) (front pay considered equitable, not compensatory).

2. *See* Meritor Sav. Bank v. Vinson, 477 U.S. 57, 64 (1986) ("when a supervisor sex-

ually harasses a subordinate because of the subordinate's sex, that supervisor 'discriminate[s]' on the basis of sex"); Canada v. Boyd Group, Inc., 809 F. Supp. 771, 780 (D. Nev. 1992) ("once a plaintiff establishes a prima facie case of hostile environment sexual harassment[,] she is entitled to a presumption of intentional discrimination").

3. 42 U.S.C. §1981a(b)(1) (2003).

4. *See* State Farm Mut. Auto. Ins. Co. v. Campbell, 538 U.S. 408, 416 (2003).

5. 42 U.S.C. §1981a(b)(3).

6. *State Farm*, 123 S. Ct. at 1519.

7. 42 U.S.C. §1981a(b)(3)(A)-(D).

8. *Id.*; *see also* Williams v. Pharmacia Opthalmics, Inc., 926 F. Supp. 791, 793 (N.D. Ind. 1996), *aff'd*, 137 F.3d 944 (7th Cir. 1998) (reducing $1.25 million jury award of compensatory and punitive damages to $300,000 cap).

9. *See, e.g.*, EEOC v. W & O Inc., 213 F.3d 600, 614 (11th Cir. 2000), *reh'g en banc denied* (finding that "each aggrieved employee represented by the EEOC in a Title VII action may receive up to the statutory cap"); Rau v. Apple-Rio Mgmt. Co., 85 F. Supp. 2d 1344, 1347 (N.D. Ga. 1999), *aff'd*, 251 F.3d 161 (11th Cir. 2001) (holding that plaintiff could not receive up to cap for each claim of damage and citing cases holding same); Galliher v. Rubin, 969 F. Supp. 1329, 1331 (S.D. Ga. 1997); Dodoo v. Seagate Tech., Inc., 235 F.3d 522, 527 (10th Cir. 2000) (Title VII and ADEA claim).

10. *See* 137 CONG. REC. H9505-01 (daily ed. Nov. 7, 1991) (interpretive memo offered by Rep. Edwards); 137 CONG. REC. H9505-01 (daily ed. Nov. 7, 1991) (statement of Rep. Schroeder); 137 CONG. REC. S15472-01 (daily ed. Oct. 30, 1991) (statement of Sen. Dole).

11. *See* 137 CONG. REC. S15336 (daily ed. Oct. 29, 1991) (statement of Sen. DeConcini); 137 CONG. REC. S15472-01 (daily ed. Oct. 30, 1991) (statement of Sen. Wallop); *see also* David Benjamin Oppenheimer, *Verdicts Matter: An Empirical Study of California Employment Discrimination and Wrongful Discharge Jury Verdicts Reveals Low Success Rates for Women and Minorities*, 37 U.C. DAVIS L. REV. 511, 528–32 (2003) (detailing portions of damages debate).

12. *See* 137 CONG. REC. H9505-01 (daily ed. Nov. 7, 1991) (interpretive memo offered by Rep. Edwards).

13. 527 U.S. 526 (1999).

14. *See id.* at 538.

15. *Id.* at 535.

16. *Id.*

17. *Id.* at 545.

18. *Id.* (quoting Kolstad v. American Dental Assoc., 139 F.3d 958, 974 (D.C. Cir. 1998) (Tatel, J., dissenting)).

19. *See, e.g.*, Bruso v. United Airlines, Inc., 239 F.3d 848, 857–58 (7th Cir. 2001).

20. *See, e.g.*, Deters v. Equifax Credit Info. Servs., Inc., 202 F.3d 1262, 1270–71 (10th Cir. 2000); Miller v. Rockford Register Star, 2001 WL 637575 at *5 (N.D. Ill. 2001); Dodoo v. Seagate Tech., Inc., 235 F.3d 522, 531 (10th Cir. 2000).

21. 308 F.3d 473, 475–77 (5th Cir. 2002).

22. *Id.* at 477.

23. *See, e.g.*, Adarand Constructors, Inc. v. Pena, 515 U.S. 200 (1995); Lee v. Edwards, 101 F.3d 805, 809 n.2 (2d Cir. 1996).

24. State Farm Mut. Auto. Ins. Co. v. Campbell, 123 S. Ct. 1513, 1519 (2003); Cooper Indus., Inc. v. Leatherman Tool Group, Inc., 532 U.S. 424, 432 (2001).

25. 2003 WL 21245201, at *1 (D. Utah 2003).

26. 998 F. Supp. 840, 851 n.15 (W.D. Tenn. 1998).

27. Baker v. John Morrell & Co., 249 F. Supp. 2d 1138, 1193 (N.D. Iowa 2003).

28. 330 F.3d 1051, 1053–54, 1060 n.3 (8th Cir. 2003).

29. Barbara A. Gutek & Mary P. Koss, *Changed Women and Changed Organizations: Consequences of and Coping with Sexual Harassment*, 42 J. VOCATIONAL BEHAV. 28, 30 (1993).

30. *See id.* at 32 (citing studies reflecting same); David N. Laband & Bernard F. Lentz, *The Effects of Sexual Harassment on Job Satisfaction, Earnings, and Turnover among Female Lawyers*, 51 INDUS. & LAB. RELATIONS REV. 594, 602 (1998).

31. Gutek & Koss, *supra* note 29.

32. Vicki J. Magley et al., *The Impact of Sexual Harassment on Military Personnel: Is it the Same for Men and Women?*, 11 MIL. PSYCHOL. 283, 285 (1999) (citing studies).

33. *See* chapter 5, pp. 164–65.

34. U.S. MERIT SYS. PROT. BD., SEXUAL HARASSMENT IN THE FEDERAL GOVERNMENT: AN UPDATE 24 (1988).

35. Laband & Lentz, *supra* note 30, at 604 (increased intent to quit by over 25%).

36. *See* Jane Goodman-Delahunty & William E. Foote, *Compensation for Pain, Suffering, and Other Psychological Injuries: The Impact of Daubert on Employment Discrimination Claims*, 13 BEHAV. SCI. & L. 183, 195 (1995).

37. Gutek & Koss, *supra* note 29, at 31–32.

38. Laband & Lentz, *supra* note 30, at 599–600.

39. *See id.* at 600.

40. Paula C. Morrow et al., *Sexual Harassment Behaviors and Work Related Perceptions and Attitudes*, 45 J. VOCATIONAL BEHAV. 295, 303 (1994).

41. *See id.* at 305.

42. Magley et al., *supra* note 32, at 297.

43. *See* Bonnie S. Dansky & Dean G. Kilpatrick, *Effects of Sexual Harassment*, in SEXUAL HARASSMENT: THEORY, RESEARCH, AND TREATMENT 152, 164 (William O'-Donohue ed. 1997).

44. *See* Gutek & Koss, *supra* note 29, at 33 (citing studies).

45. Goodman-Delahunty & Foote, *supra* note 36, at 188.

46. Kimberly T. Schneider et al., *Job-Related and Psychological Effects of Sexual Harassment in the Workplace: Empirical Evidence from Two Organizations*, 82 J. APPLIED PSYCHOL. 401, 412–13 (1997).

47. *See* Dansky & Kilpatrick, *supra* note 43, at 164, 166–67 and figs. 9-1 & 9-2.

48. *See id.* at 166.

49. *See id.* at 168.

50. *See* Sharyn A. Lenhart & Diane K. Shrier, *Potential Costs and Benefits of Sexual Harassment Litigation*, 26 PSYCHIATRIC ANNALS 132, 136 (1996).

51. *See, e.g.*, Delaney v. City of Hampton, Virginia, 999 F. Supp. 794 (E.D. Va. 1998); McCleland v. Montgomery Ward & Co., Inc., 1995 WL 571324 (N.D. Ill. 1995).

52. *See, e.g.*, Lisa Bloom, *Gretel Fights Back: Representing Sexual Harassment Plaintiffs Who Were Sexually Abused as Children*, 12 BERK. WOMEN'S L.J. 1, 2–3 (1997).

53. Margaret S. Stockdale et al., *The Relationship between Prior Sexual Abuse and Reactions to Sexual Harassment*, 8 PSYCHOL. PUB. POL'Y & L. 64, 67–68 (2002).

54. Louise F. Fitzgerald et al., *Junk Logic: The Abuse Defense in Sexual Harassment Litigation*, 5 PSYCHOL. PUB. POL'Y & L. 730, 731 (1999).

55. *Id.* at 739–40.

56. *Id.* at 742 (emphasis in original).

57. *See id.* at 748.

58. *Id.* at 750.

59. Stockdale et al., *supra* note 53, at 88.

60. *Id.* at 89.

61. *See* Edith Greene et al., *Juror Decisions about Damages in Employment Discrimination Cases*, 17 BEHAV. SCI. & L. 107, 108 (1999). Two recent exceptions are a study

by Cass Sunstein and Judy Shih and a study by David Oppenheimer. *See* Cass R. Sunstein & Judy Shih, *Damages in Sexual Harassment Cases, in* DIRECTIONS IN SEXUAL HARASSMENT LAW, 324 (Catharine A. MacKinnon & Reva B. Siegel, eds. 2004); Oppenheimer, *supra* note 11. The Sunstein and Shih study is hampered by a potentially skewed data set that is "too small to allow for reliable statistical judgments." *See* Sunstein & Shih, *supra*, at 332.

62. EDITH GREENE & BRIAN H. BORNSTEIN, DETERMINING DAMAGES: THE PSYCHOLOGY OF JURY AWARDS 21–23, 32–36, 103–7 (2003).

63. *Id.* at 35; *see also* Dennis J. Devine et al., *Jury Decision Making: 45 Years of Empirical Research on Deliberating Groups*, 7 PSYCHOL. PUB. POL'Y & L. 622, 703 (2001) (noting "the typical civil jury award is not extremely large").

64. *See* Devine et al., *supra* note 63, at 706 (citing studies).

65. GREENE & BORNSTEIN, *supra* note 62, at 107.

66. *Id.* at 109 (citing studies); Mark Geistfeld, *Placing a Price on Pain and Suffering: A Method for Helping Juries Determine Tort Damages for Nonmonetary Injuries*, 83 CAL. L. REV. 773, 777 (1995) (noting dearth of evidence supporting excessiveness).

67. *See* Geistfeld, *supra* note 66, at 784–85 (citing studies).

68. *See* GREENE & BORNSTEIN, *supra* note 62, at 111 (citing and describing R. Wissler et al., *Explaining "Pain and Suffering" Awards: The Role of Injury Characteristics and Fault Attributions*, 21 LAW & HUM. BEHAV. 181 (1997)).

69. *See id.* at 113.

70. *See* Oppenheimer, *supra* note 11, at 539.

71. *See id.* at 532. Although the study included both state and federal cases, only four of the cases were brought in federal court, and the vast majority (73 cases) of opposite-sex sexual harassment cases studied were brought under state law, where there are no damage caps. Correspondence with Natalie Kwan, research assistant to Professor David Oppenheimer (on file with author). In addition, even in the cases brought in federal court, a plaintiff would likely make a claim under state law to avoid the effect of the federal damage caps.

72. *See id.* at 534.

73. *Id.* at 547.

74. *See* Sunstein & Shih, *supra* note 61, at 332.

75. *Id.*

76. *See id.*

77. *Id.* (emphasis in original).

78. *Id.* at 332–33.

79. *Id.* at 334.

80. *Id.* at 325.

81. *See* Devine et al., *supra* note 63, at 671–72, 699.

82. *Id.* at 667 (citing studies).

83. *See* GREENE & BORNSTEIN, *supra* note 62, at 191–93.

84. *See* Geistfeld, *supra* note 66, at 790.

85. GREENE & BORNSTEIN, *supra* note 62, at 155 (describing studies).

86. *See* Geistfeld, *supra* note 66, at 792.

87. Greene et al., *supra* note 61, at 114.

88. *Id.* at 114 tbl. 1.

89. Goodman-Delahunty & Foote, *supra* note 36, at 202.

90. *See id.* at 187–89.

91. *See* GREENE & BORNSTEIN, *supra* note 62, at 36 (citing C.J. DeFrances & M.F. Litras, *Civil Trial Cases and Verdicts in Large Counties, 1996* (NCJ Rep. No. 173246) (Sept. 1999); B. Ostrom et al., *What Are Tort Awards Really Like? The Untold Story from the State Courts*, 14 LAW & POL'Y 77 (1992)). *See also* Devine et al., *supra* note 63, at 703 (noting studies indicate that punitive damages are awarded in 3%–4% of all civil

cases); Theodore Eisenberg et al., *The Predictability of Punitive Damages*, 26 J. LEGAL STUD. 623, 633 (1997).

92. *See* Devine et al., *supra* note 63, at 706 (summarizing studies).

93. Eisenberg et al., *supra* note 91, at 639; *but see* Daniel Kahneman et al., *Shared Outrage, Erratic Awards*, *in* CASS R. SUNSTEIN ET AL., PUNITIVE DAMAGES: HOW JURIES DECIDE 31–42 (2002) (study of potential jurors finding punitive damage awards erratic).

94. Eisenberg et al., *supra* note 91, at 634 tbl.1.

95. *Id.* (for example, jurors awarded successful slander/libel plaintiffs punitive damages 27% of the time).

96. *Id.* at 637.

97. *See* Sunstein & Shih, *supra* note 61, at 338–42 (listing cases studied); Oppenheimer, *supra* note 11.

98. *See* Janice R. Franke, *Does Title VII Contemplate Personal Liability for Employee/Agent Defendants?*, 12 HOFSTRA LABOR L.J. 39, 60 n.139 (1994).

99. *See* Avon L. Sergeant, *Are the Legal Remedies Available to Sexually Harassed Women Adequate?*, 20 WOMEN'S RTS. L. REP. 185, 190 (1999) (likewise suggesting removal of caps).

100. Sexual harassment claims resemble torts because they involve wrongdoing that renders the defendant liable to compensate the plaintiff for injuries inflicted on the plaintiff by the defendant. Like a tort-based scheme, Title VII has the dual goals of compensating victims and deterring potential wrongdoers and future wrongdoing by the particular defendant involved. *See generally* PROSSER AND KEETON ON THE LAW OF TORTS 2–4 (W. Page Keeton, ed., 5th ed. 1984).

101. U.S.C. §2000e(b) (West 2003).

102. *See* Brennan v. Norton, 350 F.3d 399, 430 n.24 (3d Cir. 2003) ("Among the factors a jury must consider in making a punitive damages award are the offensiveness of the conduct and the amount needed, considering the defendant's financial condition, to prevent future repetition.").

103. Ivy E. Broder, *Characteristics of Million Dollar Awards: Jury Verdicts and Final Disbursements*, 11 JUST. SYS. J. 349, 353 tbl.2 (1986).

104. *Id.* at 355 tbl.4.

105. Neil Vidmar et al., *Jury Awards for Medical Malpractice and Post-Verdict Adjustments of Those Awards*, 48 DEPAUL L. REV. 265, 285 (1998).

106. *Id.* at 286.

107. *Id.* at 292, 294.

108. KEVIN F. O'MALLEY ET AL., 3 FEDERAL JURY PRACTICE AND INSTRUCTIONS: CIVIL §128.02 at 429 (5th ed. 2000).

109. *See* Nancy McCarthy, *Plain English Instructions Are Coming to Juries*, CAL. BAR J. July 2003, at 1.

110. JUDICIAL COUNCIL OF CAL., CALIFORNIA CIVIL JURY INSTRUCTIONS, 3905A (draft 2003), *available at* www.courtinfo.ca.gov/reference/4_34juryinst.htm.

NOTES TO CHAPTER 7

1. Meritor Sav. Bank v. Vinson, 477 U.S. 57, 68 (1986).

2. *Id.* at 67.

3. *See, e.g.*, Farpella-Crosby v. Horizon Health Care, 97 F.3d 803, 806 (5th Cir. 1996); Brown v. Hot, Sexy and Safer Prods., Inc., 68 F.3d 525, 540 (1st Cir. 1995), *cert. denied*, 516 U.S. 1159 (1996); Morgan v. Fellini's Pizza, Inc., 64 F. Supp. 2d 1304, 1309 (N.D. Ga. 1999).

4. Jane L. Dolkart, *Hostile Environment Harassment: Equality, Objectivity, and the Shaping of Legal Standards*, 43 EMORY L.J. 151, 210 (1994).

Index

253

About the Author

Theresa M. Beiner is Professor of Law at the University of Arkansas at Little Rock, William H. Bowen School of Law. She and her husband, Timothy Gauger, have three children.